Buffalo's Waterfront Renaissance

Citizen Activists, NGOs, and the Canalside Project

GENE BUNNELL

EXCELSIOR EDITIONS

Excelsior Editions is an imprint of State University of New York Press

For information, contact State University of New York Press, Albany, NY
www.sunypress.edu

Library of Congress Cataloging-in-Publication Data
Name: Bunnell, Gene, author.
Title: Buffalo's waterfront renaissance : citizen activists, NGOs, and the Canalside project / Gene Bunnell.
Description: Albany : State University of New York Press, [2024] | Includes bibliographical references and index.
Identifiers: ISBN 9781438499086 (hardcover : alk. paper) | ISBN 9781438499109 (ebook)
Further information is available at the Library of Congress.

I've got a mule, her name is Sal, Fifteen miles on the Erie Canal
She's a good ol' worker an' a good ol' pal, Fifteen miles on the Erie
    Canal
We've haul'd some barges in our day, Fill'd with lumber, coal and hay,
And we know ev'ry inch of the way, From Albany to Buffalo

Low bridge, ev'ry bod-y down!
Low bridge, for we're comin' to a town!
And you'll always know your neighbor, You'll always know your pal,
If you've ever navigated on the Erie Canal

We better get along on our way, ol' gal, Fifteen miles on the Erie Canal
Cause you bet your life I'd never part with Sal, Fifteen miles on the
    Erie Canal
Git up there, mule, here comes a lock, We'll make Rome 'bout six
    o'clock
One more trip an' back we'll go, Right back home to Buffalo

Low bridge, ev'ry bod-y down!
Low bridge, for we're comin to a town!
And you'll always know your neighbor, You'll always know your pal,
If you've ever navigated on the Erie Canal

—"The Song of the Erie Canal"

Contents

Part I: History and Background

Part II: The Inner Harbor

Part III: The Buffalo River

Part IV: The Outer Harbor

Part V: Conclusion

Illustrations

About the Author

Born and raised in Buffalo, Gene Bunnell came of age when the city was hemorrhaging jobs and population and entering what would be a long period of decline. Growing up in Buffalo during that time has provided him with a lens for understanding and comparing the experiences of American cities, with a particular focus on postindustrial cities.

After earning a BA degree from Wesleyan University and earning a master of city planning degree from the Harvard Graduate School of Design, he worked as an urban planner in the public sector for 15 years, first for the Massachusetts Department of Community Affairs Office of Local Assistance and then as director of Planning and Development for the City of Northampton, Massachusetts. After earning his PhD from London School of Economics and Political Science in 1993, he taught urban planning at the University of Wisconsin-Madison's Department of Urban and Regional Planning and the Department of Geography and Planning at the State University of New York at Albany, drawing on the experience and insights he gained as a practicing planner in "the real world." He is the author of three previous books: *Built to Last* (Preservation Press, National Trust for Historic Preservation 1977), *Making Places Special* (Planners Press 2002), and *Transforming Providence: Rebirth of a Post-Industrial City* (Troy Bookmakers 2017).

Preface

Long considered a place few people would want to visit, let alone reside in, Buffalo is now viewed in a much more positive light in large part due to the remarkable transformation that has taken place along the city's postindustrial waterfront. In *Across an Inland Sea*, Nicholas Howe wrote fondly about his memories of growing up in Buffalo, but he candidly admitted that "from the late 1950s through the early 1990s . . . no travel writer would have put [Buffalo] on his [or her] trophy list" (Howe 2003, 2). That clearly was not the case fifteen years later when the *New York Times* included Buffalo in its list of "52 places to go in 2018," citing the Canalside project as well as the repurposing of long-dormant grain elevators as the reasons for its recommendation.

The Canalside project, which uncovered and rewatered the long-buried historic western terminus of the Erie Canal, is the aspect of Buffalo's waterfront renaissance that at least initially attracted the greatest attention. Unfortunately, as more time has passed, fewer and fewer people know *how* Canalside came about, *how long* it took, *why* the project was so controversial, and *what* very nearly happened instead on the site.

Other environmentally beneficial waterfront outcomes were also brought about along six miles of the Buffalo River and on the Outer Harbor. *How* the transformations of those portions of Buffalo's waterfront were brought about is likely even *less* well understood than what happened at Canalside. An important reason for writing this book is so that more people know *how* Buffalo's waterfront renaissance came about—because *that* is what makes the story so important.

While working on this book I was fortunate to be introduced to Father Jud, a Catholic priest who participated in and supported Our Outer

Harbor's efforts to prevent Buffalo's Outer Harbor from being privately developed (described in chapter 13). William "Jud" Weiksnar grew up in Eggertsville in the town of Amherst, New York, graduated from high school in 1975, and attended college at the University of Notre Dame. After graduating from Notre Dame, he returned to Buffalo, earning both a law degree in 1985 and a PhD in 1988 from the University at Buffalo, after which he enrolled at the Washington Theological Union to study for a master of divinity degree.

Weiksnar became a Franciscan friar in June 1993 and was ordained a Catholic priest in May 1994. He spent the next 20 years serving churches in New York City; Boston; Washington, DC; Camden, New Jersey; Peru and Olean, New York. In 2014 he was assigned to the St. Patrick Friary in Buffalo, and in his free time set out to discover and explore the waterfront of the city he had previously lived in but had known very little about.

Father Jud's Ode to Buffalo's Waterfront

Growing up in Amherst, New York in the 1960s and 1970s, I had little firsthand knowledge of Buffalo's waterfront. I vaguely remember family rides in the station wagon on weekends when my dad would point out factories and bridges. The mentality back then, as expressed by my parents, was that the industrialization and contamination of the waterfront were justified because they provided jobs. We were not an outdoorsy family, so I never recall taking a walk along the waterfront. If I had been dropped off on Fuhrmann Boulevard, Marine Drive, or Ohio Street, I would have been completely lost.

In the 1980s, while I attended the University of Buffalo Graduate School, the extent of my exposure to the waterfront was going out to The Pier to visit a restaurant and nightclub on Fuhrmann Boulevard. I had no conception of the difference between the Outer Harbor and Inner Harbor.

After being placed in other cities for 20 years, I returned to Buffalo in 2014 when I was assigned to the St. Patrick Friary. To reacquaint myself with the city, I took a Buffalo River History Tour by boat and a walking tour of the Old First Ward as well as a "vertical tour" of the grain elevators at Silo City. I also took part in Slow Roll Buffalo community bike rides, one of the first of which stopped at Red Jacket Park along the Buffalo River. Taking part in those activities made me curious about other parts of the waterfront—the Buffalo River, the Inner Harbor, the Outer Harbor, and the grain elevators.

Because I lived just a mile from Mutual Riverfront Park, it made sense for me to get a kayak and a bike trailer to transport it. And being so close to downtown, I pulled out my old high school ice skates and have skated regularly on the Ice at Canalside since it opened in 2014. Since returning to Buffalo, I have taken over 100 kayak trips up and down the Buffalo River and also biked hundreds of times out to the Outer Harbor. My curiosity about "the waterfront" has turned to appreciation and affection.

Having lived in the Chicago, New York City, Boston, Washington, and Philadelphia areas, I can't think of anywhere else that compares with the Buffalo River late in September for its mystical combination of natural beauty and postindustrial heritage—or that can match the joy of ascending the wind-sculpture hill at Wilkeson Pointe on the Outer Harbor at sundown and contemplating Lake Erie's resurgent ecosystem.

There is no need to "develop" our waterfront so that it mirrors Toronto's or Baltimore's. I urge those making decisions about its future to listen to those who know it up close, lest we lose this truly incredible and unique treasure.

—Fr. William "Jud" Weiksnar, O.F.M., July 2, 2022

Acknowledgments

When I was in Buffalo in summer 2018 I arranged to meet Mark Goldman at the coffee shop next to Talking Leaves bookstore on Elmwood during which I gave him a copy of the book I wrote about Providence Rhode Island, *Transforming Providence: Rebirth of a Post-Industrial City.* We talked about a lot of things, but what I most remember Mark saying was "Why don't you write a book about Buffalo?"—which planted in my mind the idea of writing this book.

I want to thank the many individuals who agreed to speak with me about efforts they were personally involved in or had firsthand knowledge of that advanced Buffalo's waterfront renaissance. The names of these individuals are listed in Appendix III. I especially want to thank Lynda H. Schneekloth for her early interest in the book, for telling me how she and a small group of activists became involved with the Buffalo River, and for explaining why they established Friends of the Buffalo River. I am doubly grateful to Lynda for encouraging me to expand the scope of the book to encompass the Outer Harbor. The numerous back-and-forth email conversations I had with her over an extended period of time enabled me to piece together the story of how the waterfront renaissance eventually unfolded on the Outer Harbor.

Robert F. Shibley, dean of the University of Buffalo's School of Architecture and Planning, was kind enough to engage in lengthy and vigorous conversations with me on Zoom during the pandemic as I was beginning to consider the lessons we can learn from Buffalo's waterfront experience—which proved enormously useful in helping me clarify my own thinking. Austin Wyles, who at the time was a teaching assistant at UB's School of Architecture and Planning prepared the computer-generated maps of different portions of Buffalo's waterfront that are included in the book.

Tim Tielman provided me access to the treasure trove of documents, plans, environmental impact statements, correspondence, and other documents he compiled over many years in connection with the Inner Harbor. Having had access to that rich documentation enabled me to provide readers with a blow-by-blow account of the multiyear battle between preservationists and the state waterfront agency over how the Inner Harbor would be redeveloped. Thanks too to Donn Esmonde for providing me with hard copies of dozens of articles he wrote about the Inner Harbor project for the *Buffalo News* and for the lengthy follow-up emails he sent me that provided additional valuable insights.

Lastly, I want to express my gratitude to Barbara Conover, an experienced editor whom I was fortunate to be able to hire in fall 2021 to edit early drafts of the book. I am especially grateful to Barbara for her advice regarding how the book should be structured and how the portions of the book dealing with the different parts of Buffalo's waterfront should be organized. We never met in person, but over time we got to know each other quite well and became good friends. For roughly a year and a half we were in almost constant communication with one another via email. Barbara died unexpectedly in December 2022. I wish she were able to join me in savoring the completion of this book.

Abbreviations

ADM: Archer Daniels Midland

Aud: Memorial Auditorium

Aud Block: Portion of Canalside formerly occupied by Memorial Auditorium

South Aud Block: Southern portion of Aud Block

North Aud Block: Northern portion of Aud Block

BMC: Buffalo Maritime Center

BSA: Buffalo Sewer Authority

BSNS: Buffalo Society of Natural Sciences

BSRA: Buffalo Scholastic Rowing Association

CBA: community benefit agreement

CCF: Cabot, Cabot and Forbes

C4GB: Campaign for Greater Buffalo History, Architecture & Culture

CEJ: Center for Economic Justice

CSCA: Canal Side Community Alliance

DL&W: Delaware Lackawanna & Western Railroad

ECHDC: Erie Canal Harbor Development Corporation

EPA: Environmental Protection Agency

ESDC: Empire State Development Corporation

FBR: Friends of the Buffalo River

FBNR: Friends of the Buffalo and Niagara Rivers

FEIS: Federal Environmental Impact Statement

FTA: Federal Transit Administration

GLLA: Great Lakes Legacy Act

GLSRC: Great Lakes Science Research Center

GPP: General Project Plan (for the Outer Harbor)

ILR: School of Industrial and Labor Relations

LVRR: Lehigh Valley Railroad

LWRP: Local Waterfront Revitalization Plan

LWV: League of Women Voters

MMM: Marshall Macklin Monaghan

MOU: memorandum of understanding

NGO: nongovernmental organization

NEPA: National Environmental Protection Act

NFTA: Niagara Frontier Transportation Authority

NYPA: New York Power Authority

NOAA: National Oceanic and Atmospheric Administration

NYSDEC: New York State Department of Environmental Conservation

OOH: Our Outer Harbor Coalition

OPRHP: Office of Parks, Recreation & Historic Preservation (New York State)

PBN: Preservation Buffalo Niagara

PPG: Partnership for the Public Good

PUSH: People United for Sustainable Housing

RAP: remedial action plan

RFP: request for proposals

SEIS: Supplemental Environmental Impact Statement

SEQRA: State Environmental Quality Review Act

SHPO: State Historic Preservation Office

UDC: Urban Development Corporation (State of New York)

USACE: US Army Corps of Engineers

VCA: Valley Community Association

WPB: Waterfront Planning Board

WNYEA: Western New York Environmental Alliance

WNYLC: Western New York Land Conservancy

Figure I.1: Main parts of Buffalo's waterfront: Inner Harbor, Outer Harbor, and Buffalo River. *Source*: Map by Austin Wyles.

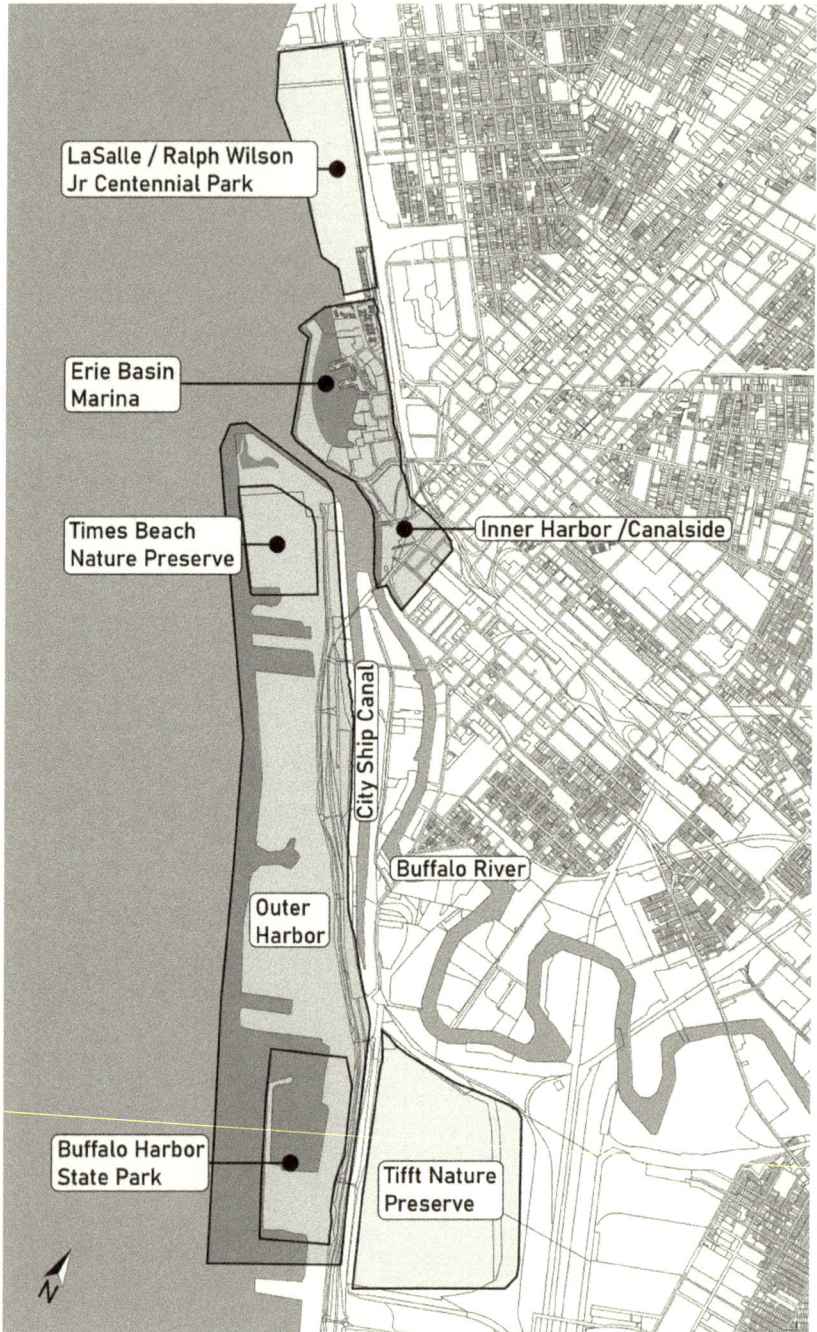

Introduction

Buffalo's waterfront renaissance was principally brought about by hundreds of local residents, citizen activists, and scores of local nonprofit/nongovernmental organizations. The overall result of the many citizen-inspired efforts and projects described in this book has been to reclaim a substantial portion of Buffalo's forlorn, industrially abandoned waterfront for public use and enjoyment, and thereby to make Buffalo a much more appealing place to live and work.

After losing more than half of its inhabitants between 1950 and 2010, Buffalo's population increased for the first time in seventy years between 2010 and 2020—from 261,310 to 278,349. "The most visible sign of Buffalo's changing fortunes are its new apartments . . . In the last decade, 224 multifamily projects, encompassing 10,150 apartments, have opened or are underway. And the pace of new housing activity appears to be quickening. A third of the total, or 78 projects, were unveiled just in 2020 and 2021" (Hughes 2022). Having weathered the negative economic impacts of the COVID-19 pandemic over a two-year period, Buffalo's prospects for the future now look much brighter.

While doing the research for this book, I contacted and spoke with dozens of individuals with firsthand knowledge of the waterfront outcomes described in the book, many of whom were directly involved in helping to bring them about. I also engaged in back-and-forth email communications with a number of those individuals. Quotes from these interviews and excerpts of these email communications are interwoven at various points in the book.

Another invaluable source of information was the e-edition of the *Buffalo News*, which provided me with a running commentary on what was happening on the waterfront. Over one hundred articles published in the *Buffalo News* are referenced in the book, including 9 editorials and 16 contributed op-eds. In addition to providing factual accounts of what was happening on Buffalo's waterfront at different points in time, such newspaper accounts also often revealed how the events being reported on were viewed by the public at the time. Two former *Buffalo News* reporters and columnists (Philip Langdon, 1973–1982 and Donn Esmonde, 1982–2015) provided me with hard copies of many of the columns and articles they wrote during their respective tenures at the newspaper. Nineteen articles posted online on *Buffalo Rising* also provided useful information and insights.

Two master of urban planning theses written by students enrolled in graduate degree urban planning programs at New York State universities served as valuable sources of information: Bradshaw Hovey's 1991 master of urban planning thesis at the University at Buffalo School of Architecture and Planning, "Taken in Again—Citizen Participation in the Buffalo Waterfront plan 1982–1987" and Jimmy Vielkind's 2012 master of urban planning thesis at the University at Albany Department of Geography and Planning, "Media Coverage of Major Land Use and Development Issues." Equally valuable was the 1983 report prepared by lawyer Frank S. Palen for the School of Law at the University at Buffalo, "City Planning in Buffalo: A History of Institutions," in which he describes in detail how planning was conducted in Buffalo in the years before the waterfront renaissance.

Structure of the Book

The chapters of this book are presented in five parts. The first five chapters in part I orient readers to the three main parts of Buffalo's waterfront and describe the impact that industrial development brought about by the opening of the Erie Canal had on the Inner Harbor, Buffalo River, and Outer Harbor. Chapter 4 describes the factors that contributed to the decline of the Inner Harbor and lower Main Street and government-funded projects that were undertaken in an effort to counteract that decline. Waterfront planning efforts undertaken in the early 1980s and early 1990s are described in chapter 5. The failure of a major waterfront planning effort undertaken by the City of Buffalo and the Niagara Frontier Transportation Authority is particularly notable because it opened the door for the first entity associated with state government to begin planning for Buffalo's waterfront.

Chapters 6 through 9 (in part II) describe the recent history of the Inner Harbor. Chapter 6 explains why Empire State Development Corporation's (ESDC) 1998 Inner Harbor Plan was so controversial and why the Preservation Coalition of Erie County filed a lawsuit against ESDC in Federal District Court. Chapter 7 describes how a new controversy was ignited in 2004 when Governor Pataki announced that preservationists and ESDC had resolved their differences, but also announced that a large-scale Bass Pro Outdoor World retail outlet would be developed in the Inner Harbor.

Two public forums held in fall 2010 in the wake of Bass Pro's withdrawal from the Inner Harbor project are described in chapter 8, which produced strong support for a lighter, quicker, and cheaper approach to activating the waterfront. Chapter 9 describes three projects initiated and carried out by NGOs with the help of the state waterfront agency that broadened Canalside's appeal as a visitor destination.

Chapters 10 and 11 (in part III) return to the Buffalo River. Chapter 10 describes the key role Friends of the Buffalo River, a fledgling nongovernmental organization, played in cleaning up the river as well as in restoring natural habitat within and along the shorelines of the river. Chapter 11 describes a number of projects that took advantage of the river's improving water quality by expanding public use and enjoyment of the Buffalo River.

Chapters 12 and 13 (in part IV) return to the Outer Harbor. Chapter 12 describes how the establishment of nature preserves at Tifft Farm and Times Beach provided the earliest indication of the public's growing recognition of the need to prevent further contamination of the Outer Harbor. Chapter 13 picks up the story from there by describing the series of plans that were developed by state agencies over a quarter century that called for the Outer Harbor to be extensively privately developed. Also described is Our Outer Harbor's eventual success in getting the City of Buffalo to adopt a new Unified Development Ordinance (the "Green Code") that prohibited developing housing on most of the Outer Harbor. The final chapter in part V highlights a number of key observations and lessons that can be learned from Buffalo's experience.

Part I
History and Background

Chapter One

The Erie Canal's Impact on
Buffalo and the Nation

Construction of the Erie Canal began in Rome, New York, on July 4, 1817, although no decision had yet been made as to where the canal would terminate and connect with Lake Erie. The village of Buffalo was far from assured that it would be chosen to serve as the canal's western terminus. The village was still trying to recover and rebuild after much of it had been burned to the ground by the British during the War of 1812. An even greater liability at the time was that it lacked a navigable harbor.

To improve the village's prospects of being chosen as the canal's western terminus, local leaders secured a $12,000 loan from the state and hired Samuel Wilkeson to undertake and oversee an ambitious project aimed at creating a navigable harbor. In the summer of 1820, Wilkeson assembled the workforce needed to carry out the project, and work began on constructing a pier 800 feet out into the lake to stop sand from continuing to build up on a sandbar that blocked the mouth of Buffalo Creek. Nevertheless, the existing sandbar still represented an obstruction to navigation.

To eliminate the obstruction altogether, Wilkeson proposed *moving* the mouth of the creek 60 rods (990 feet) to the south. To accomplish that major alteration, Wilkeson proposed that the creek be dammed in such a manner as to allow the force and weight of the water built up behind the dam to create a new channel out to the lake.

Not long after the creek was dammed, a torrential rainstorm and strong winds blowing in off the lake caused water levels in both the creek and the lake to abruptly rise. Workers and villagers toiled through the night to try to keep the dam from prematurely breaking apart. Fortunately, the dam held long enough for sufficient pressure to build up behind it before the raging current of the Buffalo Creek broke through the dam at precisely the spot Wilkeson had intended. The tremendous burst of water gouged out a new harbor entrance that was more than wide and deep enough to provide Buffalo with the navigable harbor it needed to be chosen as the Erie Canal's western terminus (R. C. Brown and Watson 1981, 31).

Construction of the Erie Canal was completed in the fall of 1825. The canal as originally constructed was only 4 feet deep and 40 feet wide, but it was an impressive accomplishment nonetheless, given the crude construction methods available at the time. Oxen plowed the ground for the canal, but the bulk of the work related to excavating the canal was carried out by Irish laborers working with primitive tools. It was also a monumental engineering achievement. Over its 363-mile length between Albany and Buffalo 83 15-foot × 90-foot stone locks and 18 aqueducts had to be constructed to enable the canal to span ravines and climb 568 feet in elevation to reach the level of Lake Erie. Along one side of the canal was a 10-foot-wide towpath, on which horses and mules pulled canal boats that could be loaded with up to 30 tons of freight.

No one was more responsible for the building of the Erie Canal than DeWitt Clinton. While serving as a state senator in 1811, Clinton introduced a bill into the New York Senate that called for a commission to be established to explore possible routes for a canal across New York State to link the Northeast with the Great Lakes via Lake Erie. Critics of the project called it "Clinton's Ditch." After the War of 1812 ended in 1814, the canal idea was revived. Clinton once again went to the state capital in Albany urging acceptance of the detailed plan that had been developed. The legislature eventually agreed in 1816 to finance the canal as a state project and appointed Clinton to the commission that had been established to oversee the project. Clinton's first term as governor of the State of New York began in 1817 and ended in 1823. He was reelected in 1825 and was governor of the state until 1828.

Governor Clinton came to Buffalo to preside over the ceremony that was held along the Commercial Slip on October 26, 1825, to mark the official opening of the canal. After the speeches were done, Governor Clinton, Samuel Wilkeson, and other dignitaries boarded the *Seneca Chief* packet boat and led a parade of boats on a celebratory journey along the newly dug canal and on to New York City. Also on board the *Seneca*

Chief for that inaugural trip were jugs of Lake Erie water. Upon arriving in New York City ten days later, Governor Clinton ceremonially poured Lake Erie water into New York Harbor, thus signifying the "wedding of the waters." On its return trip to Buffalo, the *Seneca Chief* carried jugs of Atlantic Ocean water. Soon after arriving back in Buffalo, the packet boat was towed out into the lake, and the jugs of Atlantic Ocean water were ceremonially poured into Lake Erie—symbolically completing the "wedding of the waters" of the Atlantic and the Great Lakes. "The Erie Canal was every bit as world-changing in its time as the opening of the Suez Canal and the Panama Canal" (S. Fisher, interview, June 13, 2018).

Before the canal was completed, it took two weeks or more, depending on road conditions, to travel between Albany and Buffalo by stagecoach. Packet boats that traveled on the canal reduced that travel time to three to four days. During its first year, 40,000 people traveled on the Erie Canal from Albany to Buffalo. By the 1830s, 3,000 canal boats were in service offering almost hourly departures from Albany.

Buffalo was the city that most directly benefited from the opening of the canal. When the canal opened in 1825, Buffalo was a village of just 2,400 people. Buffalo was incorporated as a city in 1832, and by 1835 Buffalo's population had quadrupled to 15,661. Even more important from a national perspective was the important role the canal played in fueling and advancing the western migration that settled the interior of the country. Thousands of immigrants traveled to Buffalo on the canal, many of them having recently arrived in the United States, and boarded ships that carried them further west on the Great Lakes.

Almost overnight, the canal made Buffalo a nationally important center of commerce and trade by significantly reducing the cost and time it took to ship goods across New York State. Having to transport goods by wagon on primitive roads severely limited the volume and weight of goods that could be shipped at one time, whereas a single Erie Canal barge could carry 30 tons of freight, "dropping the price to move a ton of freight from Buffalo to New York from about $100 to $10" (Egan 2017, 18).

When the canal opened in 1825, most of the country's wheat was grown in the east. In 1829, Buffalo handled 7,975 bushels of flour and wheat; just one year later in 1830, shipments of wheat through Buffalo reached 181,029 bushels. However, as more people moved west, grain production quickly shifted to the Midwest. The barges that initially operated on the Erie Canal were capable of carrying 1,000 bushels of wheat, which reduced the cost of shipping a ton of wheat from Ohio to New York by 90 percent.

As a result, the number of Great Lakes vessels traveling in and out of Buffalo increased dramatically. However, captains of ships entering Buffalo Harbor often had difficulty seeing the first lighthouse that had been built near the mouth of Buffalo Creek. In 1826, the US Treasury Department authorized the building of a new lighthouse a thousand feet east of the original lighthouse's location. From a base with a 20-foot diameter, the new octagonal lighthouse gradually tapered to a diameter of 12 feet at its lantern room (see figure 1.1). The lighthouse was completed and began operating in 1833. As shown in figure 1.2, the new lighthouse was readily visible to ships entering the harbor.

Figure 1.1. Buffalo Lighthouse, c. 1857. *Source*: Historic American Buildings Survey (Library of Congress). Survey number HABS NY-60. http://hdl.loc.gov/loc.pnp/hhh.ny0196. Public domain.

Figure 1.2. Steamship entering Buffalo Harbor, c. 1900. *Source*: National Archives. Public domain.

The enormous number of canal barges and ships converging on the Commercial Slip meant that large numbers of sailors roamed the streets of the Canal District between trips after spending a long time on board. (See figure 1.3 for a late nineteenth century view of the Commercial Slip.) Crew members were typically paid upon arriving in Buffalo, and many were understandably keen to spend their earnings quickly and drink as if there were no tomorrow. Most of the notorious activity was concentrated on and around Canal Street (see figure 1.4). At one point there were 75 brothels and 107 saloons on or near Canal Street, which came to be known as "the wickedest street in the world." "It was said that, during its heyday, there was a murder every day. Legends were told of saloon owners who would serve a poisoned drink, steal a man's clothes and personal items, and dump the body in the canal" (Keppel 2014a).

The Central Wharf

Just south of the Commercial Slip was the Central Wharf, a nearly unbroken line of attached buildings that overlooked a 40-foot-wide wooden

Figure 1.3. The Commercial Slip, the western terminus of the Erie Canal, as viewed from Lake Street bridge, c. 1870–1896. *Source*: Buffalo and Erie County Library. Public domain.

Figure 1.4. 1872 Buffalo Atlas map of the Canal District. *Source*: Buffalo and Erie County Library. Public domain.

plank dock and extended 1,000 feet from the Commercial Slip to the foot of lower Main Street (see figures 1.5 and 1.6). All the waterfront and shipping-related commercial activity in Buffalo during the Canal Era was conducted at the Central Wharf, which was where the merchants who oversaw and arranged for the wholesale buying, selling, and forwarding of grain and other commodities had their offices. It was also where the insurance-related and vessel-related business of the city was conducted. "It was all concentrated right there, and the men who had charge of it were there, and anybody who had any business to transact with them had to go there to do it" (Conlin 2002, 20).

The ground level of the Central Wharf was occupied by warehouses. "To transport freight cargoes that had been stacked up on the dock, horse teams had to be backed through the first story warehouses to access the dock" (Conlin 2002, 22). A 15-foot-wide wooden gallery ran continuously along the fronts of the second story of the buildings that made up the Central Wharf. "There was a set of stairs every fifty feet or so the length of the balcony. The balcony itself became a busy thoroughfare communicating between hundreds of offices" (23). Merchants and vessel owners often gathered on the upper balcony to look out toward the lake for incoming vessels. The Board of Trade moved to the center of the Central Wharf early in 1862. The increased business activity that resulted increased the demand for offices located along the connecting balcony (Conlin 2016).

Figure 1.5. Central Wharf, c. 1868. *Source*: Western New York Heritage Collection.

OLD CENTRAL WHARF, ABANDONED 1883;
AND THE PIONEER STEAM CANAL BOAT WILLIAM NEWMAN.

Figure 1.6. People on balconies of the Central Wharf, c. 1870. *Source*: Courtesy Western New York Heritage, Harvey Holzworth collection.

Enlarging the Canal

The demand to ship goods on the canal was so great that just ten years after it opened the New York State Legislature passed a bill authorizing a significant enlargement of the canal. The bill called for widening the canal to 70 feet, increasing its depth to 7 feet, and enlarging and modifying the canal's locks to accommodate larger boats to allow for a more efficient flow of barge traffic. Political arguments over how to pay for the project delayed its completion. However, by 1850 the project had been sufficiently completed to enable boats 75 feet long and 12 feet wide, capable of carrying 2,500 bushels of wheat, to operate on the canal. In 1862, once the enlargement of the canal was fully completed, boats 98 feet long and 17 feet wide, capable of carrying 8,000 bushels of wheat, could navigate on the canal.

To shorten the length of time it took boats to travel the length of the canal, the number of locks was reduced (from 83 to 75), and double locks were added (18 feet × 110 feet) to allow boats traveling in opposite directions to enter locks at the same time. The canal was also straightened in places, which had the effect of shortening the canal from 363 miles to 350.5 miles. "While boats themselves [would] not move faster, fewer miles to travel and shorter lines at fewer locks meant it would take less time to reach one's destination" (Utter 2020, 245).

The Invention of the Grain Elevator

In 1843, Joseph Dart revolutionized the grain industry by building the first steam-powered grain elevator in Buffalo. Dart's elevator was built at the entrance to the Evans Ship Canal—a privately excavated canal that was connected to and accessed from the Buffalo River. In 1847, the Evans Elevator was also built along the same canal not far from Dart's Elevator.

A key feature incorporated into the Dart and Evans Elevators was the steam-powered bucket loader that was invented by Robert Dunbar. "The heart of the new invention [was] a looped or 'never-ending' conveyor-belt, made out of canvas, upon which large buckets made out of iron had been attached at regular intervals, which had to be long enough to reach *all the way down* into the hold of a grain-laden vessel and *all the way up* to the top of the warehouse" (W. J. Brown 2015, 60). After the grain was scooped up and deposited into storage bins with the elevator, the conveyor belt could be retracted, raised up, and stored within an appendage of the elevator.

Before Dunbar's invention, "a bulk shipment arriving in Buffalo consisting of 1,678 bushels of grain stored in barrels required seven days to unload by hand. With Dart's new elevator, this same task could be accomplished in less than two hours" (Bohen 2012, 9). In 1846, over four million bushels of wheat were received at the Port of Buffalo. By 1855, 13 more stream-powered grain elevators had been built along the banks of the Buffalo River, all of which used Dunbar's moveable conveyor belt.

All of these early elevators were constructed of wood, which made them relatively easy and quick to construct, but also made them extremely vulnerable to being destroyed by fire, which happened with alarming regularity. "The wooden elevators were in constant danger of fire from steam boiler sparks and combustible grain dust. Many elevators burned and were immediately rebuilt on a larger scale" (Conlin 2008, 29). The first Evans Elevator built on the Evans Ship Canal in 1847 burned down and was immediately rebuilt in 1863; it burned down again and was again immediately rebuilt in 1864. Joseph Dart's original elevator burned down in 1863 and was replaced one year later by the Bennett Elevator, which had a much larger storage capacity.

By the 1860s, giant wooden grain elevators, which were much larger than any other structures in the city, had become the dominant feature of the city's skyline (see figure 1.7). "At a time when masonry buildings were limited to six or seven stories in height, these wooden wonders rose to heights that would not be reached until the steel-framed high-rises of the 1890s" (Conlin 2008, 28). Dart's original grain elevator, built in 1842, had a storage capacity of 55,000 bushels of grain. The Coatsworth Elevator built in the 1890s, later known as the Kellogg B Elevator, could store 650,000 bushels.

As US grain production shifted from the East Coast to the Midwest, Buffalo became increasingly important as a place to ship, store, and mill grain. So many ships were arriving in Buffalo, there wasn't nearly enough dock space in the Inner Harbor to accommodate all the vessels. To provide additional wharves and dockage areas where vessels could unload and take on new shipments, a new canal (originally called as the Blackwell Canal, now known as the City Ship Canal) was excavated in the late 1840s, which branched off from the Buffalo River and ran south roughly parallel to the Lake Erie shore. Slips of modest length initially excavated into the

Figure 1.7. Downstream view of the Buffalo River from the Michigan Street Bridge, c. 1895. *Source*: Lower Lakes Historical Society.

shoreline of the Buffalo River were soon extended to connect to the new canal, thereby creating still more dockage space and wharves (figure 1.8).

The first railroad line reached Buffalo in 1842. However, the first railroads to serve Buffalo focused entirely on carrying passengers, because New York State restricted their ability to carry freight out of fear the railroads would compete with the Erie Canal. That restriction was lifted in 1851, and soon railroads proved to be a much more economical way of transporting grain and other commodities than the canal. Between 1854 and 1860, only 20 percent of the grain in bulk that was sent from Buffalo to cities on the East Coast was shipped by rail; the other 80 percent was transported on the Erie Canal/Hudson River route (W. J. Brown 2015, 15). From that point on, however, the percentage share of grain shipped on the canal steadily declined. By 1869, the combined movement of freight on the Erie and New York Central railroads exceeded the amount shipped on the Erie Canal. By 1872, railroads carried as much wheat and corn in bulk to New York City as the Erie Canal. From then on, the amount of freight shipped on the canal steadily declined. In 1882, the property on the waterfront that the Central Wharf had occupied for a half century was abandoned and taken over by the Delaware Lackawanna and Western Railroad, which demolished it and laid down a set of tracks across the property.

Major changes were also taking place in how other properties along the waterfront were being used and developed. Consider, for example, the changes that took place on the 600-acre tract south of the Buffalo Creek that George Washington Tifft purchased in 1846. (See Early History of Tifft Farm: From Farm to Transshipment Terminal on page 19.)

By the 1890s, railroads were dominating the transshipment not just of wheat but also of iron ore, coal, timber, and many other commodities. As the amount of freight handled by rail lines through Buffalo increased, rail yards in the city were expanded. By 1900, Buffalo had become the second largest rail center in the country, second only to Chicago, and Buffalo's population had increased to 353,388, making it the eighth largest city in the United States.

Up until the 1890s, every elevator erected in Buffalo had been built entirely of wood, which made them highly vulnerable to being destroyed by explosions and fire. The first Connecting Terminal elevator built of wood in 1882 at the confluence of the City Ship Canal and Buffalo River (whose storage capacity of one million bushels of grain made it one of the largest elevators in the city at the time) was destroyed by fire in 1914. The Great Eastern Elevator, which was constructed with eight million board feet of timber, provided a dramatic example of just how vulnerable

Figure 1.8. Slips and adjuncts of the Erie Canal. *Source*: *History of the Canal System of the State of New York* by Noble E. Whitford (Albany: Brandow Publishing Co., 1906), vol. 1, opposite p. 588. Public domain.

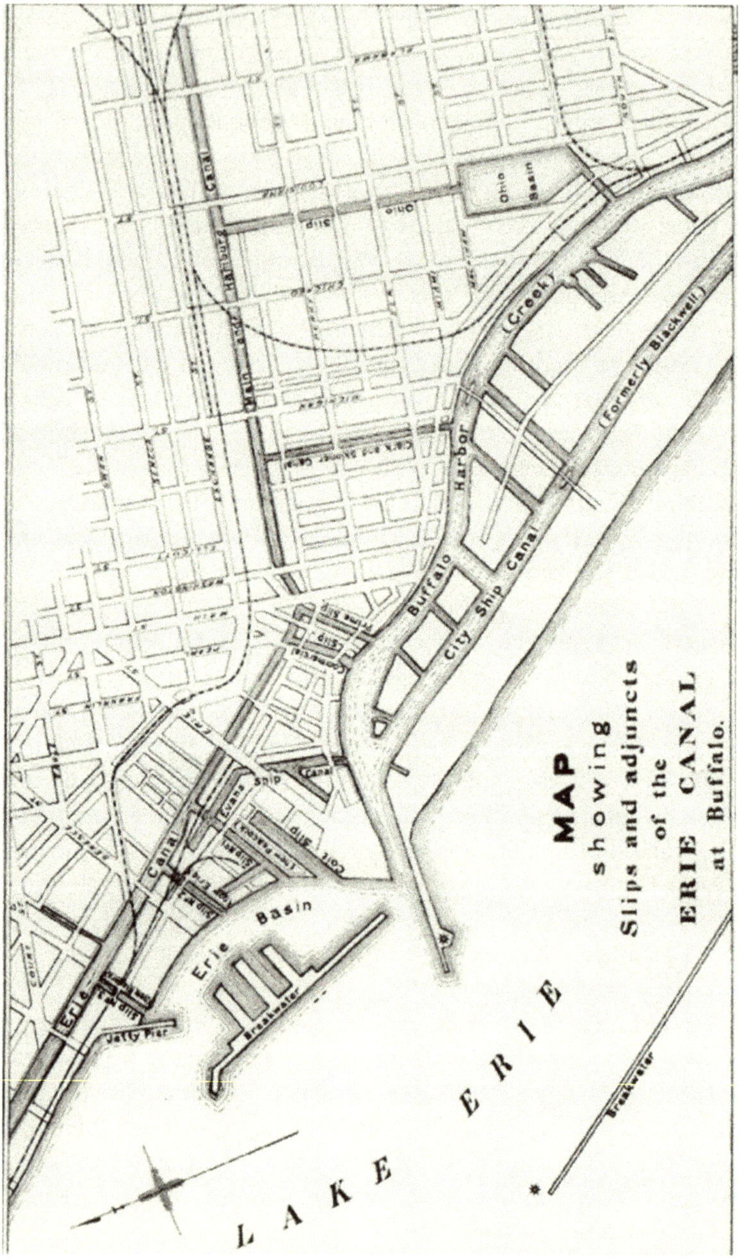

Early History of Tifft Farm:
From Farm to Transshipment Terminal

The Tifft property initially prospered as a farm, the rich bottomland providing excellent pasture for the dairy cows that supplied the family milk business. For many years, Tifft Farm's milk was sold to grocers, hotels, and vessels tied up in Buffalo Harbor. By the 1850s, Tifft Farm had become an important center for the trading of livestock. In 1883, the Buffalo Creek Railroad obtained permission from the city to extend the Blackwell Canal to the Tifft Farm property. Not long thereafter, the property was sold to a Pennsylvania company, which leased the land to the Lehigh Valley Railroad; the railroad then developed the property into a major transshipment point for coal, lumber, iron ore, and other commodities shipped to Buffalo on the Great Lakes.

A series of canals, totaling 11,400 feet in length, were excavated on the property; these canals were connected to the Blackwell Canal so that ships could access them from the Blackwell Canal. Docks and rail sidings were constructed along the Tifft Farm canals to facilitate the loading and unloading of various commodities from ships that entered the site. Elaborate docking facilities and elevated trestles were constructed along the canals to handle the unloading of coal and iron ore. In the 1880s, six lumber companies also operated lumber yards at Tifft Farm. A middle canal with docks on either site was competed in 1885. A coal trestle capable of holding 100,000 tons had a tunnel track under it for reloading into rail cars. Two years later, a freight house 450 feet long by 116 feet wide had been completed, and contracts had been signed for the building of an iron ore dock 440 feet long by 116 feet in length (Wolfe and Tifft Farm Committee 1983).

such a structure could be to fire. In 1900, just four years after the Great Eastern began operating, it burned to the ground in what was described at the time as "a grand conflagration."

New Ways of Constructing Grain Elevators

To reduce the frequency with which grain elevators were destroyed by fire, engineers began using other materials such as steel in an effort to make the storage bins in grain elevators more fireproof. In 1894, George Pillsbury, the Minneapolis flour magnate, arranged for the Great Northern Railroad to construct the largest elevator and flour mill in the world in Buffalo, which would then be operated by the Pillsbury Company (Goldman 1983, 143). The Great Northern elevator was constructed on Ganson Street along the City Ship Canal and began operating in 1897 (figure 1.9). The elevator's 99-foot-tall steel bins rested on steel girders above a concrete floor and were enclosed within a 300-foot-long, 10-story high curtain wall made of brick that made the structure look somewhat similar to earlier wooden elevators (DeCroix 2022, 26).

The same year as the Great Northern Elevator was completed, the two-million-bushel, steel-bin Electric Elevator was built along the Buffalo River at Ohio Street. The steel bins of this elevator were not surrounded by a curtain wall but rather were left outside and clearly visible. Another steel-binned elevator that left its steel bins exposed to the elements was the Great Eastern Elevator, which was built in 1901. In contrast to the Electric and Great Eastern Elevators, the Dakota Elevator, completed in 1902, concealed its steel bins behind a façade of corrugated iron panels (Leary and Sholes 1997, 29).

Figure 1.9. Great Northern Elevator and ships on City Ship Canal, c. 1900. *Source*: Library of Congress Prints and Photographs Division, http://hdl.loc.gov/loc.pnp/det.4a08420. Public domain.

By 1910, so much Midwest grain was arriving in Buffalo that there was a pressing need for more and ever larger elevators where the grain could be stored before it was milled. After the first Connecting Terminal Elevator burned down in 1913, the Pennsylvania Railroad lost no time in erecting another elevator on the same site that would be much more fireproof. The new Connecting Terminal Elevator, with fire-resistant 100-foot-tall steel-lined grain bins, was completed in 1915.

The preferred material for constructing grain elevators and making them more fireproof would eventually become reinforced concrete. A number of massive concrete grain elevators would soon be erected farther up the Buffalo River. The Concrete Central Elevator, constructed between 1915 and 1917, stretched nearly a quarter mile along the Buffalo River and was capable of storing 4.5 million bushels of grain. The Standard Elevator built in 1928 could store three million bushels. On the opposite side of the river, more concrete elevators were erected in the area that has come to be known to as "Silo City." By the 1930s, Buffalo was receiving and milling more grain than any other city in the country.

Despite the outbreak of World War II, Buffalo continued to process and ship more grain than any other port in the United States well into the 1940s. The outbreak of World War II forced American shippers to avoid Montreal and route all their grain through Buffalo. More than 200 million bushels of grain passed through Buffalo's elevators every year during World War II. "Demand for temporary storage in Buffalo was in fact so great that extensions or annexes were added to the Eastern States Grain Elevator in 1941, the Standard Elevator in 1941, the GLF elevator complex in 1942, and the Electric Elevator in 1942" (W. J. Brown 2015, 106).

By 1950 there were 46 sets of concrete grain elevators in Buffalo, the vast majority of which were located along the Buffalo River (figure 1.10). By that time, Buffalo's population had increased to 580,132, and it was expected that the city would continue to grow and prosper well into the future. Construction of the St. Lawrence Seaway began in 1954, which local officials and business leaders seemed to assume would make Buffalo a major world port. It turned out that the opening of the St. Lawrence Seaway had exactly the opposite effect, by making Buffalo much less important as a Great Lakes port.

After the Seaway opened in 1959, cargoes could be shipped directly from western Great Lakes ports to the Atlantic without off-loading them in Buffalo—thereby making the function Buffalo had historically performed as a point of transshipment unnecessary. As more and more ships bypassed Buffalo, the amount of Midwestern grain stored and milled in

Figure 1.10. 1995 photo of grain elevators along the Buffalo River taken from a plane headed to Detroit from Buffalo; on the far side of the river from left to right are the Concrete Central, Cargill Superior, Marine A, Lake & Rail, Perot, American, and Electric Elevators; on the near side of the river near the Ohio Street Bridge is the Standard Elevator. Tifft Farm Preserve can be seen in the upper left. *Source*: Photo by the author.

Buffalo's grain elevators significantly declined. "In 1966 alone, five flour mills were shut down" (Goldman 1983, 271). Three years before the Seaway had opened, 130,175,962 bushels of grain were unloaded in Buffalo; by 1971 the amount of grain unloaded in Buffalo had fallen to 54,261,253 bushels (O'Connell 1972).

Chapter Two

Industrialization and Contamination
of the Buffalo River

Grain elevators and flour mills weren't the only industries that developed and operated along the Buffalo River. Steel and coal companies, chemical companies, oil refineries, and other industries also developed along the river, which did even greater environmental harm to the river and its shoreline than the elevators and the mills.

Buffalo Union Furnace Company and Donner Steel Company both operated iron manufacturing plants along the Buffalo River; each used coke derived from northern Pennsylvania. In 1917, the two companies entered into a partnership and established the Donner-Union Coke Company. Chemicals the company produced during World War I were in high demand because the production of TNT required the use of coal chemical by-products. With the help of the US Army's Ordnance Department, Donner-Union Coke began constructing a 150-oven coke plant in Buffalo. The war ended before the plant was completed, but the army elected to finish the plant and then lease it to Donner-Union Coke. Hanna Furnace Corporation subsequently purchased the Buffalo Union Furnace Company, and the company's name was changed to Donner Hanna Coke Corporation. The new plant was opened in 1920. In 1930, Donner Hanna was acquired by Republic Steel. At one point, Republic Steel's Buffalo River factory employed 2,500 workers.

On the opposite side of the river, directly across from Republic Steel's Buffalo River plant, was National Aniline's huge Buffalo River industrial complex, the largest producer of dyes in the country; it also manufactured a wide array of resins, plasticizers, and food colorings. By World War II, National Aniline was manufacturing khaki, navy, and camouflage dyes, insect repellents, detergents, and antimalarial drugs. In 1958, the company changed its name to Allied Chemical. In 1977, Allied Chemical sold 63 acres of its property to the Buffalo Color Corporation, which specialized in the manufacture of indigo dye for blue jeans, a highly toxic substance.

At its height, Buffalo Color employed 3,000 people. The westernmost portion of the Buffalo Color property (the 19-acre Buffalo Color Peninsula) was where dyestuff was manufactured. In 1997, after being declared a Superfund site, the upland portion of the peninsula was capped to contain the contaminated soil. An impermeable slurry wall was constructed around the perimeter of the peninsula to prevent contaminated groundwater from reaching the river, and wells were constructed to collect and treat the leachate released by the buried material. In 2004, Buffalo Color declared bankruptcy. Chemicals in various stages of production were abandoned, and the property was left littered with chemical by-products.

In 2010, the Buffalo Urban Development Corporation hired Sasaki Associates and Biohabitats Inc. to prepare a master plan showing how the Republic Steel Plant property could be developed into a business park. A voluntary cleanup of the property begun in 2004 and completed in 2007 removed contaminated soil and underground storage tanks from the property. A more thorough environmental remediation of the property was later carried out after the property was designated as the South Buffalo Brownfield Opportunity Area. Tesla's 1.2-million-square-foot Gigafactory was eventually developed on the property, which began producing photovoltaic cells in modules in 2017.

The Environmental Cost of Buffalo's Industrial Growth

Buffalo reaped considerable economic benefit from all the industries that developed along the Buffalo River as a result of the city's growing twentieth-century importance as a center of commerce and industry. But that economic prosperity came at an environmental cost. Toxic materials discharged and allowed to seep into the river were killing fish and wildlife in staggering numbers. In 1967, the river was declared to be biologically dead. A year later in 1968, the river caught fire, apparently set off by a workman's torch that ignited gasoline that had been dumped into the river.

A 6.2-mile-long federal navigation channel has traditionally been maintained within the Buffalo River by the US Army Corps of Engineers (USACE) to a depth of 23 feet to enable large vessels to reach the industries that developed along the river. Unfortunately, the low hydraulic gradient of the river that was created by regularly dredging the navigation channel to that uniform depth had the unintended effect of undermining the natural processes that might otherwise have helped sustain the environmental health of the river. "The Buffalo River once ended in cattail marshes along the shoreline of Lake Erie and supported an array of wildlife, soils, vegetation, and microscopic creatures. Once it became a channelized waterway of uniform depth with a constructed shoreline, it no longer supported diverse wildlife, nor could it flood and restore the cyclical sedimentation of the land" (Schneekloth 2006b, 268).

In 1987, the International U.S./Canadian Commission identified 42 toxic hot spots in the Great Lakes region as areas of concern (AOC). One of those toxic hot spots was the Buffalo River. Designating the Buffalo River as an area of concern meant that a remedial action plan (RAP) needed to be prepared and implemented to address the identified problems. By that time, the day-to-day lives of most Buffalo residents had become increasingly disconnected from the Buffalo River, in part because fewer people were employed by companies that were still operating along the river. Also, because so much of the property along the river had been given over to industry, there were few places where people could gain access to the river, or even see the water. For the vast majority of city residents, the river was out-of-sight and out-of-mind.

Formation of Friends of the Buffalo River

Working in partnership with a local Citizen's Remedial Advisory Committee, a remedial action plan (RAP) for the Buffalo River was developed and approved in 1989 by the New York State Department of Environmental Conservation (NYSDEC) (https://www.epa.gov/buffalo-river-aoc). A number of the individuals who had served on the Remedial Advisory Committee and helped develop the RAP decided to establish a nonprofit organization called Friends of the Buffalo River (FBR) so that they could continue to speak out on behalf of the river and also make sure the RAP was properly implemented by NYSDEC.[1] The chief organizer behind forming the nonprofit organization was Ken Sherman, an ordained Lutheran minister and peace activist who was fully engaged in social and environmental justice movements in Buffalo. "He was one of the best organizers I have ever worked with," said Lynda Schneekloth (email, January 30, 2022).

NYSDEC made little progress during the 1990s in implementing the RAP it had approved in 1983, and by the early 2000s the cleanup effort had basically stalled. Meanwhile, FBR was collaborating with area residents and other nongovernmental organizations in carrying out small-scale habitat restoration projects along the river. It also endeavored to increase public interest in the health of the river by bringing people to the river for cleanups, canoe trips, and "nature hikes"—activities that NYSDEC didn't consider part of its mission.

In an effort to jumpstart the cleanup, the Environmental Protection Agency issued a request for proposals in 2002 inviting nongovernmental agencies to apply for funding to manage and coordinate the river cleanup. FBR submitted an application and in 2003 became the first nonprofit organization in the Great Lakes Basin to be awarded funding by the EPA to play such a role.

In the early 2000s, Lynda Schneekloth, a founding member of FBR, and a friend of hers launched a canoe out into the Buffalo River from the Ohio Street boat launch. What follows is Schneekloth's account of the experience.

What It Was Like Being Out on the
Buffalo River in the Early 2000s

Across the river are two enormous grain elevators and the ruins of a former industrial building, now filled with trees and grasses . . . The hollow grain elevators, dying industries and ghostly structures are the remains of the technological utopian vision that gripped Buffalo between the opening of the Erie Canal in 1825 and the closing of heavy steel plants in the 1980s. The landscape we see from the river is the land-scape of . . . a dream in disarray, visible in the ruins of the artifacts and buildings and in the overgrown wild landscapes. The quarter-mile-long Concrete Central grain elevator sits abandoned on a peninsula, surrounded by railroad tracks and grasses and shrubs that are home to deer, foxes and hawks. In spite of being so close to the central city, one hears very little except the periodic trains. The place is void of urban sounds. (Schneekloth 2006b, 253)

Chapter Three

Development and Contamination
of the Outer Harbor

The Outer Harbor was the last portion of Buffalo's waterfront to be industrially developed and in many ways was the most gravely affected by that development. It is also the least well understood portion of Buffalo's waterfront, because much of the area we now call "the Outer Harbor" didn't really exist until after 1900. Much of what existed instead were low-lying areas that were regularly flooded by storm surges coming in off Lake Erie. The Outer Harbor only achieved its present-day form after decades during which low-lying areas were progressively filled in with an unregulated, often toxic mix of waste materials to create building sites for industrial and commercial enterprises.

In 1838, construction of a seawall began that was intended to protect the Outer Harbor's vulnerable, low-lying shoreline. The seawall basically followed the present-day right of way of Fuhrmann Boulevard but very soon proved to be woefully inadequate. In 1844, a sharp drop in barometric pressure and high winds off the lake sent a massive wall of water over the seawall, flooding the waterfront and destroying all the ships and buildings in its path. A substantial portion of the seawall that had been completed up to that point was destroyed. Seventy-eight people drowned. The damaged portion of the seawall was eventually repaired and the seawall was completed in 1868, but few people believed it would provide an adequate level of protection.

In 1868, the US Army Corps of Engineers (USACE) approved building a breakwater roughly 3,000 feet offshore to intercept and break up waves before they reached the shore. Construction of the first 4,000-foot-long section of the breakwater began in 1869. Five years later, work began extending the breakwater farther south another 3,600 feet to Stony Point. When the 7,600-foot offshore breakwater was completed in 1883, the previously constructed seawall was no longer considered necessary. For many years, ownership of the seawall strip corridor was contested in court, until in April 1911 when Mayor Louis Fuhrmann was successful in winning the seawall strip for the City of Buffalo (Keppel 2023).[1] Soon thereafter, New York State approved construction of a road along the seawall corridor, originally called the Hamburg Turnpike, which led Bethlehem Steel to build a steel plant on a large tract of vacant land just over the line in Lackawanna that would employ thousands of workers.

Poorly drained swampland between the Turnpike and the lake remained undeveloped and continued to be regularly inundated by storms. In 1899, Buffalo's municipal government ceded the "underwater lands" along the coast to the owners of adjacent properties in the hope that they would fill in and develop those areas out to a newly defined harbor line. By 1925, several piers had been constructed to provide sites on which industrial facilities could be developed. The materials used to construct these piers consisted of "dredged spoils from the Buffalo River and other canals and docking areas, dumped off-spec solid and hazardous wastes associated with major industries in the area, and various City of Buffalo wastes, primarily incinerator ash" (Traynor 2018, 45).

One such man-made pier was created in the early 1920s in the northern portion of the Outer Harbor and occupied by the Buffalo Marine Construction Company, one of the largest shipbuilding companies in the city. Next to that pier was the city-owned Municipal Pier and an adjacent area which was used as a city dump.

At the other end of the Outer Harbor another man-made pier was constructed to accommodate the Saskatchewan Cooperative grain elevator, which began operating in 1925, which is known today more commonly as the Cargill Pool. (See figure 3.1, which shows the pier and Saskatchewan elevator extending out into the lake.) Rail lines of the Lehigh Valley Railroad extended alongside the elevator and along the pier where ships docked, so that grain could be offloaded either directly to the elevator itself or to awaiting rail cars. The elevator's Outer Harbor location had the advantage of enabling vessels to save time by not having to make their way through the congested Inner Harbor to grain elevators located further up the Buffalo River. In 1945 the Saskatchewan elevator was purchased by the Pillsbury Company, which operated it until 1959. Cargill purchased the elevator in 1964 and used it to store excess grain.

Figure 3.1. Buffalo's heavily industrialized waterfront, c. 1924: the canals of the Lehigh Valley Railroad's transshipment terminal at Tifft Farm are in the center of the photo; in the upper right sticking out into the lake is the Saskatchewan Cooperative elevator and beyond it is the Bethlehem Steel Works. *Source*: Public domain.

Between 1927 and 1931, the Terminal Transportation Company constructed a massive 350,000-square-foot commercial structure on another man-made pier which was also served by a rail line operated by the Lehigh Valley Railroad. In the 1940s, the building and property were acquired and operated by Merchant Refrigerator. In the 1950s, the property was acquired by Freezer Queen, a packaging company that specialized in producing frozen TV dinners. At one time Freezer Queen had over 1,000 employees. The plant failed a USDA food safety inspection in 2006 and was ordered to shut down in 2006. The structure was demolished in 2016.

By far the largest industrial facility that operated on the Outer Harbor was Ford Motor Company's 600,000-square-foot automobile assembly plant, which was built on the southern portion of the Outer Harbor. When the Ford Motor Company purchased the 94-acre site in 1930, it was largely underwater and had to be extensively filled in before the plant could be constructed. Material used to fill in the site included gravel, sand, silt, slag, glass, and metal. The steel-reinforced factory, designed by Albert Kahn and completed in 1931, soon began churning out cars and trucks. Concrete docks along opposite sides of the plant enabled it to receive materials needed to construct vehicles, and also to ship completed vehicles, via lake freighters as well as by rail. In 1953, 1,250 workers were employed at the plant. In 1956, a newly finished car or truck left the assembly line every 2.5 minutes, resulting in the production of an average of 200–300 vehicles every 24 hours.

The opening of the St. Lawrence Seaway in 1959 put an end to the 150-year-long locational advantage Buffalo had enjoyed as a place to store, mill, and transship grain, and caused many other Buffalo-based industries to rethink their rationales for having located their manufacturing operations in Buffalo. Foreseeing that the Seaway would undermine the advantage it had long enjoyed by manufacturing automobiles in Buffalo, Ford Motor Company announced that it was going to close its Outer Harbor automobile assembly plant and move its manufacturing operations to Lorain, Ohio. After Ford closed the plant and abandoned the property in 1958, the City of Buffalo assumed ownership of the property and transferred it to the Niagara Frontier Transportation Authority (NFTA), which in addition to operating the city's bus system and airport also functioned as the city's Port Authority.

The Outer Harbor as a Dumping Ground

In addition to using an unregulated mix of waste materials to construct the piers on which Outer Harbor industrial facilities were developed, the Outer Harbor was also where much of the city's trash and solid waste was disposed of during the nineteenth century. The first city dump on the Outer Harbor was developed next to the city-owned Municipal Pier, and the entire low-lying area adjacent to the pier was filled in with solid waste. Chris Andrle frequently took part in the annual cleanup of the Outer Harbor that was conducted by Buffalo Niagara Riverkeeper. "Much of the Outer Harbor from Tifft Street north to Wilkeson Pointe Park was used as a city dump. So much garbage was dumped there that it regularly floated up to the surface" (C. Andrle, email, June 22, 2021).

Another portion of the Outer Harbor that was used as a place to dump waste was Tifft Farm, which for 50 years the Lehigh Valley Railroad (LVRR) had operated as a transshipment terminal. When City Ship Canal was filled in just north of Tifft Farm in 1946, ships could no longer reach the canals and the adjacent rail sidings that had been developed there.

As a result, LVRR shut down the terminal and abandoned the property. In 1955, Republic Steel purchased the property from the City of Buffalo, and between 1955 and 1972 disposed of slag, fly ash, and other waste materials generated at its Buffalo River steel mill at Tifft Farm.

More waste material would be deposited on the Outer Harbor as a result of Governor Averill Harriman's 1958 announcement that a limited access highway would be built between the recently opened Skyway and Tifft Street interchange to make it easier for workers to get to jobs at industrial plants along the corridor. The four-lane, 1.2-mile-long divided highway, referred to at the time as the "Fuhrmann El," was constructed on an embankment that was created by depositing slag and incinerator ash along the right-of-way, placing the expressway 18–25 feet above the original Fuhrmann Boulevard (Keppel 2023). The original Fuhrmann Boulevard became a service road that was initially intended to provide access to adjoining industrial properties.

In the early 1970s, the Buffalo Sewer Authority needed to remove two million cubic yards of incinerated solid waste from Squaw Island (now known as Unity Island) so that a sewage treatment plant could be built on the island and identified Tifft Farm as the best place to dispose of the material. The City of Buffalo subsequently acquired the property, and between 1973 and 1975, the two million cubic yards of incinerated waste material were transported to Tifft Farm. (The story of how citizens and nongovernmental organizations minimized the environmental harm that was done by disposing of that waste at Tifft Farm is described in chapter 12.)

The Outer Harbor was also where most of the contaminated sediment was disposed of that the USACE dredged from the navigation channels of the Buffalo River, City Ship Canal, and Black Rock Canal. Over 1.1 million cubic yards of dredged material was deposited into a diked disposal site south of the Small Boat Harbor between 1965 and 1979. The parking area just south of the Small Boat Harbor in Buffalo Harbor State Park now sits on land that was created by that landfill. A 55-acre diked disposal area was also developed at Times Beach at the northern end of the Outer Harbor. 550,000 cubic yards of dredged material were deposited into that diked area. Chapter 12 describes why the USACE stopped depositing dredged material at Times Beach in 1977.

Chapter Four

The Decline of the Inner Harbor and Lower Main Street

At the height of the Canal Era, with large numbers of Great Lakes vessels and canal barges arriving in Buffalo every day, the Canal District was the epicenter of commercial activity in the city. However, by 1900 railroads had taken over the lions' share of the business of shipping commodities and freight across New York State. In 1903, the New York State legislature made one last attempt to extend the useful life of the canal as a means of shipping freight by approving state funding to pay for enlarging and reconstructing the canal to enable it to accommodate large self-propelled barges that could carry larger quantities of freight. Construction of the renamed New York State Barge Canal began in 1905 and was completed in 1918. The Barge Canal used portions of the Mohawk River that the original Erie Canal had bypassed so as to enter the centers of cities such as Rochester, Syracuse, and Schenectady, but mostly followed and enlarged the same channel as the original Erie Canal. The canal's western terminus was relocated to Tonawanda, and a huge storm drain (the Hamburg Drain) was placed within the walls of the Commercial Slip before it was buried and covered over.[1]

By the 1930s, the Canal District had become an impoverished Italian, predominantly Sicilian, neighborhood increasingly victimized by absentee ownership and crime. Criminal activity was so rampant that "Italian children were trained not to 'see' any crime, but just to keep on walking; they were warned, too, against answering the door at night. 'Once it got dark, you stayed in the house'" (Vogel, Patton, and Redding 2009, 3).

On January 1, 1936, a gas explosion in a tenement building in the Dante Place neighborhood killed five people and upended the lives of hundreds more. "The extent of the tragedy touched a chord in Buffalo, and the sorrow would soon give way to an anger that would call for public housing and an end to the tenements" (Vogel, Patton, and Redding 2009, 1–2). In 1949 the City of Buffalo authorized the Buffalo Municipal Housing Authority (BMHA) to apply for federal and state funding to develop a low-income housing project at Dante Place. While the Dante housing project was under construction, a scattered-site approach to developing low-income housing was approved by the Buffalo Common Council, but that approach was vetoed by Mayor Frank Sedita, who considered it politically safer to concentrate low-income housing on a cleared site in "a fairly isolated waterfront site that few people at the time lived near or were paying much attention to" (Palen 1983, 182).

Every structure that had once existed within a large area was demolished. A photograph taken by Wilbur H. Porterfield, published in the *Buffalo Courier-Express* in 1950, was accompanied by the following caption: "Blitzed London of World War II had nothing on [what happened in] the Dante Place area. Most of the tenements and buildings [were] reduced to rubble to make way for civic improvements" (Keppel 2014b).

At the same time as the Dante Place housing project was being carried out, the tracks of the New York Central Railroad were being relocated to enable the Niagara section of the New York State Thruway to be constructed through the downtown. As a result, the size of area that was subjected to widespread demolition was actually much greater than would have been required to just accommodate the housing project—further isolating the site from the rest of the downtown.

The seven 12-story brick towers that were ultimately constructed contained a total of 616 one-, two-, and three-bedroom units. Not long after the Dante housing project opened, the City of Buffalo applied for state funding to construct 1,700 low-income housing units in high-rise buildings on the city's predominantly African-American East Side. By 1960, a large proportion of the tenants at Dante Place was composed of families and households that had been uprooted from condemned housing by the East Side urban renewal project, which caused Dante Place to be viewed as an undesirable place to live. Apartment vacancies at Dante Place soared.

In an effort to stem the financial losses it was incurring due to the high rates of vacancy at Dante Place, BMHA decided to convert Dante Place into a middle-income apartment complex and move low-rent tenants from Dante Place back to the newly constructed public housing projects on the city's East Side.[2] In 1961, the conversion to a middle-income privately managed apartment development was completed, and the complex was renamed Marine Drive Apartments.

The Skyway and the Niagara Section of the Thruway

When the Buffalo Skyway was conceived in the 1950s, futuristic designs of elevated vehicle-moving systems had become highly popular, and high-level bridges were being planned and built in a number of other cities, many of them sharing the Skyway name. "The Chicago Skyway opened in 1958, crossing the Calumet River above the city's east side area. Other Great Lakes structures included the Burlington Bay Skyway Bridge (1958) and St. Catharine's Garden City Skyway (1963), both within 60 miles of Buffalo in Ontario, Canada, on the highway to Toronto" (Graebner 2007, 87). In that sense, Buffalo's Skyway wasn't so much a unique and place-specific response to a local transportation problem as it was a structure that was fairly typical of the period.

The *Buffalo News* described the Skyway as a "dream come true," in that it would enable Buffalo residents employed at the Ford Assembly Plant and at iron and steel manufacturing plants to avoid the delays they often encountered going to and from work caused by large ships making their way up and down the Buffalo River. As it turned out, the Buffalo Skyway couldn't have been more ill-timed. In 1959, four years after the Skyway was completed, the opening of the St. Lawrence Seaway led to a sharp decline in the number of ships delivering grain to elevators along the Buffalo River.

The engineers who planned and designed the Skyway didn't seem to have considered that the construction of the Skyway might make it more difficult to develop the Waterfront Redevelopment Area (see figure 4.1). The overhang of the Skyway clearly made the Inner Harbor less appealing at ground level, and the concrete structural elements required to support the Skyway constrained how the site could be redeveloped—presenting a set of "givens" that future developers would somehow have to work around.

The construction of the Niagara Section of the Thruway had a less immediate and less direct impact on the Waterfront Redevelopment Area than the Skyway. It nevertheless inflicted considerable long-term harm on the area of lower Main Street by undermining the long-standing connection

Figure 4.1. 1972 photo taken from the foot of lower Main Street showing the Skyway winding its way across the area of the Inner Harbor that 50 years later would become Canalside, with the Dante public housing project in the background. *Source*: Photo by the author.

and flow of activity between lower Main Street and downtown. The path chosen for the Thruway took it across Main Street just north of Memorial Auditorium, which meant that the highway had to be elevated so as not to obstruct vehicular traffic on Main Street. Because the Thruway at that point was a six-lane divided highway, an exceptionally wide structure was required to support it, which cast a pall upon a wide swath of the downtown. People could still walk to and from lower Main Street, but the spooky and noisy environment that the overhanging highway created at street level had the predictable effect of discouraging such movement. The long-term result was to significantly depress the amount of activity along lower Main Street.

Lost Generators of Activity

A good deal of the activity that took place along lower Main Street during the first half of the twentieth century was generated by two railroad passenger terminals that operated there. The Delaware, Lackawanna, and Western's (DL&W) passenger terminal was at the extreme southern end of lower Main Street, while the Lehigh Valley Railroad (LVRR) passenger terminal was further north. The closure of the LVRR's passenger terminal in 1952 was hastened by the NYS Thruway Authority's taking of its four-track main line by eminent domain to construct I-190 through the downtown.

After standing vacant and abandoned for eight years, the LVRR terminal was demolished in 1960 to enable construction of the 146,000-square-foot Donovan State Office Building, which opened in 1962. It was hoped that the activity generated by the new state office building, which housed 18 state agencies, would help revitalize the area.

The same year as the Donovan State Office Building opened, the DL&W railroad abandoned its passenger terminal further down lower Main Street, and the Buffalo Common Council designated 12.5 acres between lower Main Street and the Buffalo River as the Waterfront Redevelopment Area. An urban renewal plan approved in 1963 called for a new downtown neighborhood to be developed that would consist of medium- and high-density housing, a marina, a community college, and an elementary school, as well as open space and recreational amenities oriented toward the waterfront. None of these recommendations were ever acted upon.

The Waterfront Redevelopment Area remained undeveloped and unused for years, except as surface parking. In an effort to generate some activity within the area, the Buffalo Urban Renewal Agency in 1976 filed a request with the US Department of the Navy asking that it provide a decommissioned naval vessel for the purpose of establishing the Naval and Serviceman's Park at the foot of lower Main Street. Development of the park, later named Buffalo and Erie County Naval and Military Park, began in 1977. When it opened to the public on July 4, 1979, it consisted of the cruiser USS *Little Rock* and the destroyer USS *The Sullivans*. The vessels were moored end to end along the Buffalo River, which maximized their visibility but also had the effect of blocking views of the water. As it turned out, simply mooring the naval vessels along the shoreline, absent other improvements and attractions, failed to generate sufficient activity to rejuvenate the area.

In 1971, roughly half of the 18,000 workers at Bethlehem Steel were permanently laid off (Goldman 1983, 273). In 1982, Bethlehem Steel completely closed its Lackawanna steel plant, and laid off the 10,000 workers who had remained working there. That same year, another 350 people lost their jobs when National Steel Corporation closed Hanna Furnace's Outer

Harbor plant. A year later in 1983 Republic Steel permanently closed its Buffalo River steel mill.

There were also steep reductions in the number of workers employed at Trico Corporation, the world's largest manufacturer of windshield wipers—one of the largest and last remaining locally owned companies in the city. Founded in Buffalo, the company at one time employed roughly 3,000 people, most of whom were hourly workers. At the company's annual meeting in 1986, R. John Oishei, the chairman and CEO of the company and the son of John R. Oishei, who founded the company in 1917, announced that the company was going to move all its windshield wiper assembly work to Mexico and Texas. "Today we have an inability to find individuals to work for wages that would allow us to keep all our operations here. We're surely not going to stand by and watch our profits drop until we go bankrupt," Oishei said ("Trico Products Corporation," 2024). The jobs that were subsequently eliminated in Buffalo paid an average of $15 an hour, including benefits. At that time, Trico was paying workers in Mexico between $1.20 and $1.30 per hour, including benefits, while those in Texas received between $4.50 and $6.00 an hour.

Buffalo's industrial economy was in free fall. Between 1977 and 1987, 45,000 jobs—31 percent of Buffalo's manufacturing positions—were lost. The harm done by such job losses was magnified by the fact that a large proportion of the jobs that were lost had paid above-average wages. The loss of so many high-paying jobs had a devastating impact on working-class neighborhoods throughout the city. "The decline of industry struck at the core and the fiber of the community, undermining family stability, weakening neighborhoods, and permanently altering the values and beliefs many people had long lived by" (Goldman 1983, 273). It also accelerated the exodus of educated and ambitious young people out of the city.

Between 1960 and 1980, the City of Buffalo lost 36 percent of its population as well as a huge share of its manufacturing jobs, increasingly jeopardizing the fiscal stability of municipal government. At the same time, the altered socioeconomic composition of the city, and the city's increased dependence on federal and state funding, also provided an unprecedented political opportunity for the Democratic Party to solidify its hold on city government. No one was more aware of that than Frank Sedita, who was Buffalo's mayor between 1958 and 1961, and then again between 1966 and 1973. "The Republican Party became a cypher in city affairs as its members moved to the suburbs or the Sunbelt. The so-called 'Democratic Machine' was freed from electoral accountability through default, not design. The business elites, depleted by the Depression, mergers and old age, had far less clout . . . The glue for the Sedita coalition was outside [federal and state] money not subject to political control, which came in unprecedented volume . . . intended to reverse [the city's] decline" (Palen 1983, 205).

The Marine Midland Center Project

As losses of population and employment accelerated in the 1960s and 1970s, tax revenues collected by the City of Buffalo plummeted, and the financial condition of the city became increasingly precarious. As a result, the city was understandably reluctant to undertake any project that would require it to spend any of its own revenue and was eager to embrace any project that promised to increase the city's tax base—particularly one largely paid for with federal and/or state funding. It was in that context that in 1966 the city approved creation of a ten-acre urban redevelopment district just north of where the Niagara Extension of the New York Thruway crossed Main Street.

In 1967, the Boston-based real estate development firm Cabot, Cabot & Forbes (CCF) announced that a high-rise office building would be built within the redevelopment district. Marine Midland Bank, which had already been planning to expand and had been in the process of buying up properties in the area soon thereafter began negotiating with CCF to become the main tenant of the 1.2 million-square-foot project. At the 1969 groundbreaking ceremony, Erie County Executive B. John Tutuska described the project as a "major transplant" into a "rundown, disheveled, unkempt and neglected area." *Buffalo Magazine* in 1970 called the area "Buffalo's skid row." With funding provided by the US Department of Housing and Urban Development and the New York State Department of Housing, construction began in March 1969 and was completed in 1972.

It was expected that the 38-story office tower (the tallest building in New York State outside New York City) would rejuvenate the surrounding area. One reason that didn't happen was the way the project was designed. "All of the buildings' entrances [were] set back from the surrounding streets. Its engagement with the street life of the city was so minimal, it might as well be a feudal castle" (Langdon, *Buffalo News*, November 17, 1980). A large, often windswept public plaza surrounded two sides of the office tower. A good way of judging the design of a public plaza is the extent to which people are drawn to and delight in spending time in it.

By that measure, the public plaza leading to and surrounding the Marine Midland Center office tower was an abysmal failure. Writing seven years after the project was completed, *Buffalo News* columnist Philip Langdon observed that "it's possible that much of the seating on that broad expanse has never been touched by a human posterior. Even the winos stay away" (Langdon 1980). A metal plate I discovered in 1989 embedded in the plaza declared "Private Property, Permission to Use Revocable at Any Time" (figure 4.2).

Another troubling aspect of the Marine Midland Center project was that it further undermined the long-standing connection between lower Main Street and the rest of the downtown (see figure 4.3). The 38-story tower was placed *on top* of Main Street, leaving only a relatively small opening at the base of the tower. Not long after Metro Rail began operating, the portal at the base of the office tower was reserved for the exclusive use of Metro Rail (see figure 4.4). No longer able to travel straight down Main Street to the Inner Harbor, drivers had to circle around the project to reach lower Main Street. Pedestrians could still walk through the portal, but doing so was far from a pleasant experience. Venturing through the portal in the winter could actually be a harrowing experience because wind speeds accelerate considerably when forced to pass through the narrow opening at the base of the tower.

Figure 4.2. 1989 photo of metal plate with message embedded in plaza of Marine Midland Center: "Private Property, Permission to Use Revocable at Any Time." *Source*: Photo by the author.

Figure 4.3. Marine Midland Center office tower and Donovan State Office Building as viewed from the foot of lower Main Street in 1972. The desolation of the surrounding area makes clear that the two large-scale projects failed to revive lower Main Street. *Source*: Photo by the author.

Figure 4.4. 1989 photo of the entrance to the Marine Midland Center office tower from Seneca Street. In the far right, cars can be seen passing through the opening at the base of the tower—which was later closed to traffic and used exclusively by Buffalo Metro Rail. *Source*: Photo by the author.

One Small Waterfront Success

One small project undertaken by a newly established local nonprofit organization *did* have a remarkably positive effect by enhancing the public's appreciation of the Inner Harbor: the restoration of the lighthouse that had been erected in 1833 at the entrance to Buffalo's Inner Harbor. In retrospect, the project was all the more significant and propitious because it demonstrated there was strong public support in Buffalo for honoring and preserving aspects of Buffalo's distinguished waterfront history.

In the 1950s, the Army Corps of Engineers announced it planned to demolish the 1833 lighthouse at the entrance to the Inner Harbor, which had been decommissioned in 1914, as part of a proposed river-widening project. The public outcry that resulted stopped that from happening. The lighthouse was added to the National Register of Historic Places in 1979. Unfortunately, formally recognizing the lighthouse's historic significance did not result in any affirmative steps being taken to maintain and repair the long-neglected structure.

In 1985, a commander with the US Coast Guard called Michael Vogel at the *Buffalo News,* where he worked, to voice his concerns about structural cracks that were appearing in the abandoned historic lighthouse at the entrance to Buffalo's Inner Harbor and to bemoan the fact that he had no funding in his budget to restore the lighthouse. "I thought he was looking for a newspaper article to raise public awareness about the deteriorated condition of the lighthouse. Instead, he asked me to consider forming a not-for-profit organization to save the lighthouse" (Vogel, email, February 20, 2019). Vogel was employed by the *Buffalo News* and needed to obtain their permission to do that. Once he obtained it, he established the Buffalo Lighthouse Association, and, except for the six years when he was editorial page editor, he has headed the group from the start.

"We essentially completed the restoration of the lighthouse, having raised and spent about $800,000 to $900,000 as part of that effort. We also raised and spent another $180,000 restoring the 1903 South Buffalo Lighthouse on the breakwater at the other end of the harbor. We took ownership of that light station from the federal government in 2011, while the 1833 lighthouse is leased from the Coast Guard and is still part of the Coast Guard base. We commissioned a replica third-order lens and relit the landmark in 2016" (Vogel, email, February 20, 2019).

Chapter Five

Early Waterfront Planning Efforts

In 1982, the City of Buffalo undertook a waterfront planning process aimed at developing a plan to guide the future use and development of the city's waterfront. Because of the city's limited financial resources, it asked the Niagara Frontier Transportation Authority (NFTA) to join with it in carrying out the process to augment the amount of funding available to pay for consultant services. Gail Johnstone, Buffalo's director of planning, had already applied for and secured a half-million dollars in funding from the state and federal governments, which made it possible to carry out a fairly thorough planning process.[1] Getting NFTA to agree to participate in the waterfront planning process provided the city with an additional $200,000 to pay for consultant services, but this ended up not being worth the added aggravation.

Far from helping to advance the planning process, NFTA's involvement proved to be an ongoing source of friction, because NFTA controlled the property formerly occupied by Ford's Outer Harbor assembly plant, which the city had transferred to NFTA to operate as a port facility after Ford abandoned the property.[2] Once NFTA got out of the port business, the city thought it should have the land back. However, NFTA "was chronically squeezed for cash and saw the Outer Harbor parcel as a means for them to develop a new revenue stream that could help fund its other operations" (Hovey 1991, 49).

City of Buffalo/NFTA Waterfront Planning Process, 1982–1987

The Waterfront Planning Board (WPB) created by the City of Buffalo and NFTA to oversee the waterfront planning effort met for the first time in March 1982 and approved the hiring of Marshall Macklin Monaghan (MMM), a Toronto firm as the main consultant. The Caucus Partnership of Buffalo was selected as the subcontractor to manage the citizen participation component of the process.[3] Gail Johnstone endorsed the idea of holding numerous public workshops in different parts of the city to solicit comments and suggestions from citizens and make it as easy as possible for citizens to actively participate in and contribute to the planning process.

In December 1984, MMM was fired as the lead consultant. Among the reasons given by the WPB for the firing were that the individuals they thought they had hired to carry out the project were no longer working for MMM; also, the individuals who now represented MMM didn't appear to be able to "figure out how to approach the project" (Hovey 1991, 66). In fairness, it needs to be said that the planning process that had been embarked upon was remarkably ambitious, encompassed a geographically expansive and diverse waterfront area, and required taking into account the varied and often conflicting interests of a large number of competing constituencies. That set of circumstances could have easily challenged even the most capable consultant team. Fourteen months after it fired MMM, the WPB approved an official statement of the goals of the waterfront planning effort and hired Wallace Roberts Todd (WRT) to replace MMM as the lead consulting firm.

In July 1985, a second round of public workshops began, aimed at soliciting comments and suggestions from citizens. At the first of those public workshops, D. Ward Fuller, a transplanted San Franciscan, president of the American Steamship Company headquartered in Buffalo, and a member of the WPB spoke up and asked: "Why not do something unique and creative and idiosyncratic to Buffalo?" When invited to elaborate on the idea, Fuller said that one way of doing that could be to develop and organize the plan around a concept he called "Canal Street"—a theme that would capture and draw attention to Buffalo's unique history as the western terminus of the Erie Canal and the nineteenth-century jumping off point for the Great Lakes and the upper Midwest.

Fuller's idea struck a responsive chord, but how that concept might be physically manifested remained sketchy. Fuller thought it might involve "some kind of canal-like waterway around which a variety of museums, restaurants, shops, and other attractions might be developed" (Hovey 1991, 78–79). In a subsequent public workshop, the 'foot of Main Street' was identified by participants as the most appropriate site for such a project . . . "But Mayor Griffin, who didn't want to risk being too ambitious and failing to get something done, remained cool to the idea" (Hovey 1991, 80).[4] In January 1987, the *Buffalo News* published a special section of its newspaper entitled "Buffalo Poised for Rebirth," which included a map showing the proposed site of "Canal Place" at the foot of lower Main Street. In April of that year, the WPB voted to support the Canal Street concept, but Mayor Griffin still hadn't been won over. At a subsequent meeting of the WPB, Griffin asked, "Where will visitors park?" When informed that three parking ramps would be built, Griffin retorted " 'Who's paying for that?' " (Ciotta 1986).

At the next meeting of the WPB, WRT told board members exactly how they proposed to physically express the idea of "Canal Street." Unfortunately, the approach they proposed had little or no physical connection or relevance to the actual historic western terminus of the Erie Canal. Instead, what they proposed was to develop a "Great Lakes Park" consisting of scale models of the lakes fashioned in concrete. They also floated the idea of constructing a navigable canal through downtown. In the words of Planning Commissioner Fred Fadel, "If the consultants had been any good they would have taken [Fuller's] idea, worked it back and forth, and come up with something good. Instead, they took the idea and came back with something that would not fly, either technically or politically" (Hovey 1991, 82).

The citizen input obtained through the various public workshops provided the basis for a number of the recommendations and proposals that found their way into the draft plan. Among the actions recommended in the plan were constructing a "Gateway Bridge" across the Buffalo River to link the downtown and the Outer Harbor; reconstruction and beautification of Fuhrmann Boulevard on the Outer Harbor; providing greater direct access to the waterfront; a major mixed-use development on the NFTA property on the Outer Harbor; and the above-described Great Lakes–themed Canal Place "mega-project" on lower Main Street (Hovey 1991, 86).

Public hearings held to solicit public comments on the plan did not go well. Members of the longshoremen's union protested NFTA's role in relocating the authority's bulk cargo facility. Other constituencies voiced their own narrow and specialized agendas and failed to endorse the overall plan wholeheartedly. In the end, nobody "owned" the plan, and none of the citizens who had participated in the planning process "represented a constituency potent enough to demand that the plan go forward" (Hovey 1991, 132). Gail Johnstone, the city's planning director, believed that the adverse publicity generated by the public hearings "probably killed the implementation of the waterfront plan" (89). Fuller believed that the way WRT chose to express the Canal Street idea was the primary reason the entire plan failed. The Canal Street idea had drawn a great deal of public support and could have been reworked, but the mayor apparently wasn't interested in saving the plan.

In March 1987, Buffalo's Division of Planning delivered the draft of the waterfront plan to Mayor Griffin. However, the mayor failed to acknowledge having received the plan and never explained what happened to it. After hundreds of hours of consultant meetings with community leaders and neighborhood groups, and after having spent more than $700,000 in professional fees, it was as if the mayor had burned the plan. As far as the public was concerned, the plan just vanished. A final version of the plan was never completed.

After sabotaging the product of the five-year-long waterfront planning process, Mayor Griffin had this to say: "I don't want to hear about a lot of pie-in-the-sky things to do. I want to see housing, and I want to see office buildings, and I want to see restaurants. . . . I'm not much for plans. I never was. If I had to do it over again, I wouldn't have had this master plan" (Ciotta 1987, A-1). Planning Director Johnstone resigned in August 1987.

One reason why Mayor Griffin had so little interest in what he considered "pie-in-the-sky" planning was that he was pursuing a dream of his own—that of bringing professional baseball back to Buffalo. The Buffalo Bisons minor league franchise in the Triple-A International League had long been the pride of Buffalo baseball fans. Mid-season in 1970, however, the franchise was abruptly moved to Winnipeg, leaving Buffalo without professional baseball for the first time since 1912. In 1978, Mayor Griffin organized a group of investors which purchased the Jersey City A's of the Double-A class Eastern League for $55,000, and the team began playing as the Buffalo Bisons in War Memorial Stadium in 1979. Rich Products heir Robert E. Rich Jr. purchased the Bisons for $100,000 in 1983 and upgraded the team to the Triple-A American Association in 1985 by buying the Wichita Aeros for $1 million and moving the franchise to Buffalo.

The site chosen for the new ballpark was a 13-acre parking lot at Washington and Swan Streets. The property was acquired by the city through eminent domain, which then hired HOK Sport to design the stadium. The new roughly 16,000-seat ballpark opened and hosted its first baseball game on April 14, 1988 (see figure 5.1). $22.5 million of

Figure 5.1. Bronze statue honoring former Buffalo Mayor Jimmy Griffin outside Buffalo's downtown ballpark. *Source*: Photo by the author.

the $42.4 million cost of the stadium was paid by New York State, $12.9 million came from the City of Buffalo, $4.2 million from Erie County, and $2.8 million from the Buffalo Bisons. In addition, the City of Buffalo and Erie County paid $14 million to construct an 816-space parking garage behind the right field fence on Exchange Street to serve the ballpark and businesses and office buildings nearby such as Marine Midland Center.

The Horizons Waterfront Commission and the 1992 Action Plan for the Erie County Waterfront

One year after Mayor James Griffin sabotaged the product of City of Buffalo's own ambitious waterfront planning, Erie County's newly elected County Executive Dennis T. Gorski (a Democrat) launched another waterfront planning effort aimed at developing a waterfront plan not just for the City of Buffalo but for *all* of Erie County. To help advance Gorski's waterfront planning initiative, Governor Mario Cuomo (also a Democrat) authorized the establishment of the Horizons Waterfront Commission as a subsidiary of New York State's Urban Development Corporation (UDC).[5] In September 1988, Erie County Executive Gorski, Mayor Griffin, Vincent Tese, chairman and CEO of UDC, and other state and local government officials gathered on the deck of the USS *Little Rock* to sign the intergovernmental agreement that established the Horizons Waterfront Commission and cleared the way for UDC to provide the funding the commission would need to pay for staff and consultant services.

County Executive Gorski placed the county's Director of Planning Richard Tobe in charge of determining how the commission should be structured. When I interviewed him, Tobe recalled that Gorski had instructed him to structure the commission so as to have the best chance of garnering the support of most if not all of the municipalities with shorelines along Lake Erie and the Niagara River, and also to avoid the appearance of state control over the process (Tobe, interview, February 7, 2018).

A 16-member board of directors was established, with each municipality in the county with shorelines along Lake Erie and the Niagara River represented by a voting member. Governor Mario Cuomo appointed Edward C. Cosgrove, a Buffalo attorney, as the chairman of the commission. Thomas D. Blanchard, who had previously been executive vice president of the Greater Norfolk Corporation in Norfolk, Virginia, was appointed president of the commission and started in his new position on November 1, 1989. Eighteen nonvoting members, also appointed to the commission's board, represented various government agencies that might need to be involved in helping implement waterfront projects recommended by the commission.

In 1992, the Horizons Commission issued its "Action Plan for the Erie County Waterfront," which identified and described a large number of possible open space and recreation projects that could provide residents with greater opportunities to use and enjoy shoreline areas for recreation. To underscore that all portions of the county stood to benefit, it organized and listed the recommended projects separately for the northern, central, and southern portions of the county's shoreline.

The Horizons Commission's 1992 Action Plan had remarkably little to say about what should happen in the area of Buffalo's Inner Harbor—apparently not wanting to risk the ire of Mayor Griffin. In sharp contrast, the

Action Plan had a great deal to say about what could and should happen on Buffalo's Outer Harbor, which Buffalo's previous waterfront planning process had largely ignored. Instead, the plan called for undertaking a dizzying array of fairly ambitious and very different kinds of projects in different parts of the Outer Harbor. Richard Tobe, who had staffed the Horizons Commission, admitted that the commission was "mesmerized" by the possibilities Buffalo's Outer Harbor presented (Tobe, interview, February 7, 2018). On the portion of the Outer Harbor controlled by NFTA, the Action Plan envisioned a large number of three- to five-story and six- to ten-story residential structures in a park-like setting that would contain a total of up to 1,500 new housing units, as well as a considerable amount of new retail and commercial space. The plan also called for a waterfront park, an amphitheater, a marina, and thousands of parking spaces.

Perhaps the most remarkable project called for in the plan was to develop a "Great Lakes Science Research Center," referred to as "the Nowak Project" in honor of long-time Western New York Congressman Henry J. Nowak, who had conceived of the project.[6] As described in the Action Plan, the Great Lakes Science Research Center (GLSRC) would be "a multi-purpose tourist attraction" which would include "aquaculture and hydroponic facilities, a fish hatchery, a fresh-water aquarium, weather research facilities, a hazardous waste center and planetarium" (Horizons Commission Action Plan, 3–21). The GLSRC was to be developed in the northern third of the Outer Harbor; a nature preserve and visitor center, hotel and conference center, shops and restaurants, and a marina were also to be developed in close proximity

After the Action Plan was issued, the commission belatedly realized that the action agenda its consultants had set out for the Outer Harbor was too ambitious and would require that it forego all the other projects that had been recommended for waterfronts in other municipalities in the county. "We ultimately concluded that the Outer Harbor was simply too big an undertaking, would have cost too much and take too much time. We decided instead to focus attention on accomplishing a number of much smaller projects in various towns throughout the county" (Tobe, interview, February 7, 2018). One such project, which was carried out, was the development of a public beach along the shore of Lake Erie in the Town of Evans.

In 1993, the Horizons Commission turned its attention to Buffalo's Inner Harbor, where a new arena was under construction at the end of lower Main Street. When the new arena opened in the fall of 1995, all the sporting events and trade shows that had been held at "the Aud" would shift to the new arena, and Memorial Auditorium would be made redundant. There was a very real fear that once Memorial Auditorium was shuttered it might stand empty and deteriorate for years.

The Horizons Waterfront Commission's Crossroads Harbor Plan

In an effort to identify a practical way of reusing Memorial Auditorium and also capitalize on the impact the new arena might have on lower Main Street, the Horizons Commission prepared the Crossroads Harbor plan which was unveiled in August 1993 by the Horizons Waterfront Commission Chairman Joseph E. Goodell at an evening event attended by approximately 200 people.[7] The Crossroads Harbor plan represented a significant departure from commission's previous 1992 Action Plan, which called for developing a Great Lakes Science Research Center (the "Nowak project") on the Outer Harbor. Instead, the Crossroads Harbor plan proposed developing an aquarium and related Great Lakes exhibits in Memorial Auditorium, which the plan renamed Buffalo Harbor Center.

To increase the Aud's appeal as a visitor attraction, the plan called for carving an inlet into the shoreline to bring the waterfront right up to the edge of the structure, despite the fact that doing so would have obliterated the historic western terminus of the Erie Canal. Despite that oversight, Congressman Nowak secured $20 million in government funding to advance the idea (T. Blanchard, email, January 20, 2020). Nowak's political instincts must have told him, given the pressing need to find a way of reusing Memorial Auditorium, that developing an aquarium in the Aud was much more likely to garner political support and public funding than trying to build the GLSRC on the Outer Harbor.

To activate the area around the new arena, the Crossroads Harbor plan proposed carving a second inlet into the shoreline to bring the riverfront closer to the new sports arena, which could provide a new home for the naval vessels that were then moored further north along the shore of the river, as well as a place where visiting cruise ships and other small craft could dock. According to Thomas Blanchard, who was president of the Horizons Commission at the time, "The consultant team made a number of assumptions without discussing them with us. For example, relocating the USS *Little Rock* to a newly created inlet near the new arena would have required placing the vessel *under* the Skyway. The problem was that the USS *Little Rock* would barely fit under the Skyway." As Blanchard further explained, "With a Lake Erie storm surge of five to six feet, which was not at all unusual, the vessel could actually *lift* the bridge. When challenged on this point, the consultant responded that the ship would be bolted to the bottom" (T. Blanchard, email, January 30, 2019).

In 1994, the Buffalo Common Council expanded the boundaries of the Waterfront Redevelopment Area to include the land and rights-of-way at the foot of Main Street needed for the construction of a new arena at the foot of lower Main Street.[8] A further enlargement of the Redevelopment Area added three properties, two of which were along the east side of Lower Main Street: a city-owned surface parking lot (known as "the Webster Block") and the former Donovan State Office Building, which state government no longer used for that purpose. The third property added to the Waterfront Redevelopment Area was Memorial Auditorium.

Despite having been provided with a substantial amount of state funding to pay for consultant services and projects, the Horizons Commission produced very little of consequence during its eight-year existence. "The Horizons Commission ultimately had no constituency" (B. Fisher, interview, February 9, 2018). Not long after he took office as governor of New York, George Pataki dissolved the Horizons Commission in 1995 and placed Empire State Development Corporation (ESDC), another subsidiary of the Urban Development Corporation, in charge of planning for the redevelopment of Buffalo's waterfront.[9]

Part II

The Inner Harbor

Chapter Six

Empire State Development Corporation's 1998 Inner Harbor Plan

In June 1998, Governor George Pataki came to Buffalo to unveil what was billed as the "final revised Inner Harbor plan." Prepared for the Empire State Development Corporation (ESDC) by Jambhekar Strauss Architects, PC, the plan called for creating an esplanade along the shoreline of the Buffalo River that would extend all the way to Erie Basin Marina. The plan also called for relocating the naval vessels that comprised the Naval and Military Park closer to the mouth of the harbor to minimize the extent to which they blocked views of the water. Other actions called for included creating a large public plaza that could be used for concerts and festivals and carving four new slips into the shoreline to provide dock space for vessels visiting Buffalo as well as water taxis and recreational boats. "The plan was basically a glorified landscaping project that ignored the site's history" (Esmonde, email, May 20, 2019).

A front-page article in the *Buffalo News* praised the plan as "historically based" because it called for constructing a replica "canal slip" next to the buried Commercial Slip and the installation of a "period-style pedestrian bridge like those that once crossed the site's network of canals" (Vogel 1998, A1). However, architectural historian John H. Conlin, the former executive director of the Landmark Society and past chairman of the Buffalo Preservation Board, said he was "disappointed" that the plan called for creating a replica slip next to its historic location, rather than excavating and revealing the original. The fact that a massive storm drain had been placed within the Commercial Slip before it was closed and filled in in 1918, and that removing the drain was going to be costly, undoubtedly contributed to the decision *not* to uncover the Commercial Slip.

The Federal Environmental Impact Statement (FEIS) that ESDC was required to submit for the project was prepared by Dean & Barbour Associates. Based on the information contained in the FEIS, the Office of Parks, Recreation, and Historic Preservation (OPRHP), the State Historic Preservation Office (SHPO) for New York State advised ESDC on December 8, 1998, that it was satisfied that the project would have "no adverse effect" on resources eligible for inclusion in the National Register for Historic Places. The problem was that ESDC's consultant hadn't conducted any archaeological digs to determine what historic artifacts (portions of the walls of the Commercial Slip, remnants of former Canal District streets, foundations of Canal-era buildings, etc.) lay beneath the surface that could be adversely affected by the proposed project. "Any project like this requires an environmental impact statement to see—among other things—if there's anything of historic worth that will be affected. As absurd as it sounds, the state finished its impact statement before its archaeologist dug to see what might be buried on the site" (Esmonde 2000b, C-1).

It wasn't until early May 1999 that ESDC's archaeological consultant finally got around to doing some digging on the site and discovered a roughly 80-foot section of wall of the Commercial Slip. "When people became aware that the original Commercial Slip was buried under a parking lot on the project site, they started clamoring for the excavation and restoration of this crucial piece of interpretable artifact" (Hovey, email, January 2018). Over the next few weeks there were additional discoveries of the foundations of buildings along Lloyd Street. School groups began touring the site, and the public debate over what should happen at the Inner Harbor intensified.

On May 18, 1999, New York's SHPO issued a new Advisory Opinion informing ESDC that the Commercial Slip wall met the criteria for being listed on the National Register of Historic Places. However, approximately three weeks later, on August 6, 1999, the SHPO reiterated its formerly stated position that the project would have "no adverse effect" on historic resources and that it did not consider it feasible to preserve the Commercial Slip wall in "an exposed condition." In rendering that judgment, the SHPO appeared to agree with ESDC's contention that although the historic resources buried at the site might be archeologically important, they were likely "of minimal value for preservation in place" and therefore did not need to be uncovered. As an alternative to uncovering the walls of the Commercial Slip, the SHPO recommended that ESDC "conduct a detailed documentation of the wall that had been uncovered, rebury it, and provide for appropriate historical interpretation of the Wall through marking and signage in the project design."

In October 1999, the Preservation Coalition of Erie County, led by Tim Tielman and Susan McCartney, filed a lawsuit in Federal District Court against ESDC and the other state and federal government agencies that were also involved in the project: the Federal Transportation Administration, Niagara Frontier Transportation Authority, New York State Thruway Authority, and New York State Office of Parks, Recreation, and Historic Preservation. The legal citation for the case is "Preservation Coalition of Erie County v. Federal Transit Administration et al." because the Federal Transit Administration was officially considered the lead agency. However, the ESDC was the "project's sponsor" and was the entity that was responsible for preparing and submitting the FEIS for the project.

The Preservation Coalition argued that the actions that were proposed threatened to irreparably harm and destroy the historic western terminus of the Erie Canal, a resource eligible for listing on the National Register of Historic Places (see Figure 6.1). It further argued that the FEIS that was

Figure 6.1. Tim Tielman holding sign that says: "Canal District Do the Real Thing." *Source*: Photo by Mark Goldman. Used with permission.

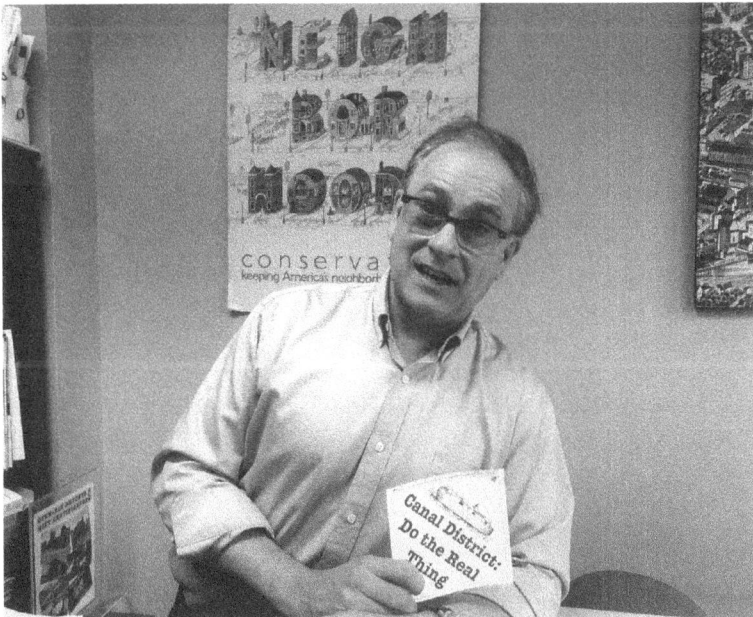

submitted for the project failed to consider alternative ways of carrying out the project that could have lessened the harm to historic resources, as was required by the National Environmental Policy Act (NEPA). The Preservation Coalition urged the court to issue a preliminary injunction to prevent the defendants from taking further actions to carry out the project. Richard Berger and Francis Amendola served as the Preservation Coalition's attorneys. The case was heard by Federal District Court Judge William M. Skretny.

Expert witnesses called by the defendants downplayed the importance of the artifacts that remained buried on the project site, characterizing them as an "archaeological resource"—officially defined as "a remnant or remain of a former element of the built environment that has lost all function related to its original intended use." Warren Barbour, PhD and Robert D. Kuhn, PhD testified that, although uncovering such an archaeological resource might be useful to researchers in terms of the information it would provide, not disturbing such long-buried remains was the most historically respectful approach.

Affidavits submitted by a number of experts and individuals on behalf of the Preservation Coalition spoke to the historical importance of the site. In his affidavit, David Gerber, professor of American history at the State University of New York at Buffalo, attributed the site's historic significance to having been "at the center of the avenues of commerce and transportation that bound the northern and western states together, stimulated the settlement of the West, and greatly assisted the rapid ascent of the United States as one of the richest and most developed nations in the world by 1860." Gerber expressed his dismay that ESDC proposed to construct a "replica slip" rather than restore the actual historic resource in its actual historic location, wanted to carry out a plan that would "obliterate historic street patterns, and render impossible the reconstruction of the Commercial Slip, which formed the heart of the historical canal terminus site" (Gerber, January 2000 Affidavit, Preservation Coalition v. Federal Transit Administration et al.).

Affidavits in support of the Preservation Coalition were also submitted by Monroe Fordham, professor of history at Buffalo State College; Mark Goldman, the author of three books on the history of Buffalo; H. David Rogers, professional engineer and principal at Ryan-Briggs Associates, PC, in Troy, New York; Greg Stein, professor of geography, Buffalo State College; and Robert Z. Melnick, professor and of landscape architecture and historic preservation at the University of Oregon, who according to Tim Tielman, offered to fly across the country to Buffalo to testify on behalf the Preservation Coalition "in exchange for airfare and chicken wings." Before joining the University of Oregon faculty, Melnick had worked for the National Parks Service and helped the agency develop the first official guidelines for identifying, evaluating, and treating historic and cultural landscapes.

In his court testimony, Melnick took issue with ESDC's characterization of the Erie Canal's buried remains as a mere "archaeological resource," as opposed to an "historic resource." "The fact that [a resource] is currently underground . . . doesn't necessarily mean that it is an archaeological resource," testified Melnick. He also took issue with the ESDC consultant's characterization of the buried remains as "ruins." "It would depend upon their condition. They could be underground and be perfectly intact or largely intact."

ESDC had argued that it decided not to uncover the buried remains of the canal's western terminus out of an abundance of caution and was motivated by a desire to avoid harming such a resource. Melnick countered that argument by observing that *not* revealing the canal's buried remains would deny the American public the opportunity to fully understand the resource. "I always go back to what's the purpose of historic preservation, and that is to provide the interested public a greater sense of how this country developed over a number of years. By denying that access, you are, in one sense, harming those people who can't see that and gain from that knowledge," said Melnick.

As Melnick's testimony neared an end, Judge Skretny asked the Preservation Coalition's co-counsel Francis Amendola if there were anything else he might want to ask Melnick on redirect examination. Amendola took advantage of the opportunity by asking a question that underscored the inadequacy of the environmental impact study that ESDC had submitted for the project.

AMENDOLA: Dean Melnick, does it have any significance at all that the excavation that resulted in the discovery and uncovering of the Commercial Slip occurred *after* [italics added] having submitted a FEIS that determined that the project would have "no adverse effect" on historic resources?

MELNICK: Yes.

AMENDOLA: Could you elaborate on that?

MELNICK: Well, it strikes me as unusual to undertake such a basic investigation following a determination [of no adverse effect]. It would seem to me that you'd want to do a more open-minded investigation of the resources, including an excavation, *prior to* arriving at such a determination [of no adverse effect]. Otherwise you don't know what [historic resources] the project will be impacting.

By far the most sensational testimony was delivered by Warren Barbour, PhD, who supervised the December 1998 site survey that provided the basis for the FEIS that ESDC submitted for the project and thus testified as an expert witness on behalf of ESDC.[1] Barbour at first stated that not much of the former Canal District and Commercial Slip remained below the surface to be uncovered. When pressed to explain why the Commercial Slip should not be uncovered, Barbour testified that after being "submerged below water level for more than one hundred twenty years" and subjected to prolonged freeze/thaw cycles during that period, the stones that had lined the Commercial Slip might "blast apart" if uncovered and exposed to the air. Barbour told the court that he had spoken with three other experts, who had independently told him they agreed it was possible stones might "blast apart" if exposed to the air. Barbour's "exploding rocks" theory was heavily relied upon by ESDC to support its contention that the Commercial Slip should remain buried—and appears to have been considered credible by the court.

While the Federal District Court was hearing testimony, the political environment that surrounded waterfront planning in Buffalo was significantly altered by the election of a new Erie County executive and a new governor. In January 2000, Joel Giambra took office as the newly elected Republican Erie County executive, and George Pataki (also a Republican) replaced Mario Cuomo (a Democrat) as governor of New York. Not long after Giambra took office, Bruce Fisher, who served under Giambra as deputy county executive, urged his brother Scot to go to Giambra's house on a Saturday and take with him a map to show Giambra where the Old Erie Canal had connected to the Buffalo River so as to make him aware of the historic resource ESDC's Inner Harbor plan was putting at risk. Since both Giambra and Pataki belonged to the same political party, it seemed reasonable to hope that if Giambra could be won over to support uncovering and preserving the historic remains of the Old Erie Canal, he would likely be listened to by the governor and state agency officials. It was a warm day, and when Fisher arrived at Giambra's house he was out in the driveway.

Fisher's visit had the desired effect of persuading Giambra that both he and the governor stood to gain politically by making it known that they favored uncovering and preserving the Erie Canal. Giambra would go on to also discover that "historic preservation was a very good 'wedge issue' that enabled him to gain favor with Democrats in the largely Democratic City of Buffalo" (Tielman, interview, February 14, 2018).

The Court Ruling and Its Consequences

On March 31, 2000, the Federal District Court issued its Decision and Order in the case of Preservation Coalition of Erie County vs. Federal Transit Administration et al. Judge Skretny agreed with the Preservation Coalition that historic resources eligible for listing on the National Register for Historic Resources did in fact exist on the project site and had not been adequately considered in the FEIS. Although he declined to issue the injunction the Preservation Coalition had requested, he ordered ESDC to prepare a Supplemental Environmental Impact Statement (SEIS) that more fully took account of historic resources at the site and directly addressed preservationists' concerns regarding the impact the project would have on historic resources.

The judge also ordered ESDC to conduct a public hearing to enable members of the public to express their concerns regarding the project and the issues that should be addressed in the SEIS. "Judge Skretny basically said the state messed up. His ruling forced the state to take another look at what's down there, and how it might be used as more than window dressing" (Esmonde 2000b).

The public hearing was held in the auditorium of Erie County Community College on May 24, 2000, and was marred by a number of irregularities. See "A Travesty of a Public Hearing" on the following page. See figure 6.2 for an aerial view of what Buffalo's Inner Harbor looked like when the May 2000 public hearing was held.

Warren Barbour had said that three experts had independently supported his "exploding rocks" theory. Dr. Rossman F. Giese, Jr. vehemently disputed that claim by stating at the public hearing that he had personally contacted each of the three geologists Barbour said he had spoken to, and

A Travesty of a Public Hearing

The beginning of the public hearing was delayed for 25 minutes while representatives of ESDC attempted to eject people with video cameras from recording the proceedings and a number of them refused to leave. Once the hearing finally began, a considerable amount of time was taken up by a lengthy presentation by ESDC and its consultants. After that, the first people who were allowed to speak were ESDC's supporters, who had showed up early to sign the speakers' list. This "front-loading" of the hearing had the effect of pushing back the opportunity of the general public to comment until fairly late in the evening. Many citizens who came to oppose the project left the hearing without getting an opportunity to speak.

Finally, around 11 p.m., Dr. Rossman F. Ross Giese, Jr., a geologist on the faculty of the University at Buffalo's Geology Department with decades of experience studying rocks rose to speak. By the time Giese spoke, almost everyone who had been there earlier, including all the representatives of the media who had come to cover the hearing, had left—with the one exception of Donn Esmonde, a reporter with the *Buffalo News*. If Esmonde had not stayed until the bitter end, the pertinent information Giese provided might have been like the proverbial tree that falls in the forest with no one around to hear it.

each one told him that they had never said any such thing (Esmonde, email, May 30, 2019).

Barbour had made it sound as though he had formally contacted each of the geologists to invite their opinions. However, one of the geologists Barbour said he had consulted (University at Buffalo professor Charles H. V. Ebert) told Giese that Barbour had approached him one day at the copy machine in the UB Geology Department office and casually asked him if he'd ever encountered a situation in which a stone wall had fallen or broken up because of weather factors. He further added that Barbour made no mention of the Commercial Slip or of any specific type of stone or context. "Ebert was later outraged to learn that Barbour had used this casual conversation as support for the notion that canal stones of Onondaga limestone, among the hardest rocks on the planet, would crack or break from weather exposure" (Esmonde, email, May 30, 2019).

Figure 6.2. Buffalo Inner Harbor in 2000: Buffalo and Erie County Naval and Military Park in its original location; the Commercial Slip still buried; Memorial Auditorium vacant and deteriorating and most of the rest of the area used as surface parking. *Source*: ECHDC. Used with permission.

What Giese said at the public hearing was a huge game-changer. "If the 'exploding rocks' story wasn't true, then ESDC was caught in a lie. Once the lie was reported in the media, the revelation would prompt a huge outcry from the public, thus motivating and providing political 'cover' for elected officials who'd previously been too cowed by the Governor and various other power brokers" (Esmonde, email, May 30, 2019.).

To corroborate what Esmonde said he heard Geise say at the public hearing, the *Buffalo News'* editor assigned reporter Kevin Collison to contact the three experts Barbour had cited to independently verify what they said they had told Barbour. All three told Collison that Barbour had "misquoted and misrepresented their views" and that they most certainly didn't support Barbour's notion that the stones of the Commercial Slip would blast apart.

Barbour's "exploding rocks" theory was regarded as credible right up until Kevin Collison's article was published on the front page of the *Buffalo News* on June 3, 2000, under the headline "The Hard Facts: The Stone Walls of the Old Erie Canal Terminus Are More Durable Than a Consultant's Report Says" (Collison 2000b).

In the meantime, Scot Fisher had hundreds of "Save, Don't Pave!" lawn signs printed up, and with the help of other members of the Preservation Coalition had them placed throughout the city. He also printed up hundreds petitions for people to sign in support of uncovering and restoring the Commercial Slip. During a single day at the Allentown Art Festival that summer Fisher reportedly collected 4,000 signatures. With the help of other board members, the petitions garnered a total of 14,000 signatures.

Ramifications of the Revelation
That ESDC's Principal Consultant Lied

Up until the May 24, 2000, public hearing, Buffalo's Mayor Anthony Masiello had publicly supported ESDC's proposed Inner Harbor project, based on its assertion that the Commercial Slip walls were too fragile to be exposed to the air. The revelation that ESDC's consultant had misled local officials caused the mayor to reconsider his support. Unfortunately, ESDC's 1998 Inner Harbor Plan was the only plan on offer at the time. Also, no one knew for sure if rewatering the Commercial Slip was feasible, nor was there any agreement as to what other actions should be taken to achieve an historically respectful Inner Harbor plan.

Tim Tielman recognized that a study needed to be conducted to answer those questions and, equally important, to specifically envision how the Inner Harbor could be redeveloped as an alternative to what ESDC had proposed. Tielman also knew that the local politician who was in the best position politically to commission such a study was Erie County Executive Joel Giambra, because both Giambra and Pataki were Republicans. Governor Pataki would therefore be inclined to believe that Giambra, as a fellow Republican, had Pataki's best interests at heart when he commissioned the study. Tielman reached out to Deputy County Executive Bruce Fisher to inquire if Giambra would support such a study.

On June 17, 2000, two weeks after Collison's "hard facts" article appeared in the *Buffalo News*, Giambra and Mayor Masiello issued a press release announcing that "a feasibility study would be conducted to assess the potential for restoring the Erie Canal Commercial Slip and other historic archaeological/architectural resources located within the 12.5-acre Inner Harbor Project site" and that the study would be completed in two months. The press release quoted Mayor Masiello as saying, "I am pleased that Governor Pataki and ESDC Chairman Gargano recognized the value of resolving this matter locally." The $200,000 cost of the study was jointly funded by the city and the county. Meanwhile, ESDC agreed to suspend further excavation and construction of the replica Canal Slip at the Inner Harbor, pending the results of the study.

Giambra and Masiello's announcement didn't receive nearly the attention it deserved, because one day before, on July 16, 2000, Adelphia Communications announced that it was going to build a 20–25-story office building on lower Main Street that would bring 1,000 new jobs to the area and anchor the Inner Harbor redevelopment project. Governor George Pataki deemed the project so important that he flew to Buffalo to be present for the announcement, which he said would "launch this region's economic renaissance into the 21st century" (Archibold 2002). When the office building project was announced, Adelphia Communications' president and CEO, John Rigas, was part owner of the Buffalo Sabres. One month later Rigas would gain majority control of Buffalo's NHL franchise.

While the general public and local media were still digesting the news about the proposed Adelphia Communications office tower project, the study that Giambra and Masiello had commissioned quickly got underway. Based on Tim Tielman's recommendation, Roy Mann, an architect and planner from Austin, Texas, was hired to lead the study. Having seen an article in *Landscape Architecture* magazine about a canal project that Mann's firm had carried out in Austin, Tielman had invited Mann to come to Buffalo to speak about the project earlier in the year and was impressed by his work. The contract was administered and overseen by Erie County's Commissioner of Environment and Planning Larry Rubin.

Mann's "Erie Canal Heritage Waterfront" report was completed in August 2000. It identified the following features as being essential to a historically respectful Inner Harbor redevelopment project: uncover, restore, and rewater the Commercial Slip; uncover and reveal buried foundations of Canal-era buildings; historically reference the Central Wharf by establishing a boardwalk from the Commercial Slip to the tip of lower Main Street; and reestablish the Canal-era street pattern of the Canal District. These key elements were then codified into a memorandum of understanding (MOU) that Erie County Executive Giambra hoped state officials and preservationists would agree to sign. The MOU also included a provision that the signatories pledged to work toward the goal of developing a historically sensitive waterfront plan that preserved as much of the remains of the old Erie Canal as possible. Based on the initial positive response to the MOU, the county executive's staff went to work planning an event to celebrate the Erie Canal's 175th anniversary at which Mayor Pataki could announce that preservationists and state officials had reached an agreement that would put an end to the long-simmering Inner Harbor controversy.

However, it turned out that officials at Empire State Development Corporation were unwilling to agree to the provision in the MOU that called for a boardwalk to extend continuously from the Commercial Slip to the tip of lower Main Street. Instead, they wanted to carve slips into the shoreline to provide berthing places for Great Lakes excursion vessels, tall ships, and other kinds of vessels to dock. Meanwhile, the Preservation Coalition's Tim Tielman told Giambra's office that *he wouldn't* sign the MOU if it didn't assure that slips *would not* be carved into the shoreline.

Tielman might have continued to insist that he wouldn't sign the MOU if it hadn't been for Deputy Erie County Executive Bruce Fisher, who assured him that it was unlikely that ESDC would have enough money to construct the slips and docks into the shoreline.[2] Three days before Governor Pataki was scheduled to come to Buffalo on October 26, 2000, to celebrate the 175th anniversary of the Erie Canal, Tielman received a call from the Governor's Office. After reiterating the reasons *why* he objected to carving slips into the historic footprint of the former Central Wharf, Tielman reluctantly said that he would agree to sign the MOU based on Fisher's assurances that the slips wouldn't ever get built. "I do not know whether Pataki's visit would have happened without something positive to announce" (Tielman, email, April 2, 2019).

Tielman was standing up for an important principle when he opposed carving slips into the historic footprint of the Central Wharf that directly overlooked the harbor. "Because of Tielman's insistence on having a boardwalk along the waterfront where the Central Wharf had stood, Canalside has become the public's waterfront. So much of the battle was about saving the waterfront for people to enjoy" (Esmonde, interview, April 29, 2019).

The "Supplemental Final Environmental Impact Statement" that ESDC filed for the Erie Canal Harbor Project in December 2004 included an exhibit that showed two wide slips being carved into the shoreline for ships to dock, which would have eliminated a significant portion of the waterfront boardwalk. Thankfully these slips were never constructed. Indeed, the waterfront boardwalk that runs uninterrupted from the Commercial Slip to the tip of lower Main Street is one of the most publicly beneficial and appreciated aspects of Canalside today (see figures 6.3 and 6.4).

Figure 6.3. Waterfront boardwalk at Canalside looking toward the Commercial Slip and USS *Little Rock*. *Source*: Photo by the author.

Figure 6.4. Waterfront boardwalk at Canalside looking toward the foot of lower Main Street. *Source*: Photo by the author.

"A Canal Conversation"

In September 2000, eight national experts in historic preservation were brought to Buffalo to participate in a two-day conference titled "A Canal Conversation"—an event conceived of and spearheaded by Kevin Gaughan, a lawyer and civic activist. Gaughan's stated aim in holding the "Canal Conversation" was to increase the public's understanding of the choices the city faced in deciding how to treat the recently discovered historic remains of the Erie Canal's terminus at Buffalo Harbor. Earlier in the 1990s, Gaughan had achieved a degree of notoriety in Western New York for his outspoken advocacy of regionalism and regional government, and for organizing a series of conferences at which invited speakers from other parts of the country spoke about how regional cooperation had made their respective areas more economically successful. Gaughan took the concept a step further by advocating that the City of Buffalo and Erie County should merge to form a single consolidated unit of government. In large part because of his efforts in that regard, the *Buffalo News* named Gaughan "Citizen of the Year" in 1998.

The first organization Gaughan approached when seeking sponsors for the "Canal Conversation" was the Baird Foundation. In her remarks at the beginning of the event, Executive Director of the Baird Foundation Catherine F. Schweitzer described the thoughts that ran through her mind when Gaughan came seeking the Baird Foundation's support: "When he first proposed the idea of the conference, The Baird Foundation was quite reticent to follow his lead. We found many objections: not enough time; too contentious; too political; too confusing; too many questions. Eventually, our reluctance became the reason to support his proposal. Perhaps the general community shared our confusion about what original material remains at the site, why it is important, and what benefits would return to the community from this large public works project. Perhaps we could learn how successful public/private alliances and partnerships have been built around similar projects" (Shibley and Hovey 2001, 14).

The Baird Foundation ultimately agreed to sponsor the event. Robert Shibley and Bradshaw Hovey at the University at Buffalo's School of Architecture and Planning were enlisted to help plan the event, organize the conference program, and select the speakers and topics to be addressed. Shibley and Hovey also produced a detailed report of the conference proceedings to assure that the educational value and significance of the event would endure long after the event itself was over.

More than 400 people attended the Canal Conversation that was held September 11–12, 2000, including Mayor Anthony Masiello and Erie County Executive Joel Giambra. A number of the invited speakers at the event emphasized the economic benefits that Buffalo could derive from heritage tourism if the Inner Harbor site were developed in a historically respectful manner. Wendy Nicholas of the National Trust for Historic Preservation told the audience that "heritage tourism is the fastest growing segment of the national tourism industry . . . and would soon become one of the most important sectors of retail activity in the country" (Shibley and Hovey, 2001, 41).

That same message had been put forward in affidavits offered in support of the Preservation Coalition's lawsuit against ESDC. For example, Monroe Fordham, professor of history at Buffalo State College, stated that "the historic building sites, streets, and remnants of the Erie Canal terminus represent a unique kind of treasure and historic natural resource for the City of Buffalo . . . [that has] the potential for being magnets for tourists in the emerging lucrative heritage tourism industry . . . if properly preserved and developed."

Should the former Commercial Slip be uncovered, restored, and filled with water? Or should the Commercial Slip remain filled in and a "replica" slip be constructed nearby, thereby allowing ESDC to develop the property as it had planned? The speakers at the Canal Conversation event assiduously avoided being seen as telling people in Buffalo what should be done. Instead, they delivered a more general message: "Celebrate it and use it to tell the riveting story of the world-renowned canal and the city it built" (*Buffalo News* editorial 2000).

By the time the Canal Conversation was held in September 2000, the Preservation Coalition had basically prevailed over ESDC, which made it all the more ironic that Tim Tielman, who had led the fight against ESDC's Inner Harbor plan, was disinvited from attending the Canal Conversation. According to Richard G. Berger, one of the two attorneys who argued the Preservation Coalition's case against ESDC in federal court, the reason Tielman was excluded was "to avoid injecting politics" into the event (Berger, interview, June 4, 2018). Tim Tielman can perhaps be forgiven for having a less than charitable view of what the Canal Conversation really represented. "The sponsors [of the Canal Conversation] basically stood on the sidelines during our seven-year campaign to save the Canal District from destruction. Once the issue was largely decided, and the mass public wave we engendered had swamped ESDC's plans, they came forward to wrap themselves in the flag" (Tielman, email, May 2, 2018).

On October 25, 2000, the 175th anniversary of the Erie Canal, Governor Pataki joined Mayor Masiello, County Executive Joel Giambra, and representatives of ESDC on the deck of the USS *Little Rock* and announced that preservationists and ESDC had signed an agreement that assured that the Commercial Slip would be uncovered and restored. He also promised that a revised, historically respectful Inner Harbor plan would be developed that called for restoring Canal-era cobblestone streets, uncovering foundations of Canal-era buildings, and restoring a long section of the former footprint of the Central Wharf. (See figure 6.5 of Donn Esmonde interviewing Governor Pataki at Canalside on October 25, 2000.) "This date 175 years ago was arguably the most important date in Buffalo's storied history," said Pataki. "On this historic occasion we announce our commitment to capitalize on the Erie Canal's worldwide appeal as a cultural and historic attraction" (Collison 2000c, A11). "It's a tremendous victory for everyone who cares about the Buffalo area's heritage," said Tim Tielman (A11).

On December 14, 2000, six months after the Federal District Court issued its decision, the parties to the lawsuit brought by the Preservation

A Remarkable Turn of Events

"What happened Thursday afternoon was so uncommon, so commendable and—until recently—so unimaginable, it bordered on surreal. Hand in hand, all together—Republicans and Democrats, city and county, preservationists and the governor of the state they were suing—skipped merrily through the looking glass. In less than five months, against all odds, the state did a near-complete turnaround on a now $40 million public project. Buried on the downtown waterfront are the walls of the Commercial Slip, the western terminus of the Erie Canal. The state was hell-bent on a plan that would have destroyed or left buried the slip walls and other historic remnants that tell not just our story, but a big piece of America's tale. 'I can't remember when—if, indeed, ever—public plan changed after the shovels were in the ground' " (Esmonde 2000j, B1).

Figure 6.5. *Buffalo News* reporter Donn Esmonde interviewing Governor George Pataki at Buffalo's Inner Harbor on October 26, 2000, the 175th anniversary of the opening of the Erie Canal. *Source*: Associated Press. Used with permission.

Coalition appeared before Judge Skretny with a proposed settlement agreement, which the court approved. The Funding Agreement that committed the $8.5 million needed to cover the cost of the compromise was finally signed by ESDC, Erie County, and the Buffalo Sewer Authority on March 12, 2003. It called for $4.5 million of the increased cost to be paid for by ESDC, and for Erie County and the Buffalo Sewer Authority to each pay $2 million toward the remaining $4 million cost. In addition to paying the cost of removing and relocating the Hamburg Drain and uncovering and restoring the Commercial Slip, funding was also provided for relocating the three naval vessels that were part of the Naval and Military Park, constructing a new naval museum, and developing a public esplanade along the Buffalo River on the footprint of the historic Central Wharf. It seemed as though the Inner Harbor project would proceed smoothly from then on. However, that wasn't to be the case, because Mayor Masiello started pushing the idea that a Bass Pro Outdoor World retail outlet should anchor the Inner Harbor project.

Chapter Seven

The Bass Pro Fiasco

Only a desperate community tosses tens of millions of dollars at a
chain retailer to occupy its plot of American history.

—Donn Esmonde, *Buffalo News*

Buffalo eventually does the right thing, after it has exhausted all the
other alternatives.

—Tim Tielman

Governor Pataki returned to Buffalo in November 2004 to announce the
release of the revised, more historically respectful Inner Harbor plan he
had promised back in October 2000. Prepared by Flynn Battaglia Architects of Buffalo, the "Erie Canal Harbor Project Master Plan" was notable
in that it was the first Inner Harbor plan that referenced the Erie Canal
in its title. The plan called for uncovering, restoring, and rewatering the
Commercial Slip, and constructing a boardwalk overlooking the harbor
on the footprint of the historic Central Wharf. It also called for a replica
of the bowstring truss footbridge that had spanned the Commercial Slip
during the Canal Era to be put in place in the same exact location, and
for a two-story masonry building to be built alongside the Commercial
Slip resembling the Coit-McCutcheon block that had once occupied the
site to serve as a museum and visitor center for the relocated Naval and
Military Park.

On the same day as the Erie Canal Harbor Master Plan was unveiled,
however, Erie Canal Harbor Development Corporation (ECHDC) also

announced it had entered into a memorandum of understanding (MOU) with Bass Pro that would lead to the development of a 140,000-square-foot Bass Pro sporting goods outlet within Memorial Auditorium, which had been vacant for eight years. Under the terms of the agreement, the state agreed to provide the company with $35 million in direct subsidies and to spend a total of $80 million on underlying infrastructure in support of the project. In return, Bass Pro agreed to spend $105 million to develop one of its huge Outdoor World Sporting Goods stores within Memorial Auditorium. As reported in the *Buffalo News*, $21 million of the $80 million committed to the project was state funding that had previously been committed to support the Adelphia Communications office building project; $17 million of the $80 million would come from funding the City of Buffalo and Erie County had previously committed to pay for a 1,000-vehicle parking structure and intermodal transportation center in the area. Another $30 million would come from federal transportation funding, which would pay for constructing a new off-ramp from the Niagara Thruway directly connected to the parking ramp and transportation center (McNeil, Linstedt, and Hammersley 2004).

Origin of the Bass Pro Idea

Buffalo billionaire Robert E. Rich, Jr., majority owner of Rich Products Corporation, frequently vacationed in Islamorada in the Florida Keys and had become good friends with Johnny Morris, the founder of Bass Pro, who also owned a vacation home there. There is every reason to believe that they often went fishing together.

It must have been during Rich's winter 2000 Florida vacation, while socializing with Morris, that Rich became entranced by the idea of attracting a Bass Pro store to Buffalo's waterfront, because not long after he returned to Buffalo from that vacation the idea somehow migrated into the mind of Mayor Masiello. By summer 2000, Mayor Masiello had begun pushing the idea of having a Bass Pro Outdoor World store anchor the Inner Harbor redevelopment project, and he had also begun working to secure state financial backing for the project.

In September 2005, Governor Pataki authorized the creation of an entirely new Urban Development Corporation (UDC) subsidiary, Erie Canal Harbor Development Corporation (ECHDC), to replace Empire State Development Corporation as the state entity principally in charge of waterfront planning and development in Buffalo. ECHDC was provided with its own separate governance structure, which called for a board of directors composed of seven voting members appointed by the governor, and two ex officio nonvoting members (the mayor of Buffalo and Erie County executive). In practice, individuals appointed to ECHDC's board by the governor as voting members were first recommended to the governor by Empire State Development Corporation's board of directors.

The political considerations that surrounded the waterfront planning that unfolded were complicated. Governor Pataki authorized creating ECHDC in an effort to secure a deal with Bass Pro that would assure that a large-scale sporting goods retail store would be developed within "the Aud." However, Mayor Masiello, who had been the first person to put forward the idea of developing a Bass Pro retail outlet in Memorial Auditorium and had actively sought state funding for the project, didn't like the idea of a state agency being in charge of developing the city's waterfront.

A City Desperate for a Silver Bullet Solution

To understand why state and local government officials were so desperate to lure a Bass Pro to Buffalo's waterfront, it is necessary to recall what had happened to Buffalo during the prior 40-year period. Between 1960 and 2000, Buffalo lost over half its population, and few public officials or leaders of the local business community seemed to have any idea how to reverse the decline. In the midst of that 40-year decline, *Buffalo News* columnist Phil Langdon rhetorically asked, "Why are opportunities for imaginative planning so rarely grasped? Partly because the depressed economy encourages a desperate lunge for whatever development can be immediately acquired" (Langdon 1981a).

Nowhere in the United States was the loss of manufacturing jobs more devastating than in Buffalo. In 1971, half of the 18,000-person workforce at Bethlehem Steel was permanently laid off (Goldman 1983, 273). Between 1977 and 1987, Buffalo lost more than 45,000 jobs, 31 percent of Buffalo's manufacturing positions, a large proportion of which paid above-average wages. For years, the wages paid blue-collar workers in Buffalo were among the highest in the nation. "But by the mid-1980s, Buffalo had suddenly become a low-wage town" (Goldman 1990, 218).

The loss of so many high-paying jobs had a devastating impact on working-class neighborhoods throughout the city. "The decline of industry struck at the core and the fiber of the community, undermining family stability, weakening neighborhoods, and permanently altering the values and beliefs many people had long lived by" (Goldman 1990, 218.). It also accelerated the exodus of educated and ambitious young people out of the city. Between 1980 and 2000, the city's population declined by 22 percent, to barely 50 percent of what it had been in 1950.

The city's financial condition was becoming increasingly dire, which at least partially explains why the city was so desperate for the "quick fix" that the Adelphia Communications project appeared to promise. By 1992, the city's fund balance had dropped below zero and the city was basically bankrupt. Tax hikes of 19.3 percent in 1992 and 9.5 percent the following year further burdened the residents and local businesses that remained in the city.

The Adelphia Communications office building project that state and local officials had been so enthusiastic about being built on lower Main Street turned out to be a mirage. In 2002, John Rigas, president and CEO of Adelphia Communications, was charged with corruption and securities violations, and Adelphia Communications filed for bankruptcy.[1] The demise of the Adelphia Communications project appears to have made local and state officials all the more desperate to lure Bass Pro to the waterfront.

"The Erie Canal Harbor Project Master Plan" issued in November 2004 didn't shed any light on whether it was a good or a bad idea to develop a Bass Pro store within Memorial Auditorium, because Memorial Auditorium wasn't included in the study area covered. The reason Memorial Auditorium wasn't included was because the Aud was still owned by the City of Buffalo, which wanted to maintain as much control as possible over how the property was redeveloped so as to maximize the financial benefit it would derive.

Around the same time as it was announced that a large-scale Bass Pro Outdoor World sporting goods outlet would be built within Memorial Auditorium, Brian Higgins was elected to Congress to represent Buffalo and Niagara Falls in the US House of Representatives. Public opposition to the proposed Bass Pro project was beginning to intensify when Higgins took office in January 2005.

People familiar with Higgins' background before he was elected to Congress knew that the two issues he was most passionate about were improving the environmental quality of Buffalo's waterfront and improving public access to the waterfront. Higgins was born and raised in South

Buffalo, a part of the city with an extensive waterfront that had once been dominated by heavy industry but was subsequently abandoned by most of those industries. Higgins commitment to improving the environmental quality of Buffalo's waterfront was clearly evident during the 1980s when he served on the board of directors of Friends of the Buffalo River (whose efforts related to the environmental cleanup of the Buffalo River are described in chapter 3).

In 1988, Higgins was elected to represent the same South Buffalo district on the Buffalo Common Council that Higgins' father had previously represented. Not long after joining the Buffalo Common Council, Higgins authored and submitted a report to the Common Council titled "From Rust Belt to Green Belt" in an effort to advance the revitalization of Buffalo's waterfront. In the report he explained why he considered it essential that the city become more proactively involved in charting a new course for the waterfront.

> In the past, random shifts in industry have defined development for our area, giving us prosperity in good times, and unemployment in bad. Many of these industrial shifts have been based on changes related to Buffalo's status as a harbor city. With the exodus of heavy industry, over which we have been able to exert almost no control, we are left with a sluggish economy, a preponderance of low-wage jobs, and a series of hazardous waste sites throughout the area . . .
>
> If we leave development of the waterfront to a new series of random, market-driven decisions, we are consigning ourselves to another boom and bust cycle. If, on the other hand, we stand up and aggressively point ourselves in a public-access, people-oriented direction, we will be building on solid ground and establishing something positive which will outlast the vagaries of economic cycles. (Higgins 1990)

One of the "big ideas" Higgins put forward in his "From Rust Belt to Green Belt" report was creating a Waterfront Greenway Trail that would extend the full length of Buffalo's waterfront—a recommendation that would later be endorsed by the Horizons Commission. Higgins resigned from his position on the Buffalo Common Council in 1993 to study for a master's degree in public administration at Harvard University's John F. Kennedy School of Government, which he earned in 1995.

By the time Brian Higgins was sworn in to serve in the US House of Representatives in January 2005, he had been thinking a long time about ways to improve environmental quality and public access to the waterfront—and about how projects that advanced those goals might be paid for. Not long after taking office, Higgins began publicly insisting that the relicensing of the Niagara Power Project should be made conditional on a commitment by the New York Power Authority (NYPA) to provide a substantial amount of money over a long period to help pay for waterfront improvements. Not long thereafter, Higgins successfully negotiated the terms of a legal agreement with NYPA whereby the Authority agreed to provide annual payments of $3.5 million for 50 years (a total of $279 million) for various projects at Canalside and elsewhere along Buffalo's waterfront.

In 2005, NYPA made its first annual payment of $3.5 million to the Canalside project. Nevertheless, considerable uncertainty remained with regard to the proposed Bass Pro project. The *Buffalo News* reported on March 7, 2005, that an agreement with Bass Pro still hadn't been finalized and that a MOU signed by Bass Pro was "not binding." Over a year and a half later, ECHDC had still not received a definite commitment from Bass Pro that it planned to develop an Outdoor World retail outlet in Memorial Auditorium.

In 2006, a cost-benefit analysis concluded that developing a Bass Pro retail outlet within Memorial Auditorium would cost substantially more than a new building. What made it so much more expensive was that 100,000 square feet of mold had accumulated within the building, and it would cost $10,000,000 or more to remove it, with no assurance that the mold would not come back. Based on those findings, the city reluctantly decided that the auditorium needed to be demolished. Because the city lacked the funds to demolish the massive structure, it agreed to transfer ownership of Memorial Auditorium to ECHDC for $1.00, with the understanding that ECHDC would pay for the cost of demolition and prepare the site for future development.

With Memorial Auditorium no longer available to house the proposed Bass Pro retail outlet, ESDC and Bass Pro quickly came up with an alternative plan. A front-page story in the *Buffalo News* on March 30, 2007, reported that a 100,000-square-foot, multistory Bass Pro Outdoor World store would be built instead on the portion of Buffalo's waterfront once occupied by the historic Central Wharf. Headlined "Bass Pro Landed—At Last," the article was accompanied by a color illustration showing what the project would presumably look like. The opening sentence of the article cleverly proclaimed: "After six years of casting its line, Buffalo has finally hooked a Bass Pro Outdoor World store for the downtown waterfront" (Linstedt 2007a, A1). Activist and historian Mark Goldman found it "incredible" that ECHDC would put forward such a plan after preservationists and state and local officials had publicly declared that they had settled their differences by signing a MOU and agreed to work together to carry out a historically respectful Inner Harbor Plan (Goldman, email, May 1, 2019).

Bass Pro's president asserted that the structure built on the Central Wharf to house the retail outlet would "pay tribute to the national importance of the Erie Canal's terminus" (Linstedt 2007a, A1). ECHDC Chairman Anthony Gioia echoed that sentiment by saying, "I can't think of a more appropriate type of retail business to be located on the water's edge than a Bass Pro Shop" (Linstedt 2007a, A1). According to ECHDC, the building would be designed to resemble the kind of buildings that formerly occupied the Central Wharf. In a 2007 op-ed piece published in the *Buffalo News*, Larry Quinn, managing partner and part owner of the Buffalo Sabres hockey franchise, argued that a Bass Pro outlet would "attract millions of people downtown and truly activate the lake and river with water-related activity . . . [and] remake downtown as the true retail and business center of the region" (Quinn 2007).

Preservationists were outraged by the proposed plan. Tim Tielman termed the proposed building "an abomination," and expressed the view that a "big-box" retail store had no place occupying such a historically important waterfront property. He also pointed out that developing such a structure on the historic footprint of the Central Wharf would violate the court-approved 2004 master plan that had designated that land for historic purposes and public access.

In September 2007, four months after the rendering of Bass Pro's proposed Central Wharf retail store appeared in the *Buffalo News,* Congressman Brian Higgins announced that the idea of building a 100,000-square-foot store on the historic Central Wharf had been scrapped. ECHDC and Bass Pro shifted back to the idea of developing the sporting goods outlet on the site of Memorial Auditorium after the structure had been cleared away. Demolition of the Aud began in 2008. ECHDC and city officials confirmed that the newly constructed Bass Pro Outdoor World store on the site formerly occupied by the Aud would be complemented by the same parking and transportation infrastructure improvements previously promised when it was expected that the store would be built *within* the Aud. (See figure 7.1 for what the Aud Block looked like after the Aud was demolished and the site was cleared.)

In 2008, Congressman Higgins renegotiated the terms of the earlier agreement he had negotiated with NYPA so as to accelerate NYPA's payments. Under the revised terms of the agreement, NYPA agreed to provide annual payments of $8.5 million per year for the next 20 years (rather than $3.5 million per year for 50 years). In the meantime, ECHDC had been making substantial progress in developing Canalside in the historically respectful manner called for in the MOU that preservationists and state and local government officials had signed back in 2005.

Canalside officially opened to the public in 2008. Although much of the site remained unimproved, many of the historically significant aspects of the redevelopment project had been completed by that time. The

Figure 7.1. The "Aud Block" after Memorial Auditorium was demolished and the site was cleared. Along the opposite side of lower Main Street are the Donovan State Office Building, the Webster Block used as a parking lot, and HSBC Arena. *Source*: ECHDC. Used with permission.

Commercial Slip had been restored and rewatered (figures 7.2 and 7.3), a replica bowstring truss bridge had been forged and put in place across the Commercial Slip (figures 7.4, 7.5, and 7.6), foundations of Canal-era buildings (such as the old Steamboat Hotel) had been uncovered (figure 7.6), a replica of the Canal-era Coit-McCutcheon block had been built (figure 7.6), and the ships of the Naval and Military Servicemen's Park had been moved downriver closer to the mouth of the Buffalo River. Nevertheless, considerable uncertainty remained as to what might else happen on the site because ECHDC appeared to still be counting on having a large-scale Bass Pro Outdoor World retail outlet anchor the Inner Harbor redevelopment project.

Figure 7.2. Workers reconstructing the stone walls of the Commercial Slip. *Source*: Photo by Eugene Witkowski. Used with permission.

Figure 7.3. Newly reconstructed and rewatered Commercial Slip, with a replica of the historic Coit-McCutcheon block under construction in the background *Source*: Photo by Eugene Witkowski. Used with permission.

Figure 7.4. *Edward M. Cotter* tugboat making its way down the ice-clogged Buffalo River on February 1, 2007, towing a barge carrying the newly forged bowstring truss bridge that would be installed at Canalside. *Source*: Photo by Eugene Witkowski. Used with permission.

Figure 7.5. Bowstring truss bridge being put in place over the Commercial Slip on a bitter cold day in February 2007. *Source*: Photo by Eugene Witkowski. Used with permission.

Figure 7.6. Bowstring truss bridge in place over the Commercial Slip; uncovered foundations of Canal-era structures and completed Coit-McCutcheon block in the background. *Source*: ECHDC. Used with permission.

NGOs Seek a Greater Voice in
How Economic Development Is Conducted

The fight against the Bass Pro project at Canalside was initially led by the Preservation Coalition of Erie County. Before long, however, NGOs concerned about other issues also became involved.

Back in 1945, at a time when Buffalo was one of the most heavily industrialized cities in the country, Cornell University established the School of Industrial and Labor Relations (ILR). Recognizing that Buffalo was the perfect place to study industrial and labor relations, the university created Cornell Buffalo ILR and established an office in downtown Buffalo in 1946.

In 2002, Trico Products Corporation, which was founded in Buffalo in 1917 and as recently as 1985 had employed 2,500 people in Buffalo, announced it was going to close its Buffalo manufacturing operations and move its manufacture of windshield wiper blades to Mexico. In reaction to the announcement, religious and labor leaders in Buffalo created the Center for Economic Justice (CEJ) in an effort to prevent further losses of jobs to low-wage locations.

In 2007, Cornell Buffalo ILR hired Buffalo lawyer Sam Magavern to oversee workplace compliance with the City of Buffalo's newly enacted "Living Wage Law." That same year, Magavern organized a conference titled "The High Road Runs through the City" that gave rise to the idea of creating an entity to provide policy advice and conduct research in support of local NGOs. "For all too long, the nonprofit sector lacked a seat at the table and voice in framing of public policy to the same extent as the private sector . . . Strengthening the voice of nonprofit, nongovernmental organizations was all the more important because they represented the interests of people at the grass-roots level who were basically holding the city together, even as more and more businesses and industries were shutting down and leaving the city" (Fleron, interview, January 28, 2019).

A new entity that was created was called Partnership for the Public Good (PPG). The formation of PPG was to some extent an outgrowth of CEJ's involvement in attempting to achieve a community benefit agreement in relation to the Bass Pro project. "CEJ was among the key groups that helped found PPG and served as the fiscal sponsor for our first grant application. CEJ's executive director Allison Duwe was a founding board member of PPG" (Magavern, email, November 11, 2022). Cornell Buffalo ILR "incubated" Partnership for the Public Good by providing it with some of its own office space rent-free. In 2007, PPG had 36 partner organizations. By 2018, the number of partner organizations had grown to over 200. Once it became established, PPG began paying Cornell Buffalo for the office space it occupied.

In 2009, as the controversy over the proposed Bass Pro project was reaching a fever pitch, CEJ mobilized community opposition to the huge taxpayer subsidies being offered to Bass Pro by creating the Canal Side Community Alliance (CSCA), a network of community and faith-based organizations that included PPG, People United for Sustainable Housing (PUSH), Voice-Buffalo, minority contractors, and locally owned businesses. An important aim of CSCA was to persuade the city to require the signing of a community benefit agreement (CBA) as a precondition for allowing any project at Canalside to proceed.

In March 2010, the Buffalo Common Council approved a nonbinding resolution in support making the transfer of land sought by Bass Pro for its project at Canalside contingent upon the negotiation of a CBA with the city that guaranteed that local residents, minorities, and women-owned businesses would benefit from the project. "While the activists did not win the *legally binding* [italics added] Community Benefit Agreement (CBA) that they sought, they succeeded in dramatically changing the course of Canalside and changing the way that economic development is discussed, understood and practiced in Buffalo" (Zhao 2017).

On June 2, 2010, the Public Accountability Initiative, a nonprofit public interest research organization released a report that documented the experiences of communities across the country that had granted huge taxpayer subsidies to Bass Pro in the hope that they would reap substantial economic benefit from the development of a large Bass Pro retail in their community. The title of the report was "Fishing for Taxpayer Cash: Bass Pro's Record of Big-League Subsidies, Failed Promises, and the Consequences for Cities across America" (Stecker, Connor, and Public Accountability Initiative 2011). According to the report, Bass Pro projects across the country had received a total of $500 million in taxpayer subsidies but had failed to produce the spin-off economic benefits that had been promised. The report's findings, which were reported by the *Buffalo News*, ignited a firestorm of media coverage because they undermined the argument for offering $35 million subsidies to Bass Pro to get it to develop a retail outlet on the waterfront. The report furthermore asserted that ECHDC's estimates of the Bass Pro project's potential to make downtown Buffalo a major tourist attraction were greatly inflated and that it was unlikely the project would generate the economic development benefits that had been promised.

On July 19, 2010, Congressman Brian Higgins issued an ultimatum, imposing a 14-day deadline for reaching a final agreement with Bass Pro. Two weeks later, at a hastily called news conference on July 30, a clearly disappointed Jordan Levy, ECHDC's chairman, announced that he had learned from Bass Pro's founder and chairman Johnny Morris that Bass Pro would be withdrawing from the project. Mayor Masiello expressed regret that Bass Pro found it necessary to withdraw from the project and cast most of the blame on the Buffalo City Council's approval of a resolution requiring the signing of a CBA as a condition for transferring city-owned land to the company.

While Mayor Masiello, Levy, and Quinn viewed Bass Pro's withdrawal as a setback, others saw it as the dawn of a new day. Representative Brian Higgins declared there was a silver lining to Bass Pro's withdrawal, declaring that "metaphorically, it was the day Buffalo learned to stand on its own . . . as opposed to putting our fate in the hands of outside interests" (Esmonde 2016).

Why It Took ECHDC So Long to
Walk Away from Bass Pro

When ECHDC was created in 2005, the voting members of the ECHDC's board of directors were primarily drawn from the world of business, as well as from the circle of professionals who worked closely with business and corporate leaders. "ECHDC's boardroom was populated by corporate power brokers who didn't know Jane Jacobs from Jane Fonda. They were picked for their business success and political donations, not for any grasp of urban planning . . . The idea was if you were successful in business, you could make good decisions about anything" (Esmonde 2016).

The corporate mind-set that voting members of ECHDC's board of directors brought to the table appears to have influenced the way they thought about how the city's waterfront should be developed. The original board of ECHDC included Maureen Hurley, executive vice president of Rich Products, one of the largest and most important companies headquartered in Buffalo. Mindy Rich, the wife of Robert E. Rich, Jr., chairman and majority owner of Rich Products, also served as a special nonvoting member (her Florida residency precluded her from holding a voting seat). The vice chair of the ECHDC's board was Larry Quinn, who was managing partner and part owner of the Buffalo Sabres hockey franchise. With a new arena having just been built nearby, Quinn had an obvious financial interest in how Canalside would be developed and was an outspoken supporter of the Bass Pro project. The chairman of ECHDC's board, businessman Jordan Levy, was also strongly in favor of the Bass project.

The fact that ECHDC's governance structure called for voting members to be appointed by the governor also hampered the proper functioning of the agency at times, because even during normal times the process of getting a governor to fill vacant positions could take a long time. When New York State government was in crisis, as it was in 2007–2008 when Governor Eliot Spitzer was embroiled in a scandal that forced him to resign in March 2008, the process took an especially long time. According to David Colligan, who served as a voting member on ECHDC's board from 2007 to 2017, it was not at all unusual for voting member positions on ECHDC's board to remain unfilled for extended periods. "My recollection is that we didn't have a full complement of voting members 50% of the time" (Colligan, interview, July 18, 2018). Also, because some voting members repeatedly failed to attend board meetings, many board meetings were conducted with no more than four or five voting members present, and it was often the same four people who constituted the quorum (Colligan, as quoted by Sommer 2017b). On the positive side, Colligan noted that the good attendance of the board's two nonvoting members, Mayor Byron Brown and County Executive Mark Poloncarz, helped fill the void created by the poor attendance of certain voting members of the board.

Newspaper Coverage of the Bass Pro Inner Harbor Controversy

The conflict between preservationists and the state agency over how the Inner Harbor should be redeveloped took roughly a dozen years to be satisfactorily resolved. Throughout that period, Buffalo was served by a vital local newspaper that was read every day by hundreds of thousands of people in Buffalo and across eight counties in Western New York. Within the newspaper industry the *Buffalo News* was generally known to have one of the highest levels of market penetration of any newspaper in the country. The *Buffalo News* benefited from a long period of stable ownership. After being locally owned and operated by the Butler family for decades, the newspaper was purchased in 1977 by Warren Buffett's Berkshire Hathaway Company, which operated it quite profitably for the next 43 years. As a result, what was published in the *Buffalo News* had a considerable impact on what people in the Buffalo area knew and thought about the Inner Harbor project.[2]

Editorially, the *Buffalo News* was initially in favor of the Bass Pro project, as were most people in the community with power, influence, and money. Over time, however, editorials and articles that appeared in the newspaper expressed a broader range of opinions and viewpoints and ultimately became much more critical of the proposed project.

Between 2010 and 2012, while on the faculty of the Department of Geography and Planning at the University at Albany, I supervised the research of a graduate student who analyzed the *Buffalo News'* coverage of the Inner Harbor redevelopment controversy. The research was conducted by Jimmy Vielkind, who at the time was also a reporter for the Albany *Times-Union* newspaper. The ten-year period Vielkind chose to analyze began in July 2001, when Mayor Masiello publicly announced his support for luring a Bass Pro retail outlet to Buffalo's waterfront and ended in October 2010, when Bass Pro announced it was dropping out of the project. Vielkind explained that he considered it important to analyze how the *Buffalo News* covered the Bass Pro issue because "good planning relies on the consideration of competing visions" (Vielkind 2012, 29).

Vielkind searched the archives of the *Buffalo News* to identify articles published during the study period that mentioned "Erie Canal Harbor" or "Aud" or "Bass Pro" anywhere in their text. That initial search yielded at total of 2,336 articles, with the annual number of articles peaking in 2007. He then analyzed the *content* of those articles to identify those that related directly to the Bass Pro project—of which there were 719. Each of those 719 articles were then cataloged as to the date of publication, the title, and the author. These articles were then further classified into one of four categories:

- *Event-driven* articles that dealt primarily with public meetings, press conferences, or protests.

- *Enterprise* articles that were either investigatory or analytical in nature, and often driven by a reporter's interest rather than any specific event, statement, or action that pertained to the development.

- *Viewpoint* articles—editorials, letters to the editor, op/ed submissions, or columns typically selected, commissioned, edited, and published by a staff member separate from the one that handled standard news articles.

- *Incremental* articles—straightforward reports regarding matters such as legal proceedings, changes in a project's design, or specifications and updates on project financing. (Vielkind 2012, 12)

Having worked as a reporter, Vielkind knew that *incremental* news articles tended to be the most common type of article to appear in newspapers. However, his analysis of the content of the articles revealed that a surprisingly large number—320 (45 percent) of the 719 total articles published in the *Buffalo News* during the study period—expressed a point-of-view and/or judgment regarding the merits of the project. Of the 320 "viewpoint" articles, 84 (26 percent) were editorials, most of which during the early part of the study period praised and welcomed the project. "It was only when public sentiment had turned clearly against the project that the tone of the *Buffalo News* editorials changed (Kelly, interview, February 7, 2018).

In addition to the editorials written by its own staff and 41 viewpoint articles submitted independently by a number of individuals, the newspaper also published scores of letters to the editor about the Bass Pro project, which facilitated a kind of back-and-forth community conversation on the subject. In 2010, the newspaper published the results of a poll it had commissioned that found that 52 percent of 401 city residents surveyed opposed the use of taxpayer dollars for the Bass Pro project, while 42 percent were supportive (Vielkind 2012, 32).

The *Buffalo News* also provided background information that enabled citizens to more thoughtfully consider and evaluate what was being proposed to take place on Buffalo's waterfront. The newspaper ran an article on the front page of its Sunday edition describing past "silver bullet" development failures. An editorial soon followed. Other enterprising stories looked at the Bass Pro deal from different perspectives, such as by comparing the incentive package to those offered in other cities. For another article, a reporter traveled to a Bass Pro store in Florida to assess what impact it had had on its surrounding area.

The most prolific beat reporter at the *Buffalo News* in terms of numbers of articles written during the study period about the Bass Pro project was Sharon Linstedt, who filed a total of 186 articles about the Bass Pro project, the vast majority of which were extremely supportive of the proposed project and *incremental and event-driven* in nature. Donn Esmonde was by far the most prolific writer of *viewpoint* articles that expressed an explicit point-of-view regarding the project, authoring 68 viewpoint articles during the study period. "Hard news" stories written by Linstedt were often followed by commentaries and analyses by Donn Esmonde, who repeatedly criticized ECHDC for being out of touch with local public sentiment. "Time and time again, the powers-that-be were obstacles to change, not the agents of it" (Esmonde 2016).

Chapter Eight

Lighter, Quicker, Cheaper

Canalside has been transformational for the city . . . and for the psychology of people who lived here for years believing nothing [good] would ever happen.

—Steven Ranalli, president,
Erie Canal Harbor Development Corporation

After spending nearly six years trying to get Bass Pro to develop an Outdoor World retail outlet on Buffalo's downtown waterfront, ECHDC was essentially back to square one. To enable members of the public to be involved in considering how to move forward at that point and what should be done next, Bruce Fisher and Mark Goldman began planning to hold two public forums.

The first public forum was organized by Bruce Fisher and held on October 23, 2010, in the auditorium of the Burchfield Penney Art Center on the campus of Buffalo State College. The second public forum titled "Imagining Buffalo's Waterfront" was organized by Mark Goldman and held at City Honors School on November 6, 2010. Among those in attendance were ECHDC board members David Colligan, Julie Barrett O'Neill, and board chair Jordan Levy, whom O'Neill and Colligan had persuaded to attend.[1] "Jordan Levy did come to the 'Imagining Buffalo's Waterfront' event, although he also left early" (Goldman, email, May 1, 2019).

Fred Kent, the president of the Project for Public Spaces, was the forum's keynote speaker. Kent wanted $6,000 to come to Buffalo to participate in the event—none of which was provided by ECHDC. Goldman paid half of Kent's fee, and the other $3,000 was paid by the Rupp Family Foundation. In his keynote address, Kent urged public officials and citizens in Buffalo to get over the heavy subsidy, "silver-bullet," lots-of-parking fixation that had dominated their thinking up to then and embrace a "lighter, quicker, cheaper" approach to activating the waterfront.

Eight months after the "Imagining Buffalo's Waterfront" event was held, a grassy lawn had been laid down and filled with multicolored Adirondack chairs, and suddenly people began being drawn to the site, prompting Mark Goldman to observe that "the major economic development success story in our community involved $3,000 worth of Adirondack chairs" (see figures 8.1–8.4).

ECHDC hired Fred Kent to advise it regarding what it should do next to activate the Inner Harbor. Kent advised the agency to place greater emphasis on programming to draw people down to Canalside. Soon a wide

Figure 8.1. "The major economic development success story in our community involved $3,000 worth of Adirondack chairs."—Mark Goldman. *Source*: Photo by the author.

Figure 8.2. After grass and trees were planted and colorful Adirondack chairs were placed on the grass, people began to be attracted to Canalside. *Source*: Photo by Mark Goldman. Used with permission.

Figure 8.3. Mark Goldman. *Source*: Photo by Mark Goldman. Used with permission.

Figure 8.4. Visitors viewing Erie Canal exhibit. *Source*: Photo by the author.

range of outdoor activities were taking place at Canalside that brought a steady stream of people to take part in fitness and exercise classes, yoga classes, children's story hours, ping-pong, and other activities. A platform stage was erected on which musicians could perform and, in summer 2015 ECHDC launched a series of weekly concerts called "Canalside Live" that brought large crowds to the Inner Harbor.

Around that same time a major change in the leadership of ECHDC took place. Jordan Levy stepped down as chairman of ECHDC's board of directors. Larry Quinn, who had been an outspoken proponent of the Bass Pro project also resigned from ECHDC's board. Robert Gioia, president and CEO of the John R. Oishei Foundation, replaced Jordan Levy as chairman of ECHDC's board of directors.

Up until that point, most of those who had advocated for preserving and uncovering the western terminus of the Erie Canal primarily thought about Canalside as a potential visitor destination. Few had thought that a mixed-use waterfront neighborhood might also be developed on the site where people could live and work.

On June 21, 2013, Friends of the Buffalo Story members Mark Goldman, Peter B. Dowd, and Scott A. Wood gave a presentation to ECHDC's board that showed five different ways a mixed-use, walkable neighborhood could be developed on the northern portion of the area formerly occupied by Memorial Auditorium, which varied considerably with respect to the amount and density of development that would take place and the amount of parking provided. The five development scenarios that were graphically illustrated in the presentation were: Urban Village, Village Square, Mid-Rise, Large-Scale, and Pearl Street Realignment. Funding for the planning and design work that was involved in preparing the presentation was provided by a grant from the Oishei Foundation.

With Bass Pro Out of the Picture, Good Things Start to Happen

Two years after Bass Pro announced it was withdrawing from the Inner Harbor project, the Liberty Hound Restaurant opened at 1 Naval Park Cove, adjacent to the Buffalo and Erie County Naval and Military Park and Commercial Slip, in 2012. The restaurant's outdoor deck overlooking the harbor soon became a popular gathering place during warm weather. Construction also began on converting the first four floors of the former Donovan New York State Office Building into a 102-room Marriott Courtyard hotel and the building's top four floors into office space. Meanwhile, ECHDC accepted the development proposal submitted by a subsidiary of the Buffalo Sabres that called for building a large-scale project called HarborCenter on the city-owned "Webster Block" that had long been used as a parking lot.

In September 2015, the $210 million HarborCenter project was completed, and its two indoor hockey rinks (with seating capacities of 200 and 1,800) began hosting college hockey games, youth hockey, and college hockey training camps, as well as practice sessions of the Buffalo Sabres. A sports-oriented brew pub/restaurant operated by Southern Tier Brewing Company anchored the corner of Scott and Washington Streets, while a Tim Hortons coffee shop occupied the corner of Main and Scott Streets across the from the Erie Canal Harbor Metro Rail station.

Canalside's appeal as a visitor destination got an unexpected boost when the Albright-Knox Art Gallery, as part of its first public art initiative, installed an unusual sculpture at Canalside—the figure of a girl in a Victorian dress and the head of a shark (shown in figure 8.5).[2] In 2018, the

Figure 8.5. Shark Girl sculpture at Canalside. *Source*: Photo by the author.

Huffington Post released its list of "35 Most Instagram-Worthy Subjects" in the Northeast, and Canalside's "Shark Girl" sculpture was no. 17 on the list.

To further enliven the area of lower Main Street during the evening, ECHDC hired Ambience Design Productions of Quebec to develop a dynamic, colorful digital display that could be projected onto the surface of the Connecting Terminal elevator across from Canalside (figure 8.6). The dynamic and brilliant multicolored lighting display has been projected

Figure 8.6. Light show projected onto the Connecting Terminal Elevator across from Canalside. *Source*: ECHDC. Used with permission.

onto the Connecting Terminal Elevator every evening since 2015 and has by now become a signature feature of Canalside.

A Portion of the Erie Canal Is
Recreated on the South Aud Block

In the fall of 2010, David Colligan, a voting member of ECHDC's board, was eating lunch at a pizza place on Chippewa Street and noticed an 1885 street map of Buffalo on the wall. He looked more closely at the map because he was curious about what had formerly been on the site of Memorial Auditorium before "the Aud" was built. "There, marked on the grid, snaked the Erie Canal. 'I had no idea that the canal ran right through there,' said Colligan" (*Buffalo News* staff 2015). (See again figure 1.7 for the path the Erie Canal followed as it approached its western terminus.) Colligan had formerly headed Buffalo's Olmsted Parks Conservancy and recognized that the path the canal had followed as it approached the Commercial Slip could serve a beneficial public use.

Colligan was well aware there had been considerable local opposition to a plan that ECHDC had developed that called for building a parking ramp on the site. He also knew that preservationists had strongly opposed having a replica Canal Slip built adjacent to where the real Commercial Slip lay buried.

Colligan approached preservationist Tim Tielman to see if they could strike a deal that would enable Tielman to support building a shallow canal that would historically reference the original path the Erie Canal had followed as it approached the Commercial Slip. The deal Colligan proposed was this: he would vote against ECHDC going forward with building the parking structure; in return, Tielman wouldn't oppose the recreational canal Colligan had in mind that would be on the historic alignment of the canal. "I thought people wouldn't mind if we recreated the canal [in a way] that was authentic to the site," said Colligan (Colligan, interview July 18, 2018). After vetting the idea of creating the replica canal with Tielman, and with the encouragement of Congressman Brian Higgins, Colligan took his replica canal idea to the ECHDC board and gained their approval.

In 2014, the replica canal Colligan had envisioned was completed and filled to a shallow depth with water. In December 2014, it was frozen for the first time and opened for public ice skating. City residents flocked to skate on the Ice at Canalside—the largest outdoor skating rink in New York State (figure 8.7). The Ice at Canalside has since also frequently hosted pond hockey and curling tournaments.

Figure 8.7. People skating at night on the Ice in 2015 at Canalside. *Source*: ECHDC. Used with permission.

The *Spirit of Buffalo* and *Queen City Bike Ferry*

Ric and Kathy Hilliman raised three children in Tonawanda. For many years they kept a 32-foot sloop at the Small Boat Harbor and enjoyed spending summer evenings and weekends sailing out on Lake Erie. Ric eventually earned his captain's license and for a number of years served as the captain of *Miss Buffalo*.

In 2006, the Hilliman's purchased a 73-foot, square-rigged topsail schooner called the *Jolly Roger* that had been built in 1992 and spent its first five years sailing out of Lewis, Delaware, before being brought to Georgetown, South Carolina. In December 2008 they formed Buffalo Sailing Adventures as a family-owned company and brought the schooner to Baltimore where it spent the winter being prepared for its journey to Buffalo via the Hudson River and the Erie Canal. The schooner arrived in Buffalo in May 2009 and was renamed *Spirit of Buffalo*. Shortly thereafter Buffalo Sailing Adventures began offering visitors to Canalside the opportunity to sail out onto Lake Erie from the Commercial Slip (figure 8.8).

Figure 8.8. The *Spirit of Buffalo* returns to the Commercial Slip after taking passengers out onto Lake Erie. *Source*: Photo by the author.

For over 60 years, the only way to get to the Outer Harbor from downtown Buffalo was by driving a car over the Buffalo Skyway. The idea that ECHDC should initiate ferry service between Canalside and the Outer Harbor was first put forward by John Montague, the founder of the Buffalo Maritime Center. However, state agency officials dismissed the idea because they doubted the ferry would attract many riders and expected it would lose money.

Montague eventually overcame these objections by showing NYS Assemblyman Sean Ryan a movie of water taxis operating in the Netherlands. Ryan managed to find enough state money to buy a flat pontoon barge with a pilot house that could serve as the bike ferry, and ECHDC finally agreed to launch the ferry service. ECHCD awarded the contract to operate the bike ferry to Buffalo Sailing Adventures, which was already operating the *Spirit of Buffalo* out of the Commercial Slip. The *Queen City Bike Ferry* began transporting people and their bikes from the Commercial Slip at Canalside to a newly created bike ferry landing at the Outer Harbor in 2015.

"The ferry proved so popular that people often had to be turned away" (Montague, email, February 19, 2019). During its first year of operation, the *Queen City Bike Ferry* drew over 55,000 passengers, and its popularity as an enjoyable and affordable way to access the Outer Harbor from Canalside has increased since then (figure 8.9). A one-way trip to or from the Outer Harbor, with or without a bicycle, costs only one dollar.[3]

Development of Housing

In August 2018, ECHDC selected Sinatra & Company to develop a pair of multistory mixed-use buildings containing a total of 62 apartments and 71,000 square feet of retail and office space on the portion of the South Aud Block closest to the Erie Canal Harbor Metro Rail station. ECHCD agreed to sell the land for the project, called Heritage Point, to the developer for $1 and to pay $2 million for preserving and restoring the adjacent Prime Slip, installing lighting, and reestablishing Canal-era

Figure 8.9. People boarding *Queen City Bike Ferry* docked in the Commercial Slip, with the *Spirit of Buffalo* docked in the background. *Source*: Buffalo Sailing Adventures. Used with permission.

portions of Lloyd Street and Canal Street. To acknowledge and preserve the historic footprint of the former Prime Slip, one of the buildings was made larger than the other, and the smaller building was designed in the shape of a triangle (Sommer 2018d).

The Heritage Point mixed-use project was significantly delayed by a combination of factors, including the COVID-19 pandemic, the time it took to negotiate and secure regulatory approval of parking arrangements for the project, and the need to remediate environmental contamination on the site before beginning construction. Supply chain issues and associated price hikes on building materials also plagued the project. By summer 2023 the construction of the first housing at Canalside was well underway (figure 8.10).

Meanwhile, the Buffalo Municipal Housing Authority (BMHA) announced plans to tear down the 72-year-old towers of the Marine Drive

Figure 8.10. Heritage Point mixed-use project under construction in July 2023, with Explore & More Children's Museum and Marine Drive Apartments in the background. *Source*: Photo by the author.

Apartment complex adjacent to Canalside and replace them with a new housing complex capable of accommodating more residents. Multiple reasons were given for tearing the towers down and starting anew: the buildings and systems were functionally obsolete and couldn't be upgraded or rehabbed in a cost-effective manner; the kitchens and bathrooms were cramped; the windows were tiny; the walls were thin and ceiling heights were less than 7.5 feet; there had been repeated problems with the heating and water pipes; and there was no air conditioning (Epstein 2023a). According to BMHA executive director Gillian D. Brown, "Marine Drive has gone from being the only thing on the waterfront to the worst on the waterfront . . . Every current resident will have the opportunity to live in the revitalized Marine Drive Apartments" (Epstein 2023a).

Chapter Nine

Three Projects That Made Canalside Even More Special

In July 2010, the same month that Bass Pro announced it was withdrawing from the Inner Harbor project, ECHDC hired Lord Cultural Resources to conduct a study to determine what type or types of cultural institutions might be added to Canalside to increase its appeal as a visitor destination and complement Buffalo's existing array of cultural institutions. The consultants interviewed and conducted workshops with over 140 people drawn from a variety of cultural backgrounds and interests. They also contacted 110 arts and cultural institutions to see if any of them might be interested in relocating to Canalside. After going through that process, the consultants concluded that a children's museum would be the best kind of cultural attraction to have at Canalside.

The Explore & More Children's Museum

As it turned out, the Explore & More Children's Museum, which had started out 25 years earlier in a 500-square-foot rented space in the basement of a school in East Aurora, was very much interested in relocating to Canalside. Barbara Leggett, Explore & More's CEO at the time, prepared and submitted the formal proposal to ECHDC that confirmed the museum's interest in relocating to Canalside. She also prepared the museum's application to the Ralph C. Wilson Jr. Foundation requesting capital funding to build the museum.

In February 2017, ECHDC approved the construction of a 43,000-square-foot building to house the Explore & More Museum on the southern portion of the "Aud Block." Construction of the museum began in March 2017. On Valentine's Day 2018, a few months before the Children's Museum opened to the public in June, the Ralph C. Wilson Jr. Foundation awarded $6 million to the museum to assure the completion of the museum and also to establish an endowment to underwrite the museum's expanded operation at Canalside. In honor of the Wilson Foundation's gift, the museum was renamed the Ralph C. Wilson Jr. Children's Museum.

In fall 2017, the museum undertook a search to hire a new CEO and hired Michelle Urbanczyk to oversee the operation of the museum's significantly expanded facility at Canalside. Prior to being chosen to lead the museum, Urbanczyk had been president of EPIC (Every Person Influences Children) and before that had been director of development for the Buffalo Society of Natural Sciences.

ECHDC's president Steven Ranalli took me on a tour of the museum a few weeks before it opened and made a particular point of showing me the Low Bridge Café below the main level of the museum that looks out onto the replica canal. We both remarked on how wonderful it would be during the winter to be in the café and look out the window and see people ice-skating on the canal a few feet away (see figure 9.1).

Figure 9.1. Explore & More Children's Museum overlooking replica canal. *Source*: Photo by Joe Cascio. Used with permission.

During its first nine months of operation the Explore & More Children's Museum averaged between 800 and 1,200 visitors a day. One of the museum's exhibits that kids enjoyed the most was a scaled-down waterway and lock system like that on the Erie Canal that had a crane they could operate to lift grain into the hold of a boat.

In March 2020, just nine months after the Explore & Museum opened, the COVID-19 pandemic arrived, forcing the museum to drastically reduce its hours of operation and lay off more than half its staff. "Many of those who had staffed the museum self-identified as wanting to stop working" (Urbanczyk, interview, June 15, 2021). For the next 15 months the museum was open only three days a week, and at only 12 percent of capacity—resulting in a steep decline in ticket revenue. Schools stopped sending children to the museum on school trips because they couldn't maintain social distance on school buses (Urbanczyk). Pandemic protocols also prevented the museum from hosting the kinds of special events that would have attracted large gatherings and generated significant additional income.

During the initial months the museum had been open, the museum built up a substantial base of membership among Canadians. But for almost two years Canadians were unable to travel freely across the border, which further reduced visitation to the museum. "We had a million-dollar reserve prior to the pandemic but had to spend most of it during the pandemic" (Urbanczyk, interview, June 15, 2021). The museum received $42,000 from Erie County—an amount that unfortunately was based on the level of funding *it would otherwise have qualified for* had it been operating in the much smaller space it had previously occupied in East Aurora. Money the museum received through the federal government's Paycheck Protection Program (PPP) also helped the museum stay open. In May 2021, the museum was awarded a $250,000 grant from KeyBank and the First Niagara Foundation, which enabled it to rehire four members of its educational staff, refill four administrative positions, and also extend its days of operation to Mondays, Wednesdays, Thursdays, Fridays, and Saturdays (Sommer 2021g).

In early December 2021, the Ralph C. Wilson Foundation announced that the Children's Museum could expect to receive an annual grant of $200,000 in perpetuity as part of the $100 million donation the foundation would be making to arts and cultural organizations throughout the region (Sommer 2021j). By Spring 2022, Urbanczyk was cautiously optimistic that the museum had weathered the worst effects of the COVID-19 pandemic.

"We're beginning to see more out-of-town visitors from places with far away zip codes. Every day for the next few months we're booked to receive field trips from schools" (Urbanczyk, interview, April 28, 2022).

Buffalo Heritage Carousel, a beautifully restored rare example of a three-row, park-style carousel manufactured in North Tonawanda in the early 1920s began operating at Canalside on Memorial Day weekend in 2021 (see figure 9.2). "The merry-go-round has a herd of 27 horses, plus a deer, lion, tiger, giraffe, ostrich, mule, and 'lake monster,' three chariots, an Erie Canal boat, and a rocking gondolier" (Sommer 2021c, A1).

Painted depictions of the *Maid of the Mist*, Niagara Falls, the Pan-American Exposition held in Buffalo in 1901, the Great Northern Grain Elevator, a Pierce-Arrow automobile, and the Buffalo lighthouse embellish the carousel's running boards. The connection to the Buffalo area is further reinforced by the fact that the restored Wurlitzer 153 band organ that plays when the carousel turns was manufactured by the Wurlitzer Company of North Tonawanda.[1]

Figure 9.2. Heritage Carousel. *Source*: Photo by the author.

The idea of installing a carousel as a way of revitalizing Buffalo's waterfront was first suggested in 2003 by Laura Briggs, a renewable energy expert who later became the chairwoman of sustainable architecture at Parsons School of Design in New York City (Sommer 2013). The idea was soon embraced by Erie County legislator Joan Bozer, herself a strong proponent of solar energy and quickly gained additional supporters such as Mark Goldman and Robert Kresse, a trustee of the Margaret L. Wendt Foundation (DeCroix 2021, 29). Bozer asked Professor Frank Santuzzi of the University at Buffalo's School of Architecture and Planning to develop a model of such a solar-powered carousel to advance the concept (see figure 9.3). It should be noted that the previously mentioned report that Lord Cultural Resources submitted to ECHDC in 2010 recommended adding a children's museum *and* a carousel.

The idea of bringing a carousel to Canalside "began to take shape and gained new life" after an article by Mark Sommer was published in

Figure 9.3. Buffalo Heritage Carousel "Powered by the Sun." *Source*: Photo by the author.

the *Buffalo News* in August 2013 (DeCroix 2021, 30). Sommer's article attracted the attention of Laurie Hauer-LaDuca, an architect and carousel enthusiast, who along with artist Helen Ronan set out to try to make the project a reality. The kind of carousel they felt would be most appropriate for Canalside was a park-style carousel that had been manufactured by the Herschell-Spillman Engineering Company in North Tonawanda, one of the most renowned manufacturers of carousels in the country during the early part of the twentieth century. In October 2013, they identified such a carousel that had been purchased directly from the manufacturer by Dominick DeAngelis in 1924 that had been operated at two sites outside Boston and after his death in 1952 had been put into storage in Mansfield, Ohio.

In August 2014, Hauer-LaDuca and a few others traveled to Mansfield, Ohio, to examine the condition of the pieces of the carousel and to meet with members of the DeAngelis family to "make the case for bringing the carousel back to the region of its birth" (DeCroix 2021, 30). Having previously rejected other lucrative offers, the family agreed to sell the carousel so that it could be brought back to Buffalo. The Margaret L. Wendt Foundation provided the $25,000 needed to place an initial deposit on the carousel, with the understanding that the remainder of the $250,000 purchase price would be provided once a suitable site at Canalside had been secured" (DeCroix 2021, 30).

In December 2014, Buffalo Heritage Carousel, Inc. was formed as a nonprofit organization to raise the funding needed to carry the project forward, thereby providing a public "face" for the project. However, the people who made up the Heritage Carousel nonprofit organization weren't politically well connected and initially had a hard time gaining the attention and support of government officials. For that reason, the Wendt Foundation's initial support was especially important, because it added credibility to their effort and opened the door to additional support—both financial and political.

Governor Cuomo eventually announced the award of $1.2 million in state funding toward the cost of building a structure to house the solar powered carousel at Canalside. KeyBank, the First Niagara Foundation, and the Margaret Wendt Foundation chipped in another $250,000. Other sources and amounts of funding toward the cost of constructing a custom-designed octagonal structure to house the carousel included $464,000 from the Buffalo and Erie County Greenway Fund and $250,000 each from the Russell J. Salvatore Foundation and the Ralph C. Wilson Foundation. The solar panels to power the carousel were donated by Tesla and manufactured at the company's Riverbend plant in South Buffalo. Every bit as important was ECHDC's and the City of Buffalo's willingness to lease 8,500 square feet at the southern end of the historic Central Wharf rent-free to Buffalo Heritage Carousel, on which the octagonal structure could be built.

Assemblyman Sean Ryan secured $600,000 in state funds to help pay for the restoration of the carousel's wooden animals and machinery, with the stipulation that riding on the carousel should not cost more than $1.00. Additional private funding toward the cost of restoring the menagerie of wooden figures that made up the historic park-style carousel was obtained from individuals who agreed to "adopt" various carousel animals.

After being in storage for over 60 years, a good deal of work needed to be done to bring the carousel back into working order. Carousel & Carvings in Marion, Ohio, began the process by restoring the carousel's frame as well as its rounding boards, mirrors, and inner scenery panels. In the meantime, a workshop was established in North Tonawanda—one street away from where the carousel was originally built by Spillman Engineering Corporation—to house the local restoration effort.

> Master carver Patrick Stanczyk led a team of volunteers in the repair, reassembly, and restoration of the wooden animals and other details. The painting [of the wooden animals] was supervised by nationally recognized carousel artist Rosa Patton, who traveled from North Carolina six times over the restoration period to train the volunteers and oversee the effort. The carousel's decorative valances, inner scenery panels [of Western New York landmarks] and two of the chariots were painted at Patton's North Carolina studio. (DeCroix 2021, 31)

> About a dozen volunteers work at different times on the carousel: stripping, disassembling, repairing and painting the wooden animals. The volunteers come from the Buffalo Snowbirds Decorative Painters, Genesee County Decorative Painters and elsewhere . . . [T]rained by Rosa Patton . . . the group is overseen by Helen Ronan, a Snowbirds member and member of the Buffalo Heritage Carousel board of directors. "I'd say 90 percent of us are over 70 years old and we travel more than 20 miles to get here and volunteer," said Christine Kasprzak

of Cheektowaga. "It's a privilege to work on these horses," said Barb Wheeler of Depew. "Just to see them come alive. They were such a mess when we started." (Sommer 2018h, B1)

Buffalo Maritime Center
and the *Seneca Chief* Packet Boat Project

John Montague moved to Buffalo in 1984, joined the design faculty at Buffalo State College, and started a boat building and design program there in 1990s. By 1993, Montague had established the Center for Watercraft Studies, which offered an academic minor in watercraft design. Soon the program had progressed from teaching students about building kayaks to learning about how to build more sophisticated boats. The program also offered public school inner-city kids the opportunity to gain hands-on experience in woodworking and boat building. After retiring in 2006, Montague continued to pursue his interest in boats by establishing the Buffalo Maritime Center as a 501(c)(3) nonprofit corporation and taking the program off-campus.

Montague first got to know Roger Allen around 1990 through the Museum Small Craft Association, a group of curators and scholars involved with maritime museums. In addition to being a master boatbuilder in his own right, Allen had founded the Florida Maritime Museum in Cortez, Florida. Allen and Montague became better acquainted over the years because Allen's and Montague's parents lived close to one another in Florida. They frequently got together when Montague traveled south to visit his parents. Allen also visited Buffalo a number of times during that period.

Shortly after the Maritime Center was established, Montague "succeeded in persuading Allen to move to Buffalo (in winter, no less!) to become the director of the Buffalo Maritime Center" (Montague, email, June 21, 2021). Allen began serving as the Maritime Center's director in December 2010. At the time, the Maritime Center was operating out of rented space on Niagara Street. The following year, in November 2011, the Maritime Center moved into its present permanent facility on Arthur Street in the Riverside neighborhood. The 27,000-square-foot building at 90 Arthur Street had originally been a foundry in 1918 that had last housed the American Diamond Tool Company, which made abrasive wheels. When that company vacated the building, M&T Bank took over the property. However, vandals had done so much damage to the property in the interim that the bank realized it was unlikely to gain much by attempting to sell the property, which made the bank receptive to the idea of donating the building to the Buffalo Maritime Center. "With a crew of volunteers and with the help of foundation grants and donations we rehabbed the building" (Montague, email, February 22, 2019).

Brian Trzeciak joined the Buffalo Maritime Center (BMC) in 2016, starting on the shop floor and eventually working his way up to become BMC's executive director. Before joining the Maritime Center, Trzeciak had worked as a community organizer with Citizen Action—a background he said proved especially useful when the Maritime Center needed to mobilize public support for its efforts.

In October 2000, John Montague and long-time Buffalonian John Sprague pitched the idea of building a canal-era packet boat in the Inner Harbor to Tom Blanchard, Empire State Development Corporation's director of Planning and Community Development. Blanchard, who had previously been president of the Horizons Waterfront Commission, told them he thought it was a great idea. Unfortunately, Sprague died in 2003, and the 2004 "Erie Canal Harbor Project Master Plan" prepared by Flynn Battaglia Architects failed to embrace the concept.

Between 2009 and 2018, Montague met with Tom Dee, ECHDC's president a number of times both individually and as a member of ECHDC's History Advisory Group in an effort to obtain his support for the packet boat project. "His general position was that people were not really interested in history, and that heritage tourism was not a driver of economic development. He essentially viewed the Canalside project as an opportunity for commercial development" (Montague, email, August 24, 2021.

In January 2018, Montague submitted an article to the *Buffalo News* to draw public attention to his idea of building a canal-era packet boat at Canalside. Rather than immediately publish Montague's op-ed, the newspaper sent reporter Mark Sommer to the Maritime Center to interview Montague, Allen, and Trzeciak in preparation for writing a feature article about the proposed packet boat project. The article Sommer wrote, which was published on May 17, 2018, reported that the Buffalo Maritime Center was planning on building a replica of the *Seneca Chief* packet boat that Governor DeWitt Clinton had boarded in Buffalo in 1825 and traveled on to New York to mark the opening of the Erie Canal. Also reported in the article was that the Maritime Center hoped to build the replica packet boat at Canalside and complete it in time to commemorate the 200th anniversary of the canal. "Building the boat in public will stir public interest and draw attention to the canal's history as a run-up to the bicentennial. The packet boat will raise consciousness about the importance of the Erie Canal not only for the development of Buffalo, but also of the nation," said Montague (Sommer2018b, D1).

Twelve days after Sommer's article appeared, Montague's op-ed appeared in which he reiterated that assembling the canal boat in public view would serve as an evolving and ever-changing public attraction that would draw people to Canalside and build a sense of community owner-ship. "By design, the pace of construction will be calculated to maximize opportunities for public participation" (Montague 2018).

After a flood of letters to the editor expressing strong support for the proposed undertaking, Montague, Allen, and Trzeciak were invited to meet with the *Buffalo News* editorial staff. Soon thereafter the *Buffalo News* published an editorial headlined "Build the Boat."

> It's an alluring prospect: The Buffalo Maritime Center wants to construct a 73-foot boat of exactly the sort that once plied the waters of the canal, using the same tools and techniques and assisted by what would surely be an eager public. Construc-tion of the packet boat would take place in public with the public's help . . . [The project] would draw onlookers eager to watch the progress over at least a couple of years. Community excitement and pride would build.
>
> The Erie Canal Harbor Development Corp., which over-sees Canalside, should throw open its doors and resources to make this project happen . . . Here's the problem: It still has not been determined where the boat would be built, and the Maritime Center still needs to raise the $325,000 it requires to fund the project. (*Buffalo News* editorial, 2018a)

Up until then, the Maritime Center had had a difficult time raising the money it needed to build the boat. "We'd been knocking on doors for years without making much headway" (Montague, interview, February 19, 2019). The $325,000 the *Buffalo News* cited in its editorial as the amount the Maritime Center needed to carry out the project underestimated the cost, which was actually more like $650,000. But once the *Buffalo News* made people aware of what the Buffalo Maritime Center was trying to do, raising money for the project became much easier.

After reading about the Maritime Center's proposed packet boat project in the newspaper, David Rogers, the CEO of the Life Storage Company who described himself as both a "history buff" and a "boating enthusiast," contacted the Maritime Center and asked to be given a tour of its facility on Arthur Street. Having served on the board of the Old Fort Niagara Association, Rogers had seen how commemoration events surrounding the 200th anniversary of the War of 1812 had stimulated interest in Buffalo's history and boosted attendance—which for Rogers underscored the importance of commemorating the 200th anniversary of the opening of the Erie Canal in a historically meaningful way.

After the tour he was given of the Maritime Center's Arthur Street facility, Rogers asked how much it was going to cost to build the packet boat. After learning it was going to cost $650,000, Rogers said he'd like to help. "We thought he might offer a modest contribution," said Montague, "but instead he said he could pay *half* the cost—$325,000" (Montague, interview, February 29, 2019). Once Rogers' generous offer to foot a substantial part of the cost of building the packet boat became known, government officials and agencies started to get behind the project. Governor Cuomo announced that $4 million in state money would be provided toward the cost of constructing a year-round building at Canalside to house the building of the packet boat. The New York State Canal Corporation offered to provide $150,000. The New York State Council on the Arts gave nearly $50,000, and $7,000 came from the Erie Canalway National Heritage Corridor. Assemblyman Sean Ryan, who had championed the project from the outset, came up with an additional $250,000 in state funding. Knowledge of Rogers' offer to cover half the cost of building the packet boat also encouraged other private donors to step forward.

The final piece of the puzzle fell into place when ECHDC approved building a structure alongside the Commercial Slip to house the *Seneca Chief* packet boat project and also agreed to cover the full cost of designing and constructing the building, which turned out to be about $5 million. ECHDC had initially been reluctant to allow such a prime location to be used for the boat-building project, because it had been planning on constructing a building on the site that would serve as an outdoor market. But the structure ECHDC originally planned to build on the site would not have been able to accommodate building a 73-foot-long canal boat. To serve that purpose, the structure needed to be at least 100 feet long.

ECHDC hired HHL Architects of Buffalo to design the building that would meet the Maritime Center's requirements. Construction of the custom-designed two-story, gabled roof structure called the Longshed began in August 2019 and was completed in October 2020. HHL worked closely with the BMC in designing the Longshed, and Montague "couldn't say enough" about the high quality of the building's construction by Savarino Companies. "The quality of the craftsmanship is over the top," said Montague (Sommer 2020a, B1). "The location on the water and the smell of cedar and sawdust offer an ideal setting for building a boat," said Trzeciak (B1). The public opening of the Longshed had to be delayed until April 2021 because of the COVID-19 pandemic, at which point docents began staffing the facility and providing members of the public their first look into the structure.

In June 2021, John Montague met me at the entrance to the Longshed, where a model of the Canal-era *Seneca Chief* packet boat was displayed.[2] He then took us up to the second-floor mezzanine, from which we could get a good view of the workspace below where the *Seneca Chief* was being assembled. Roger Allen joined us and took part in the conversation (figures 9.4–9.6).

When the *Seneca Chief* packet boat was built in the 1800s, Western New York was covered with dense virgin forests which provided wood that was ideal for boat-building. Those virgin forests no longer exist, so the BMC

Figure 9.4. The Longshed at Canalside. *Source*: Photo by the author.

Figure 9.5. *Seneca Chief* packet boat being built in the Longshed. *Source*: Photo by the author.

Figure 9.6. John Montague (on the right) along with master boatbuilder Roger Allen. *Source*: Photo by the author.

had to search far and wide to obtain the types and sizes of lumber that would be needed to produce a reasonably accurate replica of the original. The following species of trees were obtained from the following sources:

- White oak, sourced from Hudson, New York, and North Central, Pennsylvania, for the keel, frames, stern horn timbers, and bow stem

- Black locust, from local sources and sawmills, for the cabin framing

- Cyprus, sourced from the North Carolina's Great Dismal Swamp, for the hull planking

- Larch, sourced from North Central Pennsylvania and Allegany Park, New York, for hull double-planking below the waterline

Most of the timber ordered for the project came rough-cut with bark edges and had to be milled down to the required sizes. "We had most of the timber delivered and stored off-site where it dried and 'cured' before being brought to the Longshed. Rather than buying the bolts that would be needed to construct the boat, which would have been very expensive, we made our own bronze bolts (about 2,500 of them) at our foundry on Arthur Street," said Montague (email, June 6, 2021).

Progress at Canalside Revives
Vacant Marine Midland/HSBC Office Tower Complex

In 1999, the huge 1.2 million square-foot Marine Midland Center office complex was acquired by HSBC. Thirteen years later, in December 2012, HSBC announced it was going to move its employees to a newer, more modestly scaled building closer to the new downtown arena that at the time bore its name. In 2013, the building's other major tenant also vacated the complex, which prompted a complete exodus that left the city's largest commercial building entirely vacant. The owners of the project defaulted on their loan and the complex fell into foreclosure.

In October 2016, the complex was acquired out of foreclosure by Douglas Jemal, a Washington, DC–based developer, and renamed One Seneca. Jemal's decision to take on such a huge project is likely explained by the property's close proximity to Canalside and by the positive impact that the Canalside project was having on the surrounding area.

Jemal began by developing 104 apartments in the four-story portions of the complex that wrapped around the sides of the tower. In an effort to enliven the barren and sterile plaza that faced Seneca Street, a new low-rise structure was constructed to frame the edges of the plaza which it was hoped would accommodate commercial establishments and possibly restaurants that would activate the area. A lot of people thought Jemal was crazy to buy a property that had such a large amount of empty space and then add even more space to it, but Jemal felt he had to do it to counteract the dreariness of the plaza.

In February 2019, Mayor Byron Brown announced that Jemal had offered to loan the City of Buffalo $10 million to expedite the road work that would make it possible to restore vehicular traffic on Main Street up to and eventually through the opening at the base of the tower—which for years had been reserved exclusively for use by NFTA's Metro Rail. That roadwork got underway in summer 2021.

Jemal's bold undertaking aimed at reviving the huge former Marine Midland/HSBC office complex appears to have won over the admiration of preservationists who for years had abhorred the project's brutalist-style architecture. On May 16, 2019, Preservation Buffalo Niagara held its annual Preservation Awards event on the 31st floor of the One Seneca tower, which provided attendees with a stunning vantage point from which to view Canalside (figure 9.7).

Figure 9.7. Lower Main Street in July 2022: One Seneca, Marriott Courtyard and HarborCenter. *Source*: Photo by the author.

Part III

The Buffalo River

Chapter Ten

Cleaning Up the Buffalo River

As explained earlier in chapter 2, in an effort to jumpstart the stalled cleanup of the Buffalo River, the Environmental Protection Agency (EPA) issued a request for proposals (RFP) in 2002 inviting nongovernmental organizations to apply for funding to manage and coordinate the cleanup. Friends of the Buffalo River (FBR) submitted an application and in 2003 became the first nonprofit organization in the Great Lakes Basin to be awarded funding by EPA to play such a role. With the funding it received from EPA, FBR hired Jill Jedlicka to work full-time managing the implementation of the RAP and promoted Julie O'Neill to become the organization's executive director.

After an initial two-year trial period, FBR's contract with EPA was renewed and extended for ten years in 2005. That same year, the nonprofit expanded its mission to include the Niagara River and changed its name to Friends of the Buffalo and Niagara Rivers (FBNR).

Evolution of Friends of the Buffalo River

1989: Friends of the Buffalo River (FBR) is incorporated as a nonprofit organization, governed by an all-volunteer board of directors.

2001: Julie O'Neill is hired as FBR's first paid employee.

2003: FBR is awarded funding by EPA and changes its name to Friends of the Buffalo Niagara Rivers (FBNR).

2005: FBNR changes its name to Buffalo Niagara Riverkeeper (BNR).

2012: Julie O'Neill leaves BNR to become general counsel and Green Program director for the Buffalo Sewer Authority; Jill Jedlicka becomes Riverkeeper's executive director.

2017: Buffalo Niagara Riverkeeper becomes affiliated with the Waterkeeper Alliance and changes its name to Buffalo Niagara Waterkeeper (BNW).

2022: Buffalo Niagara Waterkeeper is the largest and most influential environmental advocacy organization in Western New York.

It would be hard to think of a person better suited to take on the challenge of overseeing the cleanup of the Buffalo River than Jill Spisiak Jedlicka, whose great uncle Stan Spisiak had made it his mission in life to try put an end to the common industrial practice of discharging toxic materials into the Buffalo River. Spisiak operated a jewelry store on Buffalo's East Side and described himself as "a conservationist at heart—a jeweler by necessity." During the 1950s and 1960s he issued stinging indictments of companies such as National Aniline, Buffalo Color, Republic Steel, and Socony-Vacuum (the oil refinery that became part of Exxon Mobil) for contributing to the contamination of the Buffalo River.

Local government officials were far from eager to join Spisiak's crusade against industrial polluters because the property taxes paid by the corporations that were contaminating the Buffalo River were among the highest in the city. The industrial property with the biggest assessment in Buffalo in 1965 was Republic Steel, which was assessed at $9.5 million. The industrial properties with the next highest assessments respectively were Donner-Hanna Coke Corporation ($8.8 million), Allied Chemical ($6.5 million), and the Socony-Vacuum oil refinery, which was valued at just under $4.5 million (Cichon 2019).

Stan Spisiak's Crusade against Industrial Polluters

(EXCERPTED FROM ZACH 2020)

In 1953 Spisiak attended a public hearing that was held at the Buffalo Museum of Science on the subject of water pollution and was startled to see 250 people in the auditorium—247 of whom represented or were employed by industries that were the alleged sources of the Buffalo River's contamination. All of those who spoke at the hearing, with the notable exception of Spisiak, downplayed the seriousness of industrial contamination of the Buffalo River. One speaker looked at Spisiak directly and declared, "The people should be grateful to the industries in the Buffalo River area, particularly for the fact that there are no diseases that could live in that water because of the fact that the unselective [sic] types of antibiotic material discharged had a preferable and desirable effect upon the diseases and germs that would otherwise be present."

By the 1960s, the East Side jeweler-turned-environmentalist finally found a political ally in the form of the newly elected US Senator from New York, Robert F. Kennedy, [who arranged for Spisiak to get] a hearing before the House Subcommittee on Natural Resources. It was before that subcommittee, on July 22, 1966, that the Buffalonian declared, "In my opinion, there is no longer any doubt about man's capability of destroying this world . . . Still more important is whether he can save it from a slower but more certain end . . . through the depletion and destruction of the world's limited supply of potable water." Less than a month after Spisiak delivered his eye-opening remarks to the House subcommittee, the president of the United States was in Buffalo to witness the scourge of the Buffalo River water pollution for himself.

Joined by New York Governor Nelson Rockefeller, Mayor Frank Sedita, local members of Congress and Stan Spisiak, President Johnson and the first lady boarded the US Coast Guard cutter *Ojibwa* for a tour of the waterfront, during which they passed a large number of dead fish. Spisiak placed a bucket of black, pasty sludge in front of the president and first lady and told them that the US Army Corps of Engineers was dumping 175,000 cubic yards of such sludge dredged from the Buffalo River into the lake every year.

In Fall 1966, President Johnson issued an executive order that decreed that the US Army Corps of Engineers should no longer dump sludge dredged from the bottom of the Buffalo River into the open lake but should henceforth deposit it into "diked impoundments." Most if not all the diked impoundments that subsequently received that dredged material were on the Outer Harbor.

The Importance of the Great Lakes Legacy Act

Up until 2002, federal environmental regulations required that a "responsible party" be identified as having been primarily responsible for causing the contamination of a waterway that needed to be cleaned up. In the case of the Buffalo River that was problematic because industrial operations on *many* properties had contributed to the river's contamination. Passage of the Great Lakes Legacy Act in 2002 addressed the conundrum that such "orphan" waterways presented by authorizing the creation of public-private partnerships and cost-sharing arrangements to advance a cleanup effort.

As the corporate entity that had succeeded Allied Chemical, Honeywell International knew it could be held liable for having contributed to the contamination of the Buffalo River. "Riverkeeper brought Honeywell into the cleanup effort. Instead of fighting things out in court we encouraged them to be a partner in the cleanup effort" (Jedlicka, interview, February 13, 2019).

Honeywell International's decision to become an active partner in the cleanup effort significantly augmented the funding available to carry out the project. In March 2007, EPA and Buffalo Niagara Riverkeeper signed a Great Lakes Legacy Act (GLLA) Project Agreement for a Remedial Investigation and Feasibility Study of the Buffalo River that was estimated to cost $800,000. "The agreement was subsequently amended to add Honeywell International as a non-federal sponsor, to increase the total project ceiling to $10,650,000 and also include the Army Corps of Engineers, with EPA responsible for 65% of the total project cost and the non-federal sponsors responsible for 35%" (Giancarlo, email, January 23, 2020).

The dredging of contaminated sediment from the river finally got underway in 2011. Between 2011 and 2012, sediment was dredged from the navigation channel *below* the depth that was normally maintained by the Army Corps of Engineers (see figure 10.1). The 550,000 cubic yards of sediment removed from the river during those first two years contained

Figure 10.1. Contaminated sediment being dredged from the Buffalo River near the South Park Avenue Bridge. *Source*: Buffalo Niagara Waterkeeper. Used with permission.

such high levels of PCBs, PAHs, and heavy metals that it had to be hauled off to a special confined facility near Lackawanna for permanent disposal.

Between 2013 and 2014, the dredging of the river extended beyond the navigation channel so as to remove contaminated sediment that had accumulated along the side slopes of the river. During this second phase of dredging activity, 495,000 cubic yards of contaminated sediment were removed, which brought the total amount of sediment removed to nearly one million cubic yards. However, the river was still biologically dead, because it lacked the aquatic and shoreline vegetation needed to support fish and wildlife.

Restoring Natural Habitat within and along the River

More needed to be done than just dredging and removing contaminated sediment. "To restore the environmental health of the river it was necessary to restore natural habitat within and along the shorelines of the river" (Jedlicka, interview, February 13, 2019). Taking that next step was significantly advanced when Riverkeeper, EPA, and Honeywell entered into an amended Great Lakes Legacy Act agreement for "sediment remediation and aquatic habitat restoration" that called for spending up to $48,500,000, with EPA and Honeywell splitting the total project cost 50-50 (Giancarlo, email, January 23, 2020).

Pyramid-shaped wooden in-water structures (called "porcupine cribs") containing materials conducive to plant growth were placed in the river in locations thought to be most promising for creating habitat for fish. Because of the exceptionally low rate of water flow within the City Ship Canal, before the porcupine cribs could be placed in the canal, 65,000 cubic yards of clean material was deposited along the bottom of the canal to create a 5.5-foot-thick cap of clean material to isolate the chemical contamination. Twelve porcupine cribs containing habitats conducive to fish were then placed in four different locations and gravel beds were created using stones sized to encourage the spawning of targeted fish species.

As shown in figure 10.2, restoration of in-water and shoreline habitat was also undertaken by Riverkeeper at eight widely scattered sites: the Buffalo Motor Generator Corporation property near the Michigan Street bridge; River Fest Park; the New York State Department of Environmental Conservation's Ohio Street boat launch; the Toe of Katherine Street; Red Jacket Natural Habitat Park; Riverbend I and II; the Buffalo Color peninsula; and Old Bailey Woods. At the Toe of Katherine Street, invasive species were removed from a 2.3-acre area that had experienced significant erosion, native vegetation was established, and the shoreline was stabilized. At the elbow-shaped bend in the Buffalo River known as Blue Tower Turning Basin, in-water natural habitat was restored along 1.632 linear feet of shoreline, and vertical pilings and log booms were installed to prevent debris from building up that could interfere with establishing native aquatic vegetation. At Riverbend I and II, invasive species were removed and natural habitat restored along 4,320 linear feet of the shoreline.

In July 2018, Waterkeeper Executive Director Jill Jedlicka joined officials from the US Environmental Protection Agency, the New York State Department of Environmental Conservation, the Great Lakes Commission, and about two dozen preschoolers from the Valley Community Association at the Toe of Katherine Street to celebrate having completed restoring natural habitat along two miles of the shoreline of the Buffalo River. Jedlicka noted that the site where they were gathered had once been choked by industrial pollution but "now is home to minnows and fish, rare spiny softshell turtlers, geese and deer" (Pignataro 2018b).

Figure 10.2. Habitat restoration sites along the Buffalo River. *Source*: Map by Austin Wyles.

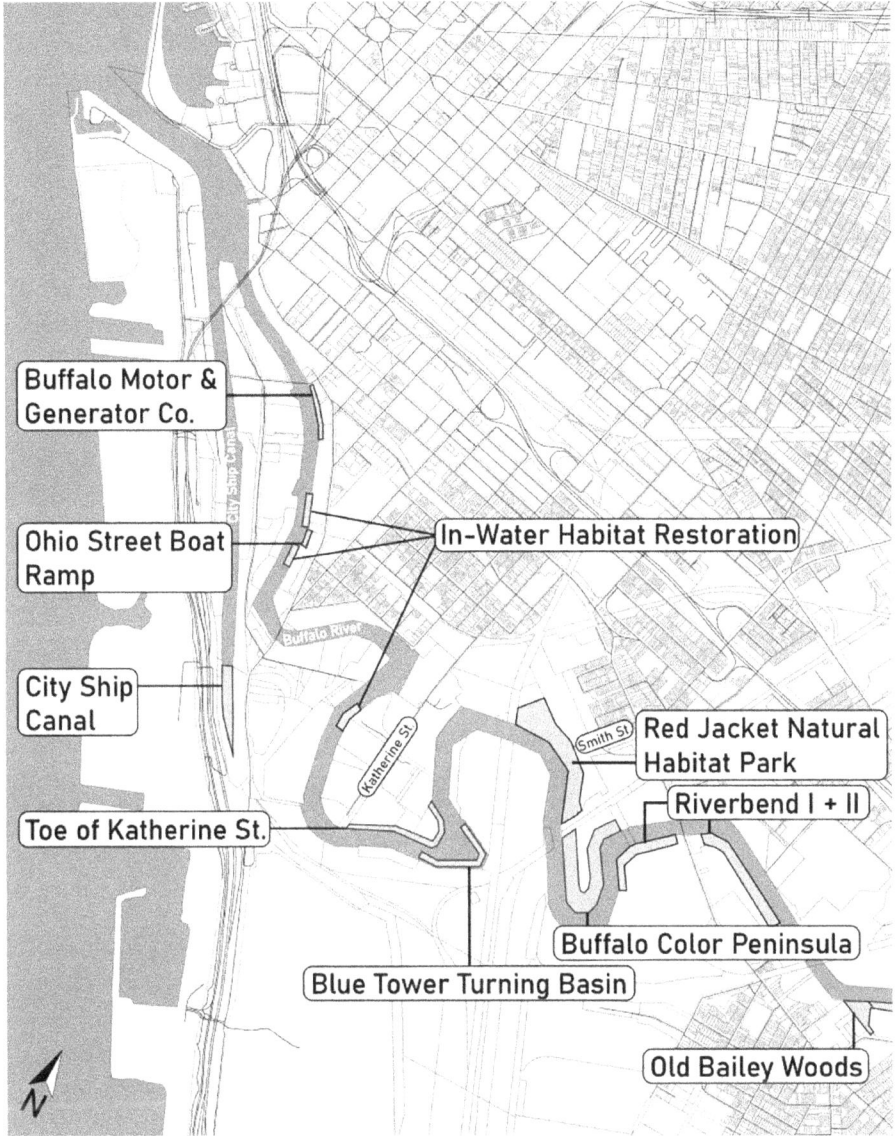

Buffalo Motor & Generator Co.

Ohio Street Boat Ramp

In-Water Habitat Restoration

City Ship Canal

Red Jacket Natural Habitat Park

Smith St

Riverbend I + II

Toe of Katherine St.

Katherine St

Buffalo Color Peninsula

Blue Tower Turning Basin

Old Bailey Woods

Buffalo River

City Ship Canal

N

Around the same time as Waterkeeper was restoring natural habitat on those eight sites, habitat for fish and wildlife was also being restored on three county-owned properties along the Buffalo River. In 2017, Erie County's Department of Environment and Planning secured $3 million in funding from the US Fish and Wildlife Service to restore natural habitat at Red Jacket Natural Habitat Park and Old Bailey Woods Natural Habitat Park. EPA also granted $2 million directly to the US Army Corps of Engineers to environmentally restore the shoreline of the county-owned park at Seneca Bluffs (see again figure 10.2).

At Red Jacket Natural Habitat Park (a 19-acre riverfront property at the end of Smith Street which the City of Buffalo transferred to Erie County in 1996), invasive species were removed, wetlands were created to provide habitat for turtles, and "a living wall" composed of densely planted native shrubs was put in place around the perimeter of the park to keep invasive plants from reinfesting restored areas (Haas, email, January 28, 2019). Submerged and emergent aquatic vegetation (water willow, pondweed, water lilies, and bulrush) was also planted by hand along 700 feet of shoreline to create habitat for fish. Trails on the property were upgraded, including one that provides excellent views of the river, and an informal kayak launch was also developed. Habitat for fish and wildlife was also restored along the shoreline of a nearby parcel owned by Niagara Frontier Transportation Authority (NFTA) on the other side of Smith Street; however, no trails were introduced onto that shoreline property due to NFTA's desire to discourage public use of the area.

~

One of the easily overlooked benefits of the major effort that has been made to improve the environmental health of the Buffalo River has been increased public interest in monitoring changes in water quality within the Buffalo River watershed.

The removal of contaminated sediment and restoration of natural habitat within and along the side slopes of the river described in this chapter were important steps toward improving the health of the Buffalo River. But more work needs to be done to protect and improve the health of the Buffalo River because Buffalo's combined sewers still discharge millions of gallons of sewage and contaminated stormwater runoff into the Buffalo River during periods of heavy rainfall. Agricultural runoff and other sources of nutrients, such as lawn fertilizer, also continue to undermine water quality.

"A Day in the Life of the Buffalo River"

In October 2013, students and teachers from a number of area schools journeyed to 11 different points along the Buffalo River and its tributaries to collect water samples and to take readings of environmental conditions such as water temperature, dissolved oxygen, pH levels, and turbidity. The event, called "A Day in the Life of the Buffalo River," was organized by Friends of Reinstein Woods in partnership with the Buffalo Audubon Society and SUNY Fredonia. The immediate aim of the exercise was to obtain a snapshot of the health of the watershed at a particular point in time. An equally important benefit of providing students with hands-on experience in collecting and analyzing data on water quality was that it was likely to make them feel a stronger connection to their watershed and to feel more personally invested in protecting water quality.

On October 4, 2014, 150 grade 4–12 students from eight area schools participated in the second annual "Day in the Life of the Buffalo River" event, revisiting the same sites where other students one year earlier had collected samples and measured environmental conditions. Each October over the course of the next four years, new groups of students came to the same 11 sites to repeat the exercise and collect additional samples and conduct additional measurements.

A heavy rainfall two days earlier, as well as an early morning thunderstorm, limited the number of students who participated in the sixth "Day in the Life of the Buffalo River" event on October 4, 2018. Despite high water levels that reduced the number of locations along the shoreline of the river where it is safe to conduct micro-invertebrate sampling and water depth measurements, 150 students from eight schools showed up to take readings of water temperature, pH levels, and turbidity. For the first time, they also measured nitrate and phosphate, high levels of which are often caused by agricultural runoff, lawn fertilizers, and wastewater discharges. On October 3, 2019, 300 students from 13 schools participated in the event, which was expanded to include field study sites in other portions of the Niagara River and Lake Erie watersheds. Reports and summaries of water quality data collected during the various annual "Day in the Life" events are available online at reinsteinwoods.org/explore/programs-services/dayinthelife/data/.

Chapter Eleven

Public Use and Enjoyment
of the Buffalo River

Not that long ago, the 1.4-mile-long stretch of Ohio Street between Michigan Avenue and the Ohio Street bridge was little more than a truck route
through a bleak, largely abandoned postindustrial landscape—which is to
say that there was little reason for motorists (except for those who lived
in the First Ward) to stop along the way. "Ohio Street was a wasteland"
(Overdorf, interview, July 3, 2019). Despite Ohio Street's proximity to the
Buffalo River, the river remained largely out of sight. The only place where
it was possible to gain access to the river was from NYSDEC's Ohio Street
boat launch, which could only be reached via an obscure, unimproved
right-of-way that extended a short distance from Ohio Street to the river.

River Fest Park

No single undertaking proved more important in jump-starting the
transformation of the Ohio Street corridor than the development of River
Fest Park. The three-acre property between Ohio Street and the Buffalo
River that the Valley Community Association redeveloped into a riverside
park was formerly occupied by a freight depot, warehouse, and loading
docks served by a rail line operated by the New York Central Railroad.
During first half of the twentieth century, one and a half million tons of
freight routinely passed through the warehouse and freight depot every
day. As a result of that activity the property became contaminated and
was declared to be a brownfield, which added considerably to the cost of
redeveloping the property.

The multiyear effort that culminated in the development of River Fest Park began back in June 2001, when Margaret "Peg" Overdorf, the executive director of the Valley Community Association (VCA) met with Rick Smith, the owner of Silo City and Rigidized Metals, to pitch the idea of holding a festival to celebrate the Buffalo River and encourage people to get out onto the river. To pull it off, however, she needed a sponsor. Would Smith's company, Rigidized Metals, agree to play that role? Smith's answer was an unequivocal yes.

Smith recalled what it was like in Buffalo and in the country at the time as follows: "The country was heading into a recession, 9/11 was just about to change the world. Buffalo was still the brunt of yet another punch line on late night TV and the huge First Ward Conagra flour milling plant had just closed its doors eliminating 70 more jobs . . . There wasn't a recreational boat to be found on the Buffalo River" (Smith, *Rigidized Metals Review Newsletter*, July 2022).

The first River Fest was held at Father Conway Park. However, Father Conway Park wasn't *on* the river, and a celebration of the Buffalo River really needed to be on the water. There *was* a site not far away that *was* on the river that Overdorf knew would be perfect to host future River Fests—but acquiring and developing a park on the site was going to require a lot of money. To help Overdorf and VCA raise the money initially needed to acquire the property, Rigidized Metals brought its "brush hog" to the site to make it look more presentable before Bob Kresse, a representative of the Margaret L. Wendt Foundation, a potential source of funding, came to look at it. Based on Kresse's recommendation, the Wendt Foundation agreed in 2007 to loan VCA $200,000 toward the cost of acquiring the property. When combined with $400,000 in state funding secured with the help of NYS Assemblyman Mark Schroeder, VCA was able to gain control of the property.

Funding for remediating environmental contamination on the property was obtained from the NYS Environmental Protection Fund and the NYS Local Waterfront Revitalization Program. Funding for constructing the capital improvements and facilities at the park was obtained from NYS Office of Parks, Recreation and Historic Preservation; Empire State Development Corporation; the Greenway Commission of Buffalo and Erie County; the Seneca Nation; and New York State Canal Corporation. Seventeen grants in all, amounting to a total of $5 million, were secured by VCA. Buffalo Niagara Riverkeeper helped Overdorf write a number of those grant applications, and the $200,000 loan from the Wendt Foundation was eventually forgiven. (See figure 11.1 for the location of River Fest Park and other parks, open space, and recreational sites along the Buffalo River.)

Figure 11.1. Parks, open space, and recreation along the Buffalo River. *Source*: Map by Austin Wyles.

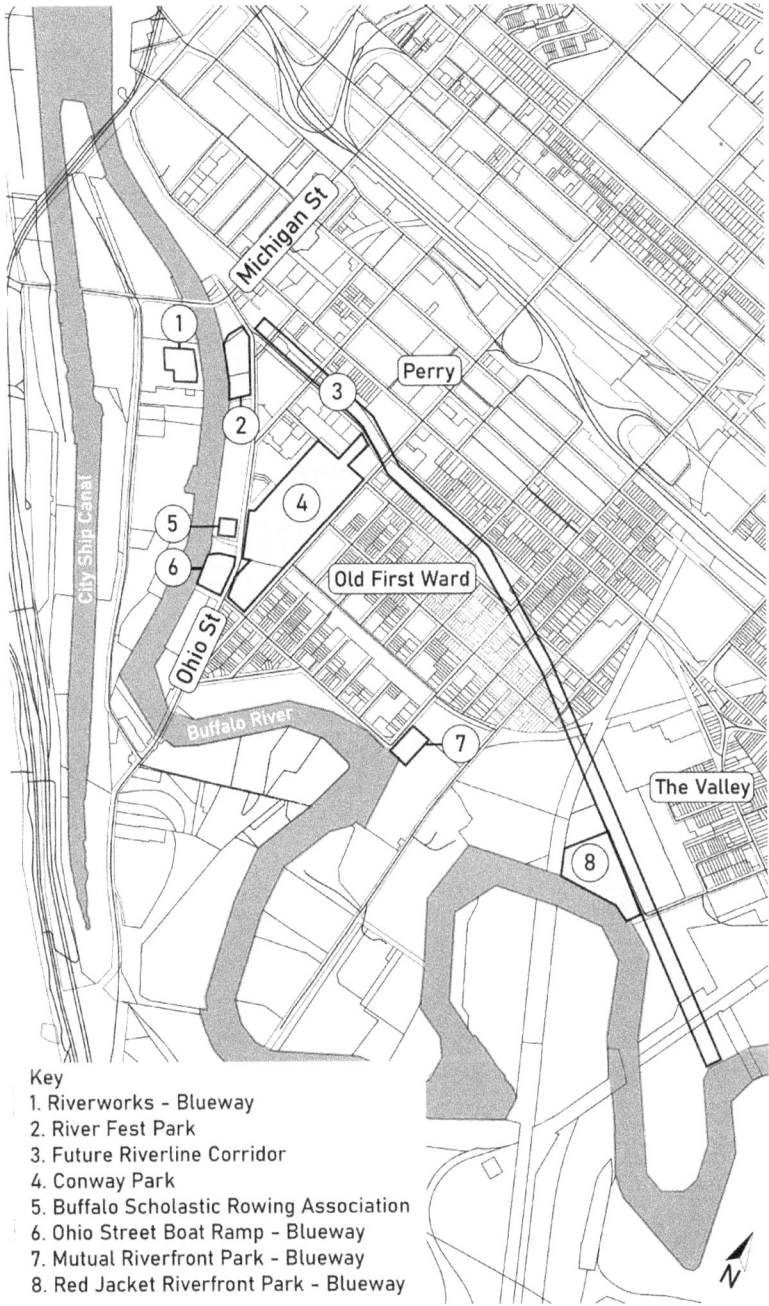

Key
1. Riverworks - Blueway
2. River Fest Park
3. Future Riverline Corridor
4. Conway Park
5. Buffalo Scholastic Rowing Association
6. Ohio Street Boat Ramp - Blueway
7. Mutual Riverfront Park - Blueway
8. Red Jacket Riverfront Park - Blueway

River Fest Park opened to the public in June 2011, and the tenth annual Rigidized Riverfest Regatta was held there for first time that summer. As shown in figure 11.2, a boardwalk extends along the football field–long riverfront portion of park. Benches placed at regular intervals along the boardwalk, most accompanied by plaques dedicated to long-time Valley residents, invite visitors to sit, relax, and gaze out at the river. One such plaque honors "Ginny & Pete Decker, Valley Born and Raised." Plaques at the base of nearby trees honor the memory of loved ones who have died, such as one that reads "In loving memory of our favorite and No. 1 Grandpa, Edward C. Smith, August 4, 1938–January 27, 2015."

On your left as you enter the park from Ohio Street is a newly constructed brick building designed to resemble the New York Central Railroad freight depot that once stood on the site. Known as Tewksbury Lodge (figure 11.3), the name chosen for the building recalls a shipping disaster (described later) that took place not far away on the Buffalo River in 1959. Occasionally open to the public for holiday brunches,

Figure 11.2. Riverfront boardwalk at River Fest Park, with the Michigan Street Bridge in the background. *Source*: Photo by the author.

Figure 11.3. Tewksbury Lodge at River Fest Park. *Source*: Photo by the author.

Recalling the Tewksbury Shipping Disaster

On January 21, 1959, after days of bitter cold and heavy snow had packed the Buffalo River and Cazenovia Creek with ice, a sudden thaw and heavy rain broke up the ice jam; strong winds then drove the ice flow down the river, shoving it into the freighter *MacGilvray Shiras*, which was tied up for the winter beside the Concrete Central Elevator. Around 10 p.m. the pressure of the ice flow snapped the mooring lines of the *MacGilvray Shiras*, causing it to break free and drift downriver until it rammed into the freighter *Michael K. Tewksbury*, which was tied up at the Standard Elevator. Both ships then passed beneath the Ohio Street Bridge, which was raised for the winter, but the Michigan Avenue Bridge couldn't be raised in time to avoid disaster. At 11:17 p.m., the *Tewksbury* smashed into the Michigan Avenue Bridge, demolishing it, wedging itself across the river, and causing an even worse ice dam. The dam created by the freighter and the bridge diverted a flow of frigid water and thick ice floes over the banks, flooding an 18-block area and bringing terror and distress and losses to hundreds of residents (Neville 2017).

Tewksbury Lodge is mostly rented out for banquets and special events such as weddings, which enables VCA to generate the revenue it needs to pay for the ongoing operation and maintenance of the park. Restrooms constructed as part of Tewksbury Lodge can be accessed by visitors to the park without having to enter the banquet hall. An outdoor shelter that incorporates many of the design features of Tewksbury Lodge was added in 2020 between Tewksbury Lodge and the river that provides a welcome place where people can picnic outdoors protected from the sun and rain.

One other structure at River Rest Park deserves mention, and that is the bandstand at the opposite end of the park that is put to good use during River Fest Park's popular series of free Wednesday night concerts. No fixed seating is provided, so most people who come to the concerts either bring folding lawn chairs or bring blankets and spread them out on the grass. No concerts were held in 2020 and 2021 due to the COVID-19 pandemic, but the concert series resumed in 2022, with 16 concerts held between May 25 and September 7.

The twentieth and likely last Rigidized Riverfest Regatta was held at River Fest Park on Saturday June 25, 2022. As explained by Rigidized Metals' Kate Gorman (email, July 1, 2022), "Attendance has dropped off over the years and only 12 people registered to participate in the 2022 regatta, so we are retiring the event." With so many people now regularly out on the river, the regattas are no longer needed to encourage people to get out onto the river.

Mutual Riverfront Park

One year after River Fest Park opened, Mutual Riverfront Park was completed further up the Buffalo River. Once again, VCA played a crucial role in making the park a reality. (See figure 11.1 for location of Mutual Riverfront Park.)

In 2010, New York Power Authority (NYPA) began using a portion of the site that became Mutual Riverfront Park to store the Lake Erie-Niagara River Ice Boom when it wasn't strung across the mouth of the Niagara River. Up until then the boom had been stored during the off-season on the northern end of the Outer Harbor.[1] However, NYPA needed to store the boom somewhere else so that ECHDC could develop Wilkeson Pointe Park—the first portion of the Outer Harbor to be developed into a public park.

No one lived near the site where NYPA had previously stored the boom on the Outer Harbor. However, the new site in the First Ward neighborhood where NYPA chose to store the ice boom was densely populated, and many of the people who lived nearby objected to its unsightliness. To appease the community, NYPA agreed to develop a park and construct a wall along the back of the property to hide the boom when it was stored there (Overdorf, email, July 20, 2021).

To its credit, NYPA enabled VCA to play an important role in planning and designing the park. With the help of NYS Assemblyman Mark Schroeder, VCA also secured a commitment from NYPA that it could control what programs and activities would take place at the park, which opened in summer 2012.

The entrance into the park from Hamburg Street is framed by a segment of the Lake Erie-Niagara River Ice Boom (figure 11.4). Two buildings were developed within the park, one of which is the Waterfront Memories and More Heritage Center where documents pertaining to the

Figure 11.4. Hamburg Street entrance to Mutual Riverfront Park framed by a section of the Lake Erie-Niagara River Ice Boom. *Source*: Photo by the author.

history of the surrounding area are kept (figure 11.5). As Peg Overdorf explained to me, one of the purposes the Heritage Center serves is as a place where people can research their family roots and possibly track down former classmates and friends. The archival material preserved at Waterfront Memories and More also tells the stories of those who lived and worked long ago along Buffalo River. Timothy Bohen grew up in the First Ward and was able to gather and verify much of the detailed information that was contained in his 2012 book *Against the Grain: The History of Buffalo's First Ward* at the Heritage Center.

The other structure developed at Mutual Riverfront Park (also shown in figure 11.5) is a boathouse whose design is reminiscent of a boathouse that the Mutual Rowing Club built nearby on South Street in 1892. At the turn of the century there were at least 22 rowing clubs in the area, the most prominent of which was the Mutual Rowing Club. A century and a quarter later, rowing and kayaking on the river have once again become extremely popular. As a result, the boathouse at Mutual Riverfront Park serves the useful purpose of providing current rowing and paddling enthusiasts a place where they can store their shells, kayaks, and canoes.

Figure 11.5. Waterfront Memories and More Heritage Center and replica 1892 Mutual Rowing Club Boathouse at Mutual Riverfront Park. *Source*: Photo by the author.

Mutual Riverfront Park provides a spectacular vantage point from which to contemplate the massive Lake and Rail Elevator at Silo City on the opposite side of the river. The only way to get a better view of that elevator and many others that line that portion of the river is to launch a kayak out onto the river, which many people are doing each year (see figure 11.6).

For a number of years, SS *Columbia*, the oldest remaining Great Lakes passenger steamship in the US was docked at Silo City across from Mutual Riverfront Park while undergoing repairs and restoration (figure 11.7). Many people who launched kayaks from Mutual Riverfront Park paddled across the river to get a closer look. Constructed in 1902, for 89 years the SS *Columbia* ferried Detroiters from downtown Detroit to an amusement park on Canada's Bois Blanc Island, an 18-mile, 90-minute excursion not unlike the excursions that tens of thousands of Buffalonians took aboard the SS *Canadiana* from downtown Buffalo to the Crystal Beach amusement park in Ontario.[2]

Figure 11.6. Kayak launch at Mutual Riverfront Park. *Source*: Photo by the author.

Figure 11.7. SS *Columbia* docked at Silo City while undergoing repairs in 2015. *Source*: Fr. William Jud Weiksnar. Used with permission.

Reinventing Silo City

The opening of the St. Lawrence Seaway in 1959, as noted in chapter 1, caused a large proportion of the ships that carried Midwestern grain to bypass Buffalo completely. As the amount of grain stored in Buffalo declined precipitously, a number of Buffalo's grain elevators shut down and were abandoned. Because the City of Buffalo was in dire fiscal distress, it couldn't afford to demolish its abandoned grain elevators. As a result, by the beginning of the twenty-first century Buffalo had the largest number of surviving, albeit unused, grain elevators of any city in the country.

As of 2004 there were 16 sets of grain elevators in Buffalo, most of them along the Buffalo River. In December 2005, that number was reduced to 15 when the Seneca Nation demolished the H-O Oats grain elevator on Fulton Street so that it could develop a casino on the property. Oat production at the H-O Oats grain elevator had ended in 1983, and a fire in 1987 destroyed a portion of the facility, but most of the structure remained intact up until the time the wrecking ball came crashing into the elevator.

In 2006, Rick Smith (figure 11.8), the owner and president of Rigidized Metals, a metal shredding company, purchased four of the elevators that were part of the group of concrete elevators popularly known as "Silo City" with the intention of using them to produce ethanol. (See figure 11.10 for location of Silo City.) When the bottom fell out of the market for ethanol, Smith dropped that idea and sold one of the four elevators

Figure 11.8. Rick Smith, owner/developer of Silo City. *Source*: Photo by the author.

(the Lake and Rail Elevator) in 2008 to a Minnesota-based hedge fund. He bought it back in 2017.

None of the concrete elevators Smith acquired was any longer used for its original purpose. Nevertheless, with each passing year the cluster of silos became increasingly popular as a visitor destination, due in no small part to Smith's ingenuity in promoting and making use of the site. Described by the *Buffalo News* art critic Colin Dabkowski as a "musta-chioed, cowboy-hatted maverick of depthless entrepreneurial vim," Smith cast a wide net in search of uses and activities that could possibly take place at the complex (Dabkowski 2018b).

One way Smith initially generated activity at Silo City was by granting permission to an outside group to turn one of the silos into a climbing facility, which drew a large number of climbing enthusiasts at a time when there weren't specialized facilities that catered to that activity, as there are now. It didn't take long for him to discover that many people simply wanted to be able walk around and explore Silo City. He arranged for tours of the grounds of Silo City to be offered on a regular basis from May through October at a modest cost. For people who were more adventurous, vertical tours of Silo City were also offered that took visitors to the upper reaches of grain elevators, which were ten-stories high (not recommended for people with a fear of heights). To sign up to take such vertical tours, people had to be physically fit enough to climb up 100 feet of stairs and up a short ladder to reach the top.

The massive scale and dramatic visual qualities of Silo City also made it a one-of-a-kind setting for film shoots and film productions, as well as an ideal place to hold photography workshops, which were held at Silo City on a fairly regular basis. The architecture critic Reyner Banham once compared Buffalo's massive grain elevators to the great cathedrals of Europe. Echoing that sentiment, Buffalo photographer Bruce Jackson observed that "there is a kind of sacred, church-like feeling to Buffalo's post-industrial landscape that you can't quite grasp until you walk into it" (Dabkowski 2018b). Those very same majestic qualities also inspired many soon-to-be married couples to want to use Silo City's elevators and grain silos as the backdrop for their weddings.

Torn Space Theater Company decided that the grain silos at Silo City were a perfect place in which to stage experimental, immersive theater productions like "In the Dark," which was performed in April 2018 within the silos of the Perot Malting House. "The unusual audio and visual effects produced by the space contributed to a production that was full of surprises" (Dabkowski 2018a).

Smith first came to appreciate the artistic possibilities the silos provided when he discovered that a note played on the piano within the Marine A grain elevator reverberated for at least nine seconds. He demonstrated the mesmerizing effect of the lingering reverberation by plunking down a pair of notes on a weathered piano in one of the silos. "We've had didgeridoos and we've had double-bassoons play here . . . We've had trumpeters and trombonists [from the Buffalo Philharmonic Orchestra] here that produced sounds that would make anybody's hair stand up . . . Some musicians have been so entranced by the sounds that were produced that they've recorded their albums in the silos," said Smith (Dabkowski 2018a).

The Just Buffalo Literary Center took advantage of the effects the silos had on sound and light by creating the Silo City Reading Series in 2013 and holding it in the Marine A elevator that was built in 1925 but which had become vacant in 1964. Each event in the series has featured readings by two poets or authors, complemented by background lighting, music, and/or other unusual sounds to enhance their dramatic effect. Ocean Vuong, one of the poets invited to read his poetry at the inaugural event in 2013 stated that "I did not expect to feel at home in the old abandoned silos in Buffalo, and yet while I was there . . . the space reminded me, with its rusted elevators and shafts, that one can find familiarity, even comfort, in making something new . . . out of what was once discarded—which is art at its most indispensable" (https://silocityreadingseries.com). Also invited to read her poems was Maggie Smith, who is reported to have said that "reading poems in a grain elevator while rain fell outside was one of the most amazing poetry experiences I've ever had" (Licata 2021, 164). The tenth annual Silo City Reading Series was held in the Marine A Elevator in 2022.

The repurposing of Silo City entered a new phase when Smith sold six of Silo City's 27 acres to Generation Development Group (GDG). In November 2020, GDG announced that it would be redeveloping the American Mill and Warehouse into 168 apartments and that it was contemplating carrying out a similar project at the adjacent Perot Malting facility that would create 92 apartments and roughly 20,000 square feet of ground floor commercial space.

When I knew I was going to be in Buffalo in July 2022, I contacted Rick Smith to see if he could meet me at Silo City so that I could see what progress had been made in converting the American Mill and Warehouse into housing (figure 11.9). Rick met me in front of Duende, a casual and

Figure 11.9. American Mill and Warehouse and Perot Malting facility at Silo City in July 2022, regenerated vegetation in foreground. *Source*: Photo by the author.

quirky place to eat and drink that opened at 85 Silo City Row in June 2018 that often hosts live music in the evening. Rick retrieved a small four-wheeled all-terrain vehicle and took me on a tour of portions of the property I hadn't known or thought much about.

Silo City earned its name because of the large number of concrete grain elevators that are grouped within a relatively small area along the Buffalo River. However, the 27-acre Buffalo River property that Rick Smith acquired in 2006 also included a substantial undeveloped area to the south of the concrete elevators. It was that portion of the property that Rick wanted me to see.

Rick drove me down one trail after another that was framed by head-high vegetation and greenery. Along the way he pointed out notable landscape features such as a meadow with a large tree in the center with a swing hanging from a limb; a dome-like structure called the Trellis, constructed of rigidized metal by students from the University at Buffalo's School of Architecture and Planning; as well as a small soccer field that has been made available to teams of young soccer players from immigrant communities in Buffalo to play on. (A game was scheduled to be played on the field later that very day.)

In 2018, Rick Smith hired Josh Smith (no relation) as Silo City's director of ecology to assure that the property was redeveloped in an environmentally responsible manner. As Josh explained, "Because of our location along two major bodies of water [the Buffalo River and Lake Erie], every square foot of the site is ecologically valuable, no matter how abused or degraded it may be. We therefore approach our management of the entire site with that in mind, even those areas that are likely to be highly utilized for human activities" (J. Smith, email, July 25, 2022).

The ecological reclamation of a large portion of the property has been aided by spreading tons of compost produced on site made from tons of food waste that otherwise would have ended up in landfills. According to Josh, the most significant ecological interventions to date had been targeted on a roughly four-acre portion of the property that was least likely to see any redevelopment.

Redesign and Reconstruction of Ohio Street

The 1.4-mile-long stretch of Ohio Street between Michigan Avenue and the Ohio Street Bridge used to serve primarily as truck route that tractor-trailers took to travel to and from the Outer Harbor. Otherwise, as stated earlier once you started driving on Ohio Street there was little reason for motorists to stop along the way. Three years after River Fest Park opened, in spring 2014, the reconstruction of Ohio Street from a four-lane industrial corridor into a landscaped, pedestrian-friendly parkway got underway. The roadway was rebuilt with permeable paving material, granite curbing was installed, and a 12-foot-wide combined pedestrian-bicycle trail was constructed the full length of the corridor. New storm and sanitary sewers, water lines, and underground utilities (electric and cable lines) were also installed to support the residential and commercial development that was expected to take place along the corridor after the project was completed. The total cost of the project was roughly $11,300,000, of which ECHDC paid $2,038,000 and the City of Buffalo $1,200,000. The balance of the project cost, $8,062,000, was funded by the Federal Highway Administration. The City of Buffalo's Department of Public Works managed the construction process. The project was completed in 2015.

While ECHDC deserves credit for having embraced and helped advance the redesign and reconstruction of Ohio Street, the entity that probably deserves the most credit for having originated the idea of recon- structing Ohio Street into a landscaped parkway and pedestrian-bicycle trail was Buffalo Niagara Riverkeeper, which commissioned Lynn Mason to prepare the 2006 Buffalo River Greenway Vision and Implementation Plan. Riverkeeper also deserves credit for the heavy emphasis that was placed on incorporating green infrastructure, tree planting, landscaping, and trails into the highway project (see figure 11.10).

The development of River Fest Park and redesign and reconstruction of Ohio Street completely transformed the corridor and caused people to appreciate its proximity to the Buffalo River. Not long after River Fest Park was completed and Ohio Street was reconstructed, two five-story mixed- use buildings were developed that created a total of 99 new housing units along the corridor. Just east of River Fest Park at 301 Ohio Street (shown in figure 11.11), 21 apartments were developed on the top three floors of the five-story building, and 10,000 square feet of commercial space was developed on each of the first two floors (See again figure 11.10 for location of 301 Ohio Street.)

Further east on Ohio Street, across from Conway Park, a handsome rust-colored, five-story mixed-use building called Buffalo River Landing was completed in 2016 that contains 78 one- and two-bedroom apart- ments on the upper four floors and commercial space on the ground

Figure 11.10. Mixed-Use Development. *Source*: Created by the author.

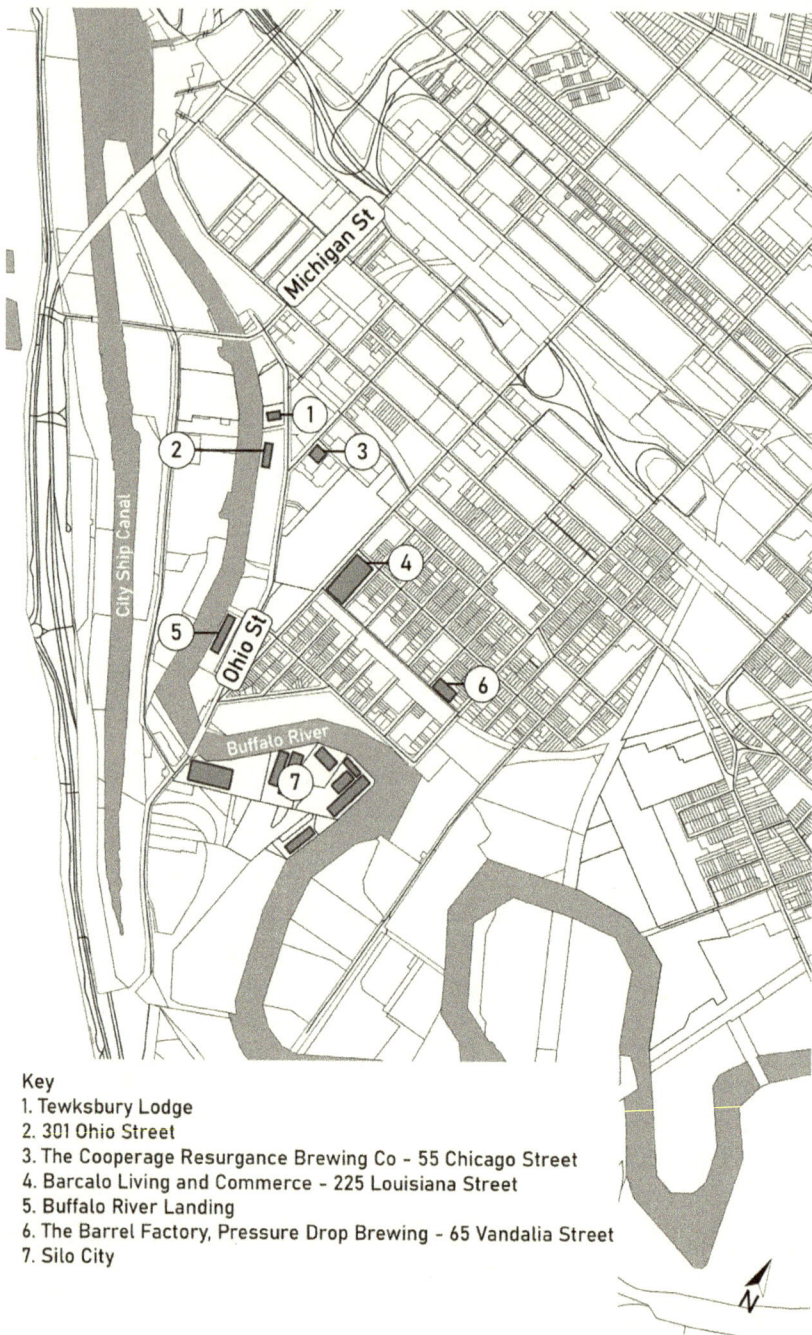

Key
1. Tewksbury Lodge
2. 301 Ohio Street
3. The Cooperage Resurgance Brewing Co - 55 Chicago Street
4. Barcalo Living and Commerce - 225 Louisiana Street
5. Buffalo River Landing
6. The Barrel Factory, Pressure Drop Brewing - 65 Vandalia Street
7. Silo City

Figure 11.11. Five-story mixed-use building at 301 Ohio Street and Tewksbury Lodge at River Fest Park as viewed from the opposite side of the river at River-Works. *Source*: Photo by the author.

floor. Designed by CJS Architects, Buffalo River Landing was financed by Community Preservation Corporation, a nonprofit affordable housing and community revitalization finance company. The building's rust-colored, rough-textured exterior makes historic reference to the large amount of industrial activity that once took place in the area. Tenants can launch their kayaks directly into the river from a dock along the shore and are also provided storage space in the building where they can store their kayaks and bicycles (figure 11.12).

Former First Ward Factory Buildings Redeveloped

In 1852, Edward and Britain Holmes established a lumberyard and planing mill on Michigan Street and "capitalized on the building boom in Buffalo by manufacturing in-demand products such as flooring, siding, ceiling, panel stuff, brackets, molding, sash, doors and blinds" (Bohen, 2012, 32).

Figure 11.12. People in kayaks paddling past Buffalo River Landing. *Source*: Buffalo Niagara Waterkeeper. Used with permission.

In 1857, they purchased an iron works on Chicago Street and devoted a portion of the property to making wooden barrels, which were in high demand because they were widely used to store and transport grain as well as many other commodities.

In September 1863, six years after they acquired the iron works, a boiler exploded, killing 20 people instantly and burying another 15 in the rubble (Walkowski 2012, 12). The Holmes brothers' barrel-making enterprise suffered an even more potentially devastating setback in July 1878 when a fire broke out that completely engulfed and destroyed the Chicago Street factory and spread quickly to nearby lumber yards and wood-framed tenements (Walkowski 2012, 14). Within two years the Holmes brothers had rebuilt and expanded the factory to twice its original size.

The E. & B. Holmes Machinery Company went on to revolutionize the process of making barrels, which up until 1880 had been done entirely by hand by a cooper, by inventing and manufacturing machinery capable of mass-producing barrels. By 1888, the Holmes brothers had obtained over 60 patents for their barrel-making machinery company.

Following the deaths of Edward and Britain Holmes, Edward's son, Edward Britain Holmes continued the business, becoming president of the company in 1906. Upon becoming the company's president following his death in 1934, his widow, Maude Holmes "steered the company away from the fading cooperage business" and toward "the more profitable production of specialty machinery" (Walkowski 2012, 16). Having no children to pass the company onto, Maude eventually sold the business to two longtime employees in January 1950, who continued to operate it at the same location under the same name until it closed for good in 2002—after which the factory sat vacant for years and fell into disrepair. In 2007, a portion of the main four-story mill building that fronted onto Chicago Street collapsed.

In 2016, what remained of the factory was nearly torn down, but Clinton Brown, a local architect, stepped forward to save and stabilize the building (Bohen 2012, 248). The redeveloped property (shown in figure 11.13) now accommodates six apartments on the third floor, office space on the second floor, and a hair salon, distillery and a brew pub operated by Resurgence Brewery on the ground floor.

When Justin and Jen Hartman were preparing the space in the Cooperage that their distillery would occupy, they discovered plans of barrel-making machinery that the Holmes company had designed and manufactured for factories in Philadelphia, St. Louis, and elsewhere. The plans have been framed and placed on the walls of the distillery so patrons can see them.

The Cooperage project also involved a significant amount of new construction. At one end of the complex is a newly constructed addition where the Resurgence Brewery brews its beer. At the other end of the Cooperage is another substantial addition occupied by Central Rock Gym—Climbing Fitness and Yoga.

Figure 11.13. The Cooperage on Chicago Street. *Source*: Photo by the author.

The entrance into Central Rock Gym is along the side of the Cooperage behind the hair salon. A staff member at the gym was kind enough to give me a tour of the facility, during which I was shown the many different types and heights of climbing surfaces that are available—vertical walls as high as 45 feet as well as various angled surfaces (see figure 11.14). A number of individuals were climbing the walls as I toured the facility, and a steady stream of men and women of different ages entered the facility preparing do the same thing.

Another recently redeveloped former barrel factory is across the street from Gene McCarthy's Old First Ward Brewery and Pub near the corner of Hamburg and Republic Streets. Eponymously named the Barrel Factory, the repurposed structure (shown in figure 11.15) houses Pressure Drop Brewery, a distillery operated by Lakeward Spirits, a cider and wine bar called Cultivar operated by Medina, New York–based SteamPunk Cider and Leonard Oakes Estate Winery, and Elevator Alley Kayak rentals and tours.

Figure 11.14. Central Rock Gym climbing wall at the Cooperage. *Source*: Photo by the author.

Figure 11.15. The Barrel Factory on Louisiana Street. *Source*: Photo by the author.

By far the most ambitious repurposing of a former First Ward factory has involved the sprawling eight-building Barcalo Manufacturing Company factory complex on Louisiana Street which "consists of both concrete and timber-framed buildings of varying heights, ranging from a one-floor foundry to a five-story structure" (Epstein 2022b). Built in phases between 1896 and 1917, the factory used to look out onto the Ohio Basin (described in greater detail later in the next section).

During its heyday, the Barcalo factory manufactured a variety of products, including metal furniture, mattresses, box springs, hand tools, and automobile parts, but became best known for its "Barcalounger" reclining chair. The factory closed its doors in 1963. The subsequent owners of the complex, the Sansone family, "managed to keep the lights on (as well as the heat on in winter) by filling it with a mix of light commercial and artist tenants" (*Buffalo Rising*, January 5, 2021).

In 2018, the Frizlen Group announced plans to redevelop the sprawling former Barcalo Manufacturing Company complex. The project qualified for historic preservation and brownfield tax credits, an abatement of the past property taxes that were due on the property was granted, and $1 million in sales and mortgage recording tax breaks were granted by Erie County's Industrial Development Agency so that the rents charged for the apartments could be kept affordable to moderate income households. However, redeveloping the factory complex proved challenging.

> The deterioration of the complex was more severe than antici-pated . . . which required extra work . . . And sharp increases in labor, material and transportation costs—prompted by the COVID-19 pandemic and the ongoing global turmoil—[drove] the project price tag up by 15% to 20%, to as much as $40 million, from $35 million previously. . . . When workers went to replace a roof they found the decking beneath was rotten, and then some of the beams below it as well . . . [which] had to be replaced. After workers took metal siding off of a three-story building they discovered it was leaning by 6 inches, so they had to completely rebuild two floors. (Epstein 2022b)

Finally completed in 2023, the redeveloped and adaptively reused for-mer factory complex now known as Barcalo Living and Commerce includes 116 housing units (including 56 two-bedroom and 7 three-bedroom units) and 30,000 square feet of commercial space for small businesses (see figure 11.16). "We want the project to include a mix of uses that both existing and new neighbors will support and enjoy," said Karl Frizlen. Among the amenities available to tenants are generous lounge areas, a large activity/

Figure 11.16. Barcalo Living and Commerce as viewed from across Father Conway Park. *Source*: Photo by the author.

assembly area, a bicycle storage area capable of storing up to 100 bikes, a dog wash station, indoor parking for 45 cars, and gated outdoor parking for 90 cars. "There will also be a curated art gallery space with permanent and rotating exhibits that pay tribute to the buildings' and First Ward's industrial heritage" (Karl Frizlen, email, April 25, 2023).

The Former Ohio Basin and Ohio Street Boat Launch

By 1851, so many barges and ships were arriving in Buffalo that the Buffalo River had become seriously congested. To alleviate the congestion, a shallow cove that became known as the Ohio Basin was dredged at a low point along the river to provide additional dock space for barges either ending or beginning their journeys on the Erie Canal, as well as a place where larger vessels could turn around. The Main and Hamburg Street Canal was privately developed to connect the Erie Canal to the Ohio Basin upstream on the Buffalo River (see again figure 1.7).

The area where the Ohio Basin was dredged intersected with several sewer lines. Because there was little or no natural flow of water in and out of the basin, the sewage that entered the basin posed a serious risk to the health of the surrounding community and became the source of a cholera outbreak. It wasn't until 1950, after two boys drowned, that the basin was filled in. Edward Barcalo, who owned the nearby Barcalo Manufacturing Company factory that overlooked the Ohio Basin, is said to have seen debris from Frank Lloyd Wright's recently demolished Larkin Administration Building being dumped into the basin as fill (Tielman, email, May 31, 2020). The area of the former basin was eventually covered over, planted with grass and trees, and renamed Conway Park in honor of Father Thomas Conway, a Navy chaplain who died in World War II.

On the opposite side of Ohio Street, directly across from Conway Park, is NYSDEC's Ohio Street boat launch, which for many years was the only point from which it was possible to gain access to the Buffalo River. At the beginning of this chapter I described the "obscure, unimproved right-of-way" that people had to find and use to reach NYSDEC's Ohio Street boat launch. In 2021, Buffalo Niagara Waterkeeper completed a major redesign and reconstruction of the Ohio Street boat launch that significantly increased the ability of people to use and enjoy the site. In addition to providing a much-needed area where people can park their cars, vehicular access into and out of the site was redesigned to make it easier to drop off paddleboats.

A railroad track pattern (shown in figure 11.17) is embedded in the walkway that leads from the parking area that references the fact that the Erie Railroad once operated a freight house on the property to transfer goods from boats docked in the Ohio Basin to railcars. Other notable design features include a pollinator garden; a wheelchair accessible walkway that extends the full length of the shoreline; and a platform, also wheelchair accessible, that arches out over the water that provides an excellent place to fish (see figure 11.18).

It is obvious that considerable thought and care was given to landscaping the site so as to create a parklike setting. On a warm summer day in 2022, I observed a small group of women sitting together in the shade of a large tree that had been thoughtfully retained amidst the reconstruction. Meanwhile, other people were fishing from the arched platform that extended out over the river.

Figure 11.17. Railroad track pattern embedded in walkway of the redeveloped Ohio Street boat launch. *Source*: Photo by the author.

Figure 11.18. The raised platform that extends out over the river provides an ideal place for fishing. *Source*: Photo by the author.

Timber guiderails incorporated into the boat launch make hand-launching of paddleboats much easier. Floating debris deflectors dampen waves and deflect floating debris and ice away from the shoreline and boat launch. NYSDEC continues to own and manage the facility.

The Buffalo Blueway

The redesign and expansion of the Ohio Street boat launch was actually just one part of a much larger initiative undertaken by Buffalo Niagara Waterkeeper aimed at developing a network of sites at places of interest from which people can conveniently launch paddleboats and kayaks into the river. Eight sites were designated as part of what was branded as the Buffalo Blueway. An online map was developed and posted at buffaloblueway.com so that before setting out on the river people could decide where they might want to paddle and what they might like to do along the way. By summer 2021, four of the eight initially designated sites had been significantly upgraded and opened to the public: RiverWorks (discussed later in this chapter); Mutual Riverfront Park; Wilkeson Pointe Park; and the one at the Ohio Street boat launch.

In 2020, Waterkeeper invited residents who lived in the vicinity of Red Jacket Natural Habitat Park to participate in a virtual online workshop conducted by Katherine Winkler, Waterkeeper's Blueway program manager, to consider and advise Waterkeeper what physical improvements should be made there. One year later, Winkler told Mark Sommer of the *Buffalo News* that "a terraced step-stone paddle launch will replace the existing gravel slope to allow easier entry and departure for boats. There will also be new benches, an improved parking area and concrete paths" (Sommer 2021d). Meanwhile, Waterkeeper was also overseeing the design of a handicapped-accessible paddleboat launch and fishing pier at Seneca Bluffs Natural Habitat Park, which like Red Jacket Park is also owned by Erie County. Winkler noted that both sites are ideally suited to becoming important components of the Blueway because they are located "in naturally quiet upstream locations that . . . avoid [the kinds of] conflicts with power boats, sailboats and commercial boating traffic found in the lower river" (Sommer 2021d).

Not far from the redeveloped and much improved Ohio Street boat launch, the Buffalo Scholastic Rowing Association (BSRA) erected a new boathouse (shown in figure 11.19) that contains four boat bays capable of storing up to 75 sculls. The boathouse also houses the stationary ergonomic machines ("ergs") that help people learn how to row. A grand opening for the new boathouse was held on August 21, 2021.

A number of different learn-to-row programs and courses are offered by BSRA for young people aged 12–16 as well as adults with different levels of proficiency and prior experience. It also provides groups of associated individuals with opportunities to engage in community-based rowing activities. BSRA was first established in 2009 and for ten years operated out of a temporary tent on the site where the new boathouse was built.

RiverWorks Sports and Entertainment Complex

Directly across from River Fest Park on the opposite side of the Buffalo River is the former Agway/GLF grain elevator complex, which has been

Figure 11.19. Buffalo Scholastic Rowing Association boathouse overlooking the Buffalo River as viewed from the Ohio Street boat launch. Source: Photo by the author.

redeveloped into RiverWorks—an imaginatively conceived facility that includes a craft brewery and restaurant, an indoor roller derby rink, ice rinks for hockey and curling, and a kayak launch that is handicapped accessible.

One of the first things the developer did was to retrofit the walls of the former elevator to enable people of different skill levels to attempt to climb the walls to heights of 35, 40, or 50 feet. Six of the former elevators' grain silos were painted to resemble a Labatt Blue six-pack. Readily visible from a considerable distance up and down the Buffalo River, the six-pack has become a widely recognized landmark along Buffalo's revitalized waterfront.

New attractions and facilities have been added over time, such as an Indiana Jones–inspired ropes course that begins with a rope bridge 110 feet up in the air atop of the Labatt Blue six-pack and takes participants back to ground level by way of four zip lines. A Ferris wheel (shown in figure 11.20) was added and began operating in 2022.

Figure 11.20. Ferris wheel and zip lines at RiverWorks. *Source*: Photo by the author.

The central building at RiverWorks, which includes bar seating and tables for casual dining, also doubles as a concert venue and occasionally hosts roller derbies. When the weather is warm, that space can be opened up to an outdoor deck that looks out directly onto the Buffalo River.

The two rinks at RiverWorks that accommodate hockey games and curling tournaments during the winter are covered by a pavilion that is open on the sides, which provides a degree of protection from the elements, but also enables the players to have the sense that they are playing outdoors. During spring and summer when it is too warm to keep the ice frozen, the rinks can be used for roller hockey and box lacrosse, as well as for boxing, wrestling, and martial arts events. The floor area within the boards of the hockey rinks can also be filled with tables and chairs to accommodate banquets.

RiverWorks was actually the first Buffalo Blueway site designated by Buffalo Niagara Waterkeeper to be fully upgraded and opened to the public. It also has the distinction of being the first handicapped-accessible

Blueway site. People who don't own a kayak or paddleboard can rent one at RiverWorks.

The Riverline—A Major Project on the Horizon

The geography of the First Ward—with natural boundaries such as the Buffalo River and man-made divisions such as canals and railroad tracks—isolated it from the rest of the city. Partly because of those boundaries, and partly because of the insular nature of the Irish who lived with the boundaries, many people in the 19th century moved around within the Ward. But hardly anyone moved out.

—Bohen 2012, 189

Because of the huge amount of shipping activity that the Erie Canal brought about along the Buffalo River, railroad companies built a number of rail corridors through the First Ward. The rail line that had the greatest and most enduring effect in separating the First Ward from other parts of the city was the one that the Delaware Lackawanna and Western (DL&W) developed that sliced through the full length of the First Ward. Even after trains stopped running on the corridor in 1960, it continued to diminish the contact that residents of the First Ward had with residents on the other side because over half of the 1.5-mile-long corridor ran along an embankment that was 20–25 feet above the grade of surrounding areas.

Abandoned rail corridors in many parts of the country have been reimagined and converted into bicycle and pedestrian trails for recreational use. However, few people until fairly recently considered the possibility that the abandoned DL&W rail corridor between Canalside and the Perry neighborhood and the Buffalo River could be reused in this way. The first person to consider that possibility was Hiroaki Hata, a professor of architecture and planning at the University at Buffalo's School of Architecture and Planning.

In the summer of 2010. Hata recruited five graduate students for a research project aimed at producing initial design schemes showing how the DL&W rail corridor could be developed into a recreational trail for pedestrians and bicyclists. One of the challenges Hata and his students faced was how and where people on opposite sides of the embankment could gain access to the trail. Hata's study came to the attention of

Congressman Brian Higgins, who asked the Western New York Land Conservancy (WNYLC) to consider trying to implement the scheme in some form. Up until that time, WNYLC, which was based in East Aurora, had mostly focused its efforts on preserving forests and farms, although many of its members lived and worked in Buffalo.

"We began thinking about the project in 2015–2016, but we really didn't know what the community wanted," said Jajean Rose-Burney, WNYLC's deputy executive director (Rose-Burney, interview, March 17, 2022). WNYLC members and staff met with residents and members of the First Ward and Valley neighborhood associations. A survey of local residents was also conducted to identify what purposes residents hoped would be served by redeveloping the rail corridor. The most frequently mentioned purposes were: walking trail 91 percent; access to nature 83 percent; bike path 76 percent; quiet places 64 percent; and gardens 54 percent.

One of the best ways to generate a wide range of ideas regarding possible ways of designing and constructing a project is to conduct a design competition. In 2018, WNYLC sponsored an international competition that invited designers to submit proposed design schemes showing how the former DL&W rail corridor could be converted into an urban nature trail and greenway. The deadline for receiving the submissions was February 15, 2019.

Ninety-eight proposed design schemes were received, which were judged in two ways: by a popular vote of members of the public who attended any one of the three public exhibitions of the proposed designs and by a seven-member jury. As an incentive for designers to submit their proposed design schemes, cash prizes of $7,500 and $3,000 respectively were promised to the first-place and second-place winners chosen by the jury. A cash prize of $3,000 was promised to the winner of the Community Choice Award. In addition to assuring that design features favored by members of the community would be recognized, involving members of the community in judging the submissions had the added benefit of increasing public interest in the project. It is important to note that members of the jury and members of the community who voted for their favorite schemes did not know who had submitted the entries; they saw only an entry number.

The winning submission based on the popular vote was submitted by Matt Rankas, a 34-year-old firefighter who studied landscape architecture at SUNY College of Environmental Science and Forestry. Rankas's trail design proposed "converting open-top hoppers that had formerly carried coal and steel into planters for small trees and shrubs and using ladles that once held molten steel to create fountains for a rain garden" (Pignataro 2019b). The first-place winner picked by the seven-member jury called for taking advantage of elevated portions of the trail and bridges along the corridor to create lookouts, one of which would overlook Red Jacket Park. WNYLC's announcement of the winners of the design competition came with the following disclaimer: the linear park when finished would probably represent an amalgam of the various design ideas that were proposed. "It was an ideas competition. The concepts submitted by the winners and even those who lost may find their ways into the final project design" (Pignataro 2019b).

W Architecture & Landscape Architecture of New York City was hired to design the trail. In the midst of the COVID-19 pandemic, the initial design concepts for the Riverline were publicly presented during a live-streamed YouTube event on Wednesday evening February 24, 2021. A virtual presentation on April 28 provided residents "one last chance to weigh in on ideas for the planned elevated urban nature trail" (Sommer 2021b).

The final concept design for the Riverline, unveiled at Tewksbury Lodge on July 19, 2021, envisions the trail beginning near the corner of Moore and Miami streets in the Perry neighborhood, where an entry plaza will be developed, and ending at the half bridge that extends out over the Buffalo River. Along the way, side trails and connections will be developed to River Fest Park, to the Ohio Street boat launch by way of Father Conway Park, and to Red Jacket Natural Habitat Park. (See figure 11.1 again for the path of the Riverline and its relation to parks and open space along the corridor.)

In June 2023, State Senator Tim Kennedy, Representative Brian Higgins, and Riverline Director Jeff Lebsack announced that New York State had awarding $225,000 WNYLC to serve as the required 20 percent local match for a $900,000 federal grant award that had previously been announced in March 2022 (Sommer, 2023c). The Riverline is expected to be developed in phases, with the one-half-mile stretch from Moore to Hamburg Street likely being the first portion to be constructed (Sommer 2021h). NFTA owns the former rail corridor and is expected to lease the land to WNYLC.

Part IV

The Outer Harbor

Chapter Twelve

Outer Harbor Waste Disposal Sites
Reclaimed as Nature Preserves

During the second half of the twentieth century, many of the major industries that had been established and operated on the Outer Harbor significantly scaled back or completely shut down their operations. As less and less manufacturing took place on the Outer Harbor, it increasingly came to be a place to dispose of all kinds of waste material.

The Tifft Farm Nature Preserve: 1946–2023[1]

In 1946, the Buffalo Creek Railroad filled in the City Ship Canal just north of Tifft Farm at the point where its tracks crossed the canal. As a result, ships could no longer enter the Tifft Farm canal system, and the Lehigh Valley Railroad was forced to close and abandon its Tifft Farm transshipment terminal. In 1955, Republic Steel purchased Tifft Farm from the City of Buffalo for $265,000, and between 1955 and 1972 used the property as a place to dispose of slag, fly ash, and other waste material generated by its Buffalo River steel mill.

In the early 1970s, the Buffalo Sewer Authority (BSA) needed to remove and relocate two million cubic yards of incinerated solid waste from Squaw Island (now known as Unity Island) so that a sewage treatment plant could be built on the island and identified Tifft Farm as the most feasible place to dispose of the material. The BSA's initial idea was that the waste material would be deposited and spread one yard thick over the entire site.

Tony Pierzchala, a long-time resident of the area and a board member of the South Buffalo Valley Association (the neighborhood association that preceded today's Valley Community Association), was the first person to speak out in opposition to what the BSA was planning to do. Pierzchala had grown up knowing Tifft Farm as a wild area, and he knew that if incinerated waste material were spread across the entire property it would entirely obliterate the site's most valued environmental qualities—such as the 75-acre cattail marsh and adjoining upland area. Father Hugh Carmichael, a South Buffalo clergyman, and others soon joined Pierzchala in calling for the city and the BSA to follow a less injurious approach.

In 1972, in response to the growing public outcry, the City of Buffalo established a Citizens Advisory Committee (CAC) to advise it and the BSA as to how the waste material should be disposed of at the site. The membership of the CAC included Tony Pierzchala and other members of the South Buffalo Valley Association, as well as representatives of local sportsmen's clubs, members of the Sierra Club, members of the Audubon Society and Buffalo Ornithological Society, and other citizens drawn from a variety of backgrounds. One of the most influential members on the Citizens Advisory Committee was Robert Andrle, a prominent member of the Buffalo Ornithological Society.

Well before he became a member of the Citizens Advisory Committee, Andrle had forged a strong professional and personal interest in Tifft Farm. He first became involved with Tifft Farm around 1941, when he started working for the City of Buffalo Health Department in rat control when the city was using Tifft Farm as a dump. As an ornithologist, Andrle would later specialize in studying gulls, which were naturally drawn to the dump. On his first date with Patricia Yates, who became his wife of 64 years, he took her to the Tifft Farm dump to watch the gulls.

In an article published in 1973, Andrle described the environmental qualities of Tifft Farm and the industrial landscape in which it existed as follows: "Of the extensive wild marshlands that once occupied the low-lying areas along Lake Erie near the mouth of the Buffalo River, only remnants remain. Cut by roads, railroads, buildings, and canals, filled by waste materials from an industrial economy and a burgeoning population, and considered by some as useless 'swamps,' these natural wetlands have received short shrift at the hands of man. The preservation of such rich aquatic habitat . . . was for a long time a concept alien to most in the Buffalo area" (Andrle, 1976, 39).

With a $15,000 gift from an anonymous donor obtained through the Greater Buffalo Development Foundation, which was matched by a grant from the NY State Department of Environmental Conservation, the CAC was able to hire a consultant to help it develop a master plan to guide how the waste material would be distributed on the site. The CAC then formed a subcommittee, called the Technical Advisory Committee, which was composed of members who possessed specialized knowledge and expertise in subject areas that were deemed essential to oversee the work of the consultant. Over the two years it took to develop the master plan, Andrle and other members of the Technical Advisory Committee devoted an enormous amount of time and effort assisting the consultant by conducting a number of detailed investigations essential for a workable and acceptable plan. During that period, Andrle also laid out the system of trails and blinds that would subsequently be developed at Tifft Farm, designing them so as to provide visitors with access to areas where they could observe wildlife, while at the same time providing sheltered areas for wildlife.

The members of the CAC unanimously agreed that the natural feature that most needed to be preserved was the 75-acre cattail marsh. To assure that the cattail marsh would not be disturbed, the committee developed and approved a plan that called for the waste material brought to the site to be "added to a previously filled section of 50 acres, contoured into hills and revegetated" (Wolfe and Tifft Farm Committee, 1983). The remainder of the 250-acre area, consisting of ship canal remnants and small waterways, and a mix of fields, shrubs, tree groves, and woodlands that provided habitat for whitetail deer, gray fox, mink, muskrats, and cottontails, also needed to be kept off-limits to the waste material that was to be brought to the property.

The master plan approved by the CAC was presented to Mayor Frank Sedita by a delegation headed by Theodore L. Hullar of the Sierra Club. The mayor told the group that he supported the plan and the Buffalo Common Council officially approved it in 1972. With those approvals having been secured, the City of Buffalo purchased the Tifft Farm property from Republic Steel.

When the final arrangements were made for bringing the waste material to Tifft Farm, Robert Andrle was associate director of the Buffalo Museum of Science. He died in 2017, and I never had the opportunity to interview him. However, I was able to speak with his son Chris, who was often at his side at Tifft Farm during the period when many of the actions that fundamentally shaped the property were taken. "I was there when they brought the incinerated waste to Tifft Farm. It was a huge operation, with dump trucks arriving around the clock from Squaw Island, and barges being brought from Squaw Island to the foot of Tifft Street, and then trucked under the Father Baker Bridge into the site. As Andrle further explained, "A spectacular amount of debris and trash also needed to be removed from the site beforehand. The City provided a huge number of trucks and volunteers to carry out the cleanup" (C. Andrle, interview, June 24, 2021).

Between 1973 and 1975 two million cubic yards of incinerated waste were brought to Tifft Farm. The waste material was bulldozed into four mounds in the southwest quadrant of the site, which were enclosed in clay and surrounded by a 22-foot-deep clay wall to prevent leachate from migrating into adjacent areas. A system of drain pipes was installed at the base of the clay wall to transmit leachate discharged from the mounds into the municipal sewage system and ultimately to the sewage treatment plant that was built on Squaw/Unity Island.

Soil excavated from other portions of the property was used to cover the mounds, and wildflowers and trees were planted. Chris Andrle recalls helping his father plant a number of those trees. Portions of the former canals on the site were enlarged to form three small lakes, which were named after Tony Pierzchala's three daughters, Kirsty, Beth, and Lisa.

During that same 1973–1975 period, Lincoln Nutting, a naturalist and educator who at the time was president of the Buffalo Audubon Society, shot a 16-mm film that "captured in celluloid the remarkable recovery of a disturbed landscape from its earlier days as a transshipment terminal . . . and later as an industrial and municipal dump . . . all in the shadow of the grain elevators along the Buffalo waterfront" (Gall 2014, 2). On top of the hundreds of hours he spent shooting the film outdoors, Nutting also spent hundreds more volunteer hours editing the film.

In August 1976, the Citizens Advisory Committee that had overseen the creation of the nature preserve officially became Tifft Farm Inc., a nonprofit corporation, which assumed the responsibility of managing and operating the 264-acre preserve. Robert Andrle was a founding member of the board of directors of Tifft Farm Inc. In 1977, Tifft Farm Inc. obtained funding from the state's municipal wetlands restoration program to create an additional open-water area near the cattail marsh by dredging along the marsh's southwest perimeter. A pump and a culvert connecting this open water area to the lake-canal system were installed to control the water level in the marsh. In 1978, Robert Andrle, his son Chris, and other volunteers stacked the logs that were used to build Tifft Farm's first visitor center.

In April 1982, Tifft Farm Inc. merged with the Buffalo Society of Natural Sciences (BSNS), and the Tifft Farm Nature Preserve became a department of the Buffalo Museum of Science. Five members of Tifft Farm Inc.'s board were added to the BSNS board of managers, one of whom was Robert Andrle. In February 1983, Wayne Gall was hired as BSNS's first administrator for the Tifft Farm Preserve. Not long after he started working at the preserve, Gall discovered 29 partially buried drums containing industrial waste that years earlier had been disposed of on the property, a number of which had broken open and leaked.[2] The preserve was promptly closed to the public, and 116 drums were excavated and removed from the site. The preserve reopened to the public in October 1983.

Between 1985 and 1987, Lincoln Nutting committed hundreds more hours to producing a second film titled "Through the Seasons at Tifft Nature Preserve." Shot at Tifft Nature Preserve, this second 16-mm film shows how animal and plant life had colonized on the recycled landscape since the mid-1970s.

Zachary Goodrich became the steward of the Tifft Nature Preserve in 2017. When I spoke with him at the end of 2019, Goodrich reflected on how difficult it has been to try to reclaim and preserve a natural landscape on a fairly small property that has long been surrounded by a much larger heavily industrialized area. "The small size of the preserve, and its lack of connectivity to a larger natural environment has made it difficult to a fully restore and maintain natural processes within the land-scape" (Goodrich, interview, December 24, 2019). Nevertheless, the cattail marsh, woodlands, grasslands, and ponds that have survived and flourished within the 264-acre preserve provide habitat for beaver, muskrat, turtles, amphibians, and a wide variety of species of birds. Five miles of trails and boardwalks within the preserve enable visitors to discreetly observe those species and wildlife in their natural habitats without disturbing them. "Discovery Summer Camps" held at Tifft Farm for children ages 3–5, 5–8, and 9–12 often provide those children with their first opportunity to experience nature in a meaningful way. The preserve has also worked closely with city schools to arrange for and schedule field trips to the preserve to increase students' awareness of natural processes and bring them into contact with aspects of the natural environment they might not otherwise observe and experience.

The Times Beach Nature Preserve: 1930–2023

As noted in chapter 1, the first lighthouse that marked the entrance to Buffalo's newly created harbor was built so close to the mouth of the Buffalo Creek that ships approaching Buffalo often had difficulty seeing it through all the smoke generated by the village. A year after the Erie Canal opened, the US Treasury Department authorized the construction of a new lighthouse farther out in the lake. In 1826, a conical pile of heavy stone was put in place to mark the place where the new lighthouse was to be built. A quarter mile-long rock parapet wall (called the "Lighthouse Pier") was then built to connect the point where the original lighthouse stood to where the new lighthouse was to be constructed (see figure 12.1).

"From the day it was built the long rock pier started catching the littoral drift of water-borne sand, which built up along the southern sloped side of the pier because water flowed along the shoreline from south to north toward the head of the Niagara River" (Vogel, email, July 2, 2021). By the 1920s, the littoral drift of sand had built up such that the area

Figure 12.1. Late 1800s glass-plate photograph showing the quarter-mile-long lighthouse pier connecting the point where Buffalo's first lighthouse had stood to where the c. 1833 lighthouse was to be built. *Source*: Buffalo Lighthouse Association. Public domain.

behind the pier was filled with sand. So much sand had accumulated at the northern tip of the Outer Harbor that by 1930 the *Buffalo Times* proposed that the area be used as a municipal beach for swimming and sunbathing. The beach was formally opened to the public in 1932 and named Times Beach because the newspaper had proposed the idea of using the area for public bathing. City residents used Times Beach as a place to swim until the 1940s, at which point increased awareness of the health risks of being exposed to contaminated material by bathing in the area caused it to be closed to public swimming. As shown in figure 12.2, the low-lying area behind the Lighthouse Pier was eventually filled in to enable the buildings and facilities of the US Coast Guard Base and Lifesaving Service to be built there.

In the late 1950s, the City of Buffalo entered into a memorandum of agreement with the US Army Corps of Engineers (USACE) that authorized it to construct a 55-acre diked disposal area along the portion of the former Times Beach shoreline that looked out directly onto Lake Erie and to use

Figure 12.2. By the time this aerial photo was taken in 1962, low-lying areas behind the lighthouse pier had been filled to enable the Coast Guard Station to be built. *Source*: US Coast Guard. Public domain.

it as a place to dispose of sediment dredged from the navigation channels of the Buffalo River, City Ship Canal, and Black Rock Canal. Over 550,000 cubic yards of sediment and silt were eventually disposed of at Times Beach.

Robert Andrle, the ornithologist who had helped establish the Tifft Farm Preserve, spent a considerable amount of time bird-watching at Times Beach, because its location made it an important place for migrating birds to rest and feed as they moved along the northern and southern shores of Lake Erie. In the course of his observations, he noticed that by discharging dredged material in the form of a slurry through pipes into the center of the Times Beach diked disposal area, the USACE had inadvertently created a set of environmental conditions that were extremely beneficial to migrating birds—namely, a roughly semicircular area of silt that sloped very gradually into deeper water. "The silt flat's littoral and shallow water zones—unique in this region—attract the kinds and numbers of birds that do not usually occur elsewhere. At least 186 species of birds have been identified at Times Beach during the past few years" (Andrle 1973, 48).

Andrle observed that three types of habitat also existed at Times Beach: "A deeper area up to about 2 meters in depth beyond the shallow water zone, a low-lying silt flat where herbaceous plants flourish, and an upland zone containing tall herbs, grasses and stands of shrubs and trees" (Andrle, 1973, 48–50). Wetlands and native plants along the shoreline of Times Beach also provided habitat for coastal fish and wildlife.

Andrle realized that if the USACE filled the diked disposal area at Times Beach entirely with dredged material, it would put an end to the unique set of conditions that made the site so attractive and nurturing to migrating birds. In 1977, at Andrle's urging, the Buffalo Ornithological Society issued a formal request to the USACE that it stop disposing of dredged material at Times Beach and support establishing a nature preserve. The USACE had the authority to continue using Times Beach as a place to dispose of dredged sediment. Nevertheless, it agreed to stop depositing dredged material at Times Beach because a new diked disposal area at the southern end of the Outer Harbor near Stoney Point was about to become available for that purpose. Another reason USACE was willing to stop depositing dredged material at Times Beach was because it wanted to study the long-term environmental impact that depositing contaminated material had had on the site.

The study that the USACE conducted in 1981 found high levels of nine organic pollutants to be present in the soils of Times Beach. Three wells were installed on the site in 1982 to monitor the groundwater. In

1983, groundwater samples indicated elevated concentrations of heavy metals and organics. Heavy metal contamination was also identified in the surface water. After leaving the staff of the Buffalo Museum of Science in 1984, Robert Andrle assisted the USACE by carrying out lengthy studies of the effects that toxins at Times Beach had had on the food chain.

Around that time, Paul MacClennan, the environmental reporter for the *Buffalo News* who broke the story about the contamination at Love Canal in Niagara Falls, connected with Andrle, and the two of them began discussing the idea of trying to establish a nature preserve at Times Beach. Because the property was owned by the City of Buffalo, Andrle and MacClennan approached George Arthur, the president of the Buffalo Common Council, to seek his support for establishing Times Beach as a nature preserve. The undertaking got a boost when the USACE entered into an agreement with the city, the Buffalo Ornithological Society, and the Audubon Society whereby the parties agreed that the unique environmental conditions that existed at Times Beach should be maintained and allowed to naturally evolve.

It took much longer to establish a nature preserve at Times Beach than it had at Tifft Farm, even though by the end of the 1970s Andrle had already developed a site management plan for Times Beach. "The Times Beach Preserve took much longer because so many different governmental entities were involved" (C. Andrle, interview, June 24, 2021). It wasn't until 1989 that the Times Beach Oversight Committee was established to exercise a degree of responsibility for the ongoing management of the area, and it wasn't until May 2005 that the City of Buffalo formally designated Times Beach as a nature preserve. The major hurdle that had long stood in the way of securing the city's final approval for establishing the nature preserve was removed when Erie County agreed that it, and not the city, would be responsible for maintaining and managing the preserve.

The nature preserve opened to the public in 2002. (See figure 13.4 for location and boundaries of Times Beach Nature Preserve.) In 2008, the Friends of Times Beach became responsible for managing the day-to-day operations of the preserve. With the help of Congressman Brian Higgins, $2.5 million in Great Lakes Restoration Initiative funding was secured for an environmental remediation project that removed invasive species from the site. In 2012, the NY State Department of Transportation spent $900,000 installing an elevated boardwalk, decorative fencing, and interpretive signage (Magavern 2019, 13).

Migrating and breeding pollinators, such as bees and butterflies, had historically depended heavily on the flora and fauna at Times Beach to sustain them. Thousands of migrating Monarch butterflies used to arrive at Times Beach in a single day, but none had arrived in 2013. In 2015, Times Beach Nature Preserve became formally associated with the Pollinator Conservation Association, an already legally established 501(c)(3) nonprofit corporation, which meant that the Times Beach Nature Preserve was finally able to receive tax-deductible contributions. In 2015, the Friends of Times Beach and Pollinator Conservation Association planted a pollinator garden to provide sources of food and habitat for bees, butterflies, and other pollinators. In 2017 and 2018 hundreds of Monarchs were once again observed at Times Beach. Around that same time, the *Queen City Bike Ferry* began dropping people off at a dock directly across from the entrance to the Times Beach Preserve.

Chapter Thirteen

The Fight for the
Future of the Outer Harbor

Perhaps the most surprising and gratifying manifestation of Buffalo's waterfront renaissance has been what has unfolded on the Outer Harbor. After having initially developed a plan that called for the Outer Harbor to be extensively privately developed, the Erie Canal Harbor Development Corporation (ECHDC) did an about-face by essentially agreeing with environmental activists and NGOs that the best way of using the Outer Harbor would be as a park. It stopped short, however, of calling for the area to be officially designated as a state park, as had been done for the southern portion of the Outer Harbor, which had been developed into Buffalo Harbor State Park.

A Quarter Century of State Agency Plans

As described in chapter 5, the Horizons Waterfront Commission's 1992 Action Plan for the Erie County Waterfront was the first state agency plan to recommend that Buffalo's Outer Harbor be extensively privately developed. Almost all of the development called for in that plan would have taken place on land that was owned by Niagara Frontier Transportation Authority (NFTA). Two decades later, NFTA still controlled that land.

Brian Higgins, who had formerly represented South Buffalo on the Buffalo Common Council and was elected in 2004 to the US House of Representatives, had long urged NFTA to transfer its Outer Harbor property to Erie Canal Harbor Development Corporation (ECHDC), which he deemed better suited to redevelop the Outer Harbor. In December 2012, as progress was finally being made toward developing the Inner Harbor in a publicly beneficial manner, Higgins called upon NFTA to transfer the hundreds of acres of the Outer Harbor it controlled to ECHDC at a cost not to exceed $2.00.

In January 2014, ECHDC's board voted to pay NFTA $2.00 for 354 acres of the Outer Harbor, while NFTA retained its ownership of the 50-acre area around Terminals A and B in the hope that it would end up being paid much more than $2.00 for that portion of the Outer Harbor. Governor Andrew Cuomo directed ECHDC to redevelop the area around and south of the Small Boat Harbor into Buffalo Harbor State Park (see figure 13.1) and to issue a request for proposals (RFP) to select a consulting firm to develop a master plan to determine how the remaining acreage would be redeveloped.

According to ECHDC's President Thomas Dee, "The master plan [was] necessary so that the development community has an idea about what may or may not work on the Outer Harbor property" (Fink 2014). Seven design firms responded to the RFP, and in May 2014 ECHDC selected Perkins&Will, an architectural firm headquartered in Chicago to prepare the plan.

Environmental activist Lynda Schneekloth suspected that the impetus for developing the master plan came from the governor's office. "Andrew Cuomo was intent on running for re-election as governor and must have thought he could gain favor with the business community and major contributors by succeeding in having the Outer Harbor privately developed" (Schneekloth, interview, June 6, 2021).

The Waterfront Development Advisory Committee was established by ECHDC to provide public input to the consultants as they developed the plan. However, members of the Advisory Committee were frustrated by the way the consultants conducted their meetings with the committee. "It was a very controlled process and there appeared to be no way to have your voice heard" (Schneekloth, email, December 17, 2018).

The Advisory Committee was presented with three alternatives, which varied only with respect to how the same amount of development would be distributed throughout the Outer Harbor. Each alternative called for developing approximately 2,100 new housing units (mostly condominiums), with retail and commercial space mixed in. One of the alternatives showed five-story condominiums, shops, and restaurants being developed around the detention pond of the Times Beach Nature Preserve, as well as being developed on the adjacent area that later became Wilkeson Pointe Park. (See

Figure 13.1. Map of the southern half of the Outer Harbor: Buffalo Harbor State Park, the former Freezer Queen property, and Terminals A and B. *Source*: Map by Austin Wyles.

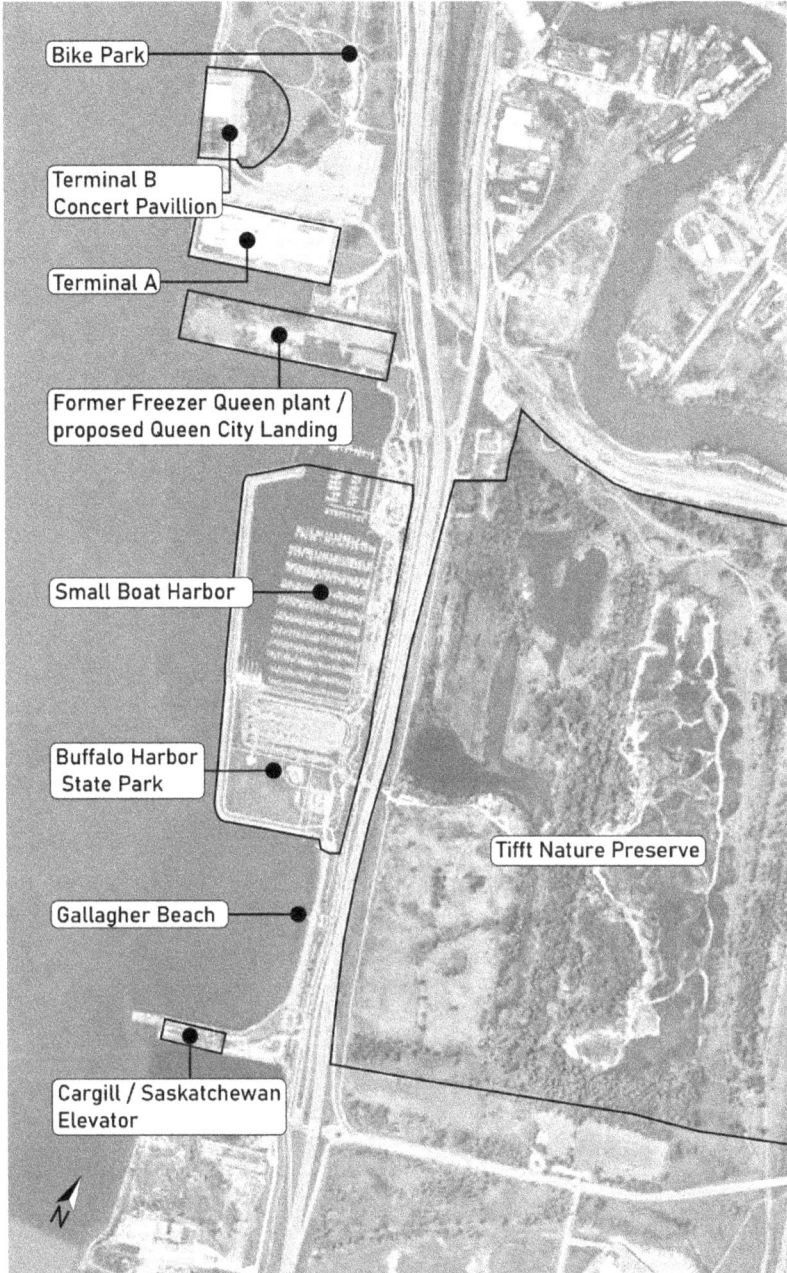

again figure 13.4.) NYS Assemblyman Sean Ryan, whose district encompassed most of the City of Buffalo, said, "I never saw a big push for housing. I saw the opposite, I saw a big push for green space" (Telvock 2014). ECHDC's preferred version of the "Blueprint: An Update on Planning for the Future of Buffalo's Outer Harbor" was publicly unveiled in September 2016.

The Sierra Club-Niagara Group, League of Women Voters of Buffalo/ Niagara, Buffalo Niagara Riverkeeper, and the Western New York Environmental Alliance all questioned whether the "Blueprint plan" truly reflected the wishes of the people. As Mark Sommer observed, the plan had drawn "a sharp rebuke from the public and local politicians" (Sommer 2019b, A1).

To be fair, the plan *did* show a large portion of the Outer Harbor as being left as open space and undeveloped. But there was no guarantee that the green space shown in the plan would remain that way in perpetuity. As ECHDC's President Thomas Dee put it, "I don't know that I am prepared to say that everything that's green will stay green forever. I don't think that's good planning" (Telvock 2014).

The conventional wisdom at the time was that money could be made developing "high-end" housing on the Outer Harbor. Thomas Dee, who was ECHDC's president between 2008 and 2018, told me that "a lot of people" had told him they'd "love to live on the Outer Harbor" (Dee, interview, January 31, 2019). "The real estate bonanza that developers hoped to profit from was based on the notion that people would "pay a lot of money to live next to the lake *without knowing the risks* [italics added for emphasis]" (Wooster, interview, June 12, 2021). ECHDC must have also believed that a lot of money could be made developing housing on the Outer Harbor because a provision was included in its contract with Perkins&Will that specified that the development called for in the plan needed to be able to be privately financed and *not* require a public subsidy. In other words, all sewer and water lines, roadways, and other facilities required to support the development would need to be paid for by the developers.

A financial analysis carried out afterward determined that the development called for in the plan would *not* be feasible to privately finance and would, in fact, require a substantial public subsidy. Because that finding violated a key provision in ECHDC's contract with Perkins&Will, the agency was forced to walk away from the plan. Environmentalists had dodged a bullet but knew they could not count on being on the winning side the next time around.

To be better prepared to oppose future efforts by ECHDC to advance the private development of the Outer Harbor, a number of nongovernmental organizations and stakeholder groups formed Our Outer Harbor (OOH), a coalition of organizations that included:

WNY Environmental Alliance
Buffalo Niagara Waterkeeper
League of Women Voters of Buffalo Niagara
Times Beach Nature Preserve
Wellness Institute of Greater Buffalo
Pollinator Conservation Association
Sierra Club Niagara Group
Trout Unlimited
21st Century Park Outer Harbor
Erie County Federation of Sportsmen's Clubs
Partnership for the Public Good
Preservation Buffalo Niagara

In the meantime, a sea change had been taking place in how members of the general public viewed the Outer Harbor, as was evidenced by the following post on *Buffalo Rising*: "Environmental and natural habitat resources/amenities should not be playing second fiddle [in the Outer Harbor]; rather they should be emphasized as part of the overall orchestration of this phenomenal opportunity" (*Buffalo Rising*, September 17, 2014).

In February 2016, ECHDC paid NFTA $3.5 million to gain ownership of the last remaining 50 acres of the Outer Harbor that NFTA had controlled for over 50 years—the area occupied by Terminals A and B. In September 2016, ECHDC also acquired the 14-acre First Buffalo Marina property that included the Connecting Terminal elevator that the agency had begun illuminating in 2015 as an attraction for Canalside.[1] Once ECHDC had acquired those two portions of Outer Harbor, the only privately owned part of the Outer Harbor between Terminals A and B and the Coast Guard Station was the former Freezer Queen property.

Outer Harbor Planning Becomes More Participatory

In September 2016, ECHDC hired Trowbridge Wolf Michaels, Landscape Architects (TWM) of Ithaca, New York, to prepare another plan for the Outer Harbor that, according to ECHDC board chair Robert Gioia, would employ the "lighter, quicker, cheaper" approach that had proved so successful in activating Canalside (Sommer 2016a). David Colligan, a voting member of ECHDC's board of directors commented, "I think we are headed in the right direction. We are trying to do what the public wants us to do" (Fink 2016). ECHDC promised that three public meetings (described as "open houses") would be held at different stages in the planning process to allow members of the public to review and comment on what was being considered before the plan was finalized.

The first open house was held on July 11, 2017, at the Canalside VIP Tent. An enlarged printout of a Google Earth photo of the Outer Harbor was spread out on a long table, and people were encouraged to write words and phrases on Post-it notes and place them on the map to indicate what they hoped would, or would not, take place there. Among the comments written on the Post-it notes were: "No Condos," "Keep it green," and "Encourage ecological restoration" (see figure 13.2). Among the comments placed on the map in the area of Terminal B were: "Keep it natural," "Preserve views of the lake," and "Great place for storm-watching."

Figure 13.2. Post-it notes with comments placed by attendees on a large-scale Google Earth map of the Outer Harbor. *Source*: Photo by Anna Scime. Used with permission.

Figure 13.3. Attendee at July 11, 2017, open house being interviewed. *Source*: Photo by Anna Scime. Used with permission.

People who attended the open house were asked to complete a brief survey, either in writing or online. After the results of the survey were tallied, ECHDC reported that the main thing members of the public wanted was to maintain usable green space and create more and better public access to the water.

In anticipation of ECHDC's second scheduled open house, the OOH Coalition held a public meeting on Wednesday, September 28, 2018, that was attended by more than 200 people. The meeting was held at River-Works in a large open space around which a number of proposals for the Outer Harbor prepared by various organizations were displayed.

Jay Burney of the Times Beach Nature Preserve began the program by showing a short video about the Bell Slip, which was described as "one of the most unique and ecologically sensitive places on the Outer Harbor." After short presentations by Tim Tielman representing the Campaign for Greater Buffalo, Joanne Kahn from the 21st Century Park on the Outer

Harbor, and Lynda Schneekloth representing the WNY Environmental Alliance, an open mic was held to enable people to comment on what they had heard and share their thoughts regarding what they hoped would happen on the Outer Harbor. People could also write their comments on cards that were handed out and then collected. A summary of the public comments that were received was posted online at www.ourouterharbor.org/2016-Riverworks-meeting.html.

The 12 organizational members of the OOH Coalition then unanimously adopted ten "shared principles" to serve as a "checklist" when reviewing plans and projects that might be proposed for the Outer Harbor, which were:

- Retain public ownership of public lands

- Be truly public and inclusive

- Be water based and water dependent

- Protect and restore natural environments and habitats

- Avoid sprawl (do not divert resources from the City proper)

- Be consistent with City policies, including the Green Code, Comprehensive Plan and Local Waterfront Redevelopment Plan (LWRP)

- Promote health, physical activity, and access to the natural world

- Be based on a transparent and democratic process

- Be sustainable, based on conserving our natural and cultural heritage

- Be climate smart, based on a clear assessment of risk and resilience factors

ECHDC's second open house was held at the Lexus Club at KeyBank Center on November 19, 2018. Attendees were shown three options for each of the three following portions of the Outer Harbor: the area between Wilkeson Pointe and the Bell Slip; the First Buffalo Marina; and Terminal B. They were then asked to comment on and compare the options and rank them in order of preference by placing color-coded stickers on the poster boards that displayed each alternative. None of the options showed any housing being developed. Not long after the second open house was held, Steven Ranalli, who had recently replaced Tom Dee as ECHDC's president, informed OOH that any plans the agency had formulated in the past to encourage the development of housing on the Outer Harbor were "off the table."

In January and March 2019, ECHDC met and reviewed its latest plans for the Outer Harbor with representatives of the First Buffalo River Marina, Buffalo Niagara Waterkeeper, WNY Environmental Alliance, WNY League of Women Voters, 21st Century Park for the Outer Harbor, Industrial Heritage Committee, and Campaign for Greater Buffalo. ECHDC's preferred plan for the Outer Harbor was unveiled at the third and final open house that was held on May 2, 2019, at the Burchfield Penney Art Center.

The Green Code and Proposed Queen City Landing Project

In December 2016, the City of Buffalo replaced the badly out-of-date zoning code it had been enforcing and relying on since 1953 by adopting a new Unified Development Ordinance, which was popularly referred to as the "Green Code." The origin of the effort to draft a new zoning code for the City of Buffalo can be traced back to 2007, when the Smart Growth Committee of a group that called itself the New Millennium Group organized a conference to promote the idea that the city should adopt a new zoning code that would "emphasize walkable neighborhoods, encourage preservation of historic neighborhoods, eliminate minimum parking requirements for all projects and add clarity to the development process" (Sommer 2017a).

The process of drafting the new code finally got underway in 2010. Chris Hawley, a senior planner in the City of Buffalo's Office of Strategic Planning who had also been a member of the New Millennium Group, played an instrumental role in drafting the new code. After city planning staff members held dozens of public meetings in different parts of the city listening to residents' concerns and suggestions, the Buffalo Common Council unanimously approved Buffalo's new Green Code in 2016.

Passage of the Green Code represented a tremendous victory for the Our Outer Harbor Coalition. Before the Green Code was adopted, most of the Outer Harbor had been zoned M3—Heavy Manufacturing.

Once the Green Code was adopted, most of the Outer Harbor was zoned D-OG (greenspace and parks). The First Buffalo Marina was zoned N-3E (Mixed-Use Edge), and Terminals A and B were zoned N-1S (Secondary Employment). Rezoning so much of the Outer Harbor for greenspace and parks or natural areas didn't come about without a fight. "The battle over the vision of what the Outer Harbor should become was hard fought, with developers still insisting that it should be privatized and with members of the public and NGOs saying 'No!'" (Schneekloth, email, April 2019).

OOH failed to persuade Common Council Member Christopher Scanlon to drop his objection to prohibiting the development of housing on the 20-acre former Freezer Queen property, which developer Gary Burchheit purchased in 2007 for $3 million at a court-ordered foreclosure auction. Because the former Freezer Queen property was located in Scanlon's district, other members of the Buffalo Common Council looked to Scanlon to determine how they would vote on the matter. As a result, when the Common Council officially adopted the Green Code, the Green Code rezoning wasn't applied to Burchheit's property.

With the door left open to the possibility that housing might be developed on the Freezer Queen property, Burchheit submitted a plan to the city that called for a 23-story, glass-walled apartment tower to be built on the property called Queen City Landing. A revised plan reduced the proposed height of the apartment tower from 23 to 20 stories. However, the proposed project still included 35,000 square feet of ground floor commercial and restaurant space and 19,000 square feet of banquet and restaurant space on the sixth floor.

According to Jay Burney, a member of OOH's steering committee, it didn't make sense to allow the development of a large number of housing units on the Outer Harbor when hundreds of acres in core neighborhoods of the city were vacant and in need of being redeveloped. "Encouraging the development of housing on the Outer Harbor will weaken market demand for developing the vacant land that is available for redevelopment within the city proper," said Burney (interview, January 20, 2019).

The vulnerability of the Outer Harbor to being inundated by tsunami-like events (known as seiches) which are occurring with increased frequency due to climate change was another reason for opposing housing on the Outer Harbor.[2] "Last month [in February 2019], a polar vortex closed access to the Outer Harbor, with high winds, cold and ice. High winds and bands of lake-effect snow have often forced the closure of the Skyway and of roads leading in and out of the Outer Harbor, making it difficult if not impossible to get into or out of the area for extended periods. Imagine being a resident stuck in a shoreline glass tower out there during such a storm" (Wooster, interview, March 21, 2019). "The Outer Harbor took a huge hit. Flood waters and debris crossed several parts of Fuhrmann Boulevard, . . . and Buffalo Harbor State Park and the proposed Queen City Landing development site [were] overtopped by raging waters" (Burney 2019).

Another reason for opposing the project was that the apartment tower was to be built in the flyway of migrating birds in the Niagara River Globally Significant Important Bird Area. The site was also adjacent the Small Boat Harbor, a 165-acre NYSDEC-designated "Significant Coastal Habitat," which provided food resources for many species of waterfowl and migratory birds. (See again figure 13.1, map of southern portion of the Outer Harbor.) Constructing a 20-story apartment tower on a peninsula that had been created by depositing contaminated sediment and waste materials into submerged areas of the shoreline posed a significant risk to coastal habitat because it would require driving pilings deep down into that waste material, which could discharge and spread contaminants into adjacent waters.

In February 2020, Burchheit "doubled down on his bet by submitting a new concept plan to the city that called for adding two more six-story apartment buildings and a cluster of 32 townhouses on the rest of peninsula—adding another 178 housing units on top of the 206 units in the apartment tower (Epstein 2020a, B1, B2). A month later in March 2020, as the COVID-19 pandemic began to grip the area, the developer issued a public statement to the effect that the proposed $180 million Queen City Landing development project would no longer proceed through the city's review process and that all work on the project was being postponed indefinitely. In July 2022, the property was put up for sale with an asking price of $12 million.

∾

Wilkeson Pointe Park was the first portion of the Outer Harbor to be developed into a public park. ECHDC assembled the 22 acres for the park, which was opened to the public in 2013, by combining a parcel it had acquired from NFTA in 2008 with a parcel that had been owned and used by the New York Power Authority to store the Lake Erie-Niagara River Ice Boom when it wasn't strung across the mouth of the Niagara River. The $2.8 million cost of developing the park was paid for with money obtained through the agreement that Representative Brian Higgins negotiated with NYPA in connection with the federal relicensing of the Niagara Hydroelectric Power Plant.

Two years after Wilkeson Pointe Park opened, ECHDC gained control of 350 acres of the Outer Harbor that had long been controlled by NFTA and developed the southern portion of that area into Buffalo Harbor State Park, which opened to the public in May 2015. At that point New York's Office of Parks, Recreation and Historic Preservation (OPRHP) became responsible for managing and maintaining the park, which included the adjacent 1,000-slip Small Boat Harbor.

Meanwhile, a growing public consensus seemed to be emerging that the entire Outer Harbor should become a public park. In August 2019, Partnership for the Public Good issued a 57-page report authored by Sam Magavern titled "Buffalo's Outer Harbor: The Right Place for World-Class Park"(Magavern 2019).

The 2020 Outer Harbor General Project Plan

On November 9, 2020, ECHDC adopted the "Outer Harbor Civic and Land Use General Project Plan" (GPP), which called for most of the Outer Harbor north of Terminal A (the site of the former Ford Motor Company assembly plant) and between Fuhrmann Boulevard and the lake to be developed into a park. The plan called for investing a total of $150 million over 20 years, removing invasive species, adding topsoil and new plantings to restore and diversify the landscape, adding shoreline trails and boardwalks, and providing restrooms and other amenities in portions of the Outer Harbor for the public's convenience. The first phase, expected to last five years and cost $45 million, would be paid for with money from the state's "Buffalo Billion" economic development program, New York Power Authority, and the federal government.

No in-person public hearing was held prior to ECHDC's approval of the 2020 Outer Harbor plan. Instead, a two-month comment period was provided during which people and organizations could submit written comments to ECHDC. Of the 242 written comments that were received, a number criticized the planned expansion of the bike park in the Lakeside Complex.[3] "Many of our members are concerned that [mountain bikes] take up too much valuable coastal land compared to the general public's needs and see potential conflicts between fast bikes and families with children and dogs and other slow walkers" (Our Outer Harbor Coalition, January 16, 2018). However, by far the most heavily criticized action called for in the plan was building an amphitheater and event facility that would draw huge crowds and hundreds of cars to the Outer Harbor. "There should be no amphitheater or facilities for mass events built anywhere on the Outer Harbor," wrote Tim Tielman. "The Outer Harbor should be designated as a public park, with an emphasis on serving the biodiversity of the Lake Erie shore and the resiliency of the Lake's coastline," wrote Patrick Burke, NY State Assembly.

As noted in chapter 8, ECHDC began holding concerts at Canalside in 2011 to generate some activity at the Inner Harbor, which proved wildly popular and drew large crowds. However, as Canalside became more built out, and as new attractions (such as the Children's Museum and Heritage Carousel) were added, the concerts were no longer needed to activate Canalside. ECHDC therefore decided it made sense to move them to the Outer Harbor.

ECHDC approved spending $13 million to develop a concert pavilion on the southern portion of the Outer Harbor by stripping the vacant Terminal B cold storage warehouse building down to its metal frame and constructing a canopied stage on the slab "to create an open-air structure with a view of Lake Erie in the background" (Sommer 2021i). Rather than provide permanent seating, the plan called for people to sit on a four-acre lawn that sloped down toward the stage.

According to Steven Ranalli, the concert venue ECHDC planned to build would be much less elaborate than other outdoor concert venues that people in Western New York might be familiar with. "People may think of Darien Lake or Artpark, which [have] giant stages with permanent seating . . . and canopies over the crowd. . . . That is not what we're building (Sommer 2021e).

Aside from the proposed amphitheater/pavilion, the 2020 General Project Plan (GPP) for the Outer Harbor went a long way toward achieving the environmentalists' aim of assuring that the Outer Harbor would be primarily used for outdoor recreation and enjoyment. For example, the plan called for adding five miles of new pedestrian and bicycle trails, and boardwalks and promenades along large portions of the shoreline.

The 171-acre area covered by the General Project Plan (GPP) was divided into seven subareas: First Buffalo Marina, Wilkeson Pointe, Michigan Pier, The Meadows, Bell Slip, Lakeside Complex, and Terminal B (as shown in figure 13.4). The actions that would be undertaken in each of the respective subareas were described in the plan as follows:

In the First Buffalo Marina Subarea (16 acres): The *Queen City Bike Ferry* from Canalside will be re-routed. Instead of dropping people

Figure 13.4. Outer Harbor 2020 General Project Plan subareas. *Source*: Map by Austin Wyles.

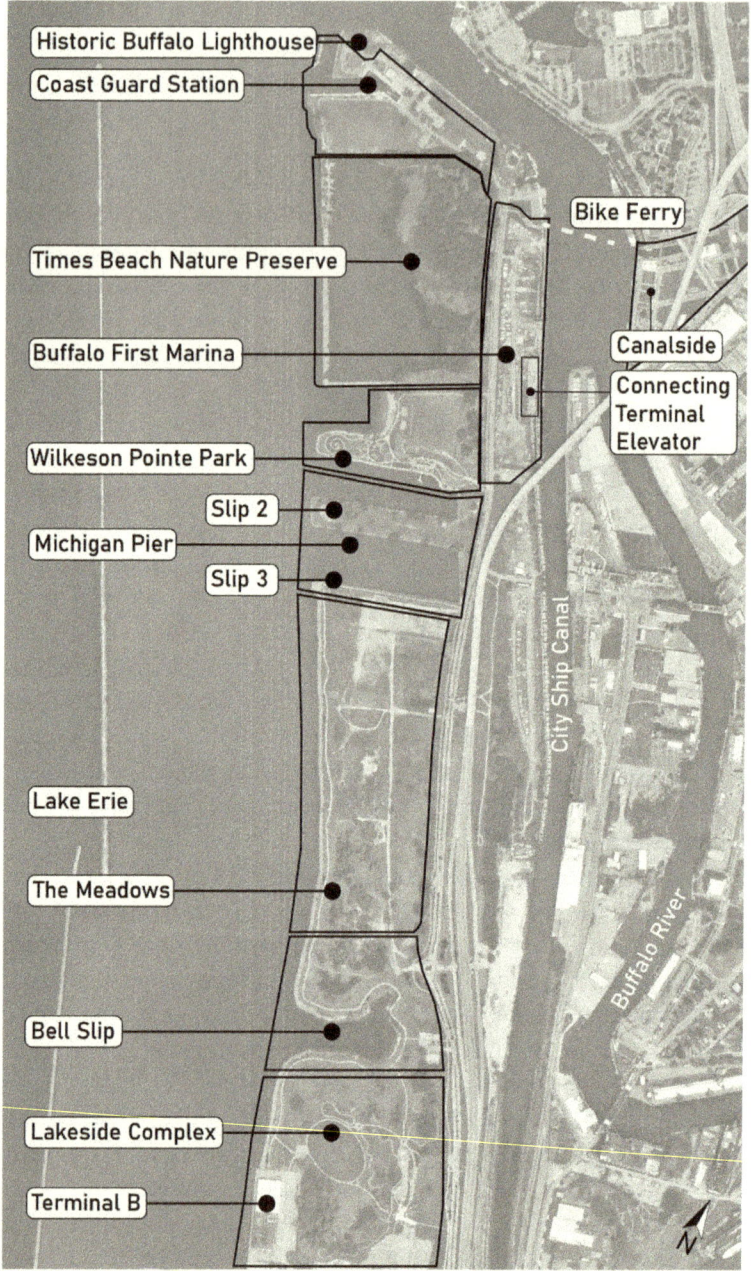

Historic Buffalo Lighthouse
Coast Guard Station
Bike Ferry
Times Beach Nature Preserve
Buffalo First Marina
Canalside
Connecting Terminal Elevator
Wilkeson Pointe Park
Slip 2
Michigan Pier
Slip 3
City Ship Canal
Lake Erie
The Meadows
Buffalo River
Bell Slip
Lakeside Complex
Terminal B
N

across from the Times Beach Nature Preserve, in future the ferry will drop people off at a new ferry landing developed in the center of the First Buffalo Marina property closer to the Connecting Terminal elevator. The new ferry landing area will include an upland beach, decks, and a comfort station with food, beverages and restrooms. A multiuse trail will be developed to connect the new ferry landing to Wilkeson Pointe Park.

Fewer boats will be stored at the marina, and fewer boats will be left on sitting on the site year-round. A network of boardwalks and paved and unpaved trails will be developed throughout the First Buffalo Marina site. The ground level of the main portion of the Connecting Terminal Elevator will be improved and made accessible to the public. An exhibit will be developed within the Connecting Terminal annex to inform the public about Buffalo's grain elevator history.

In the Michigan Pier Subarea (29.3 acres): a major environmental restoration effort will be undertaken in Slip 3 in an effort to bring muskellunge, largemouth bass, northern pike and yellow pike back to the slip. "Before big lake freighters, industry and pollution took over, the area just south of Wilkeson Pointe Park was a thriving marshy shoreline. However, having been deepened long ago to 30-feet to accommodate large commercial freighters, by the end of the 20th century Slip 3 [see figure 13.5] had

Figure 13.5. Bird's-eye view of Slip 3. *Source*: Derek Gee/Buffalo News. Used with permission.

become a 'dead zone' that no longer supported the plant life fish needed to spawn" (Pignataro, 2018a, A1).

"Clean sediment dredged from the Buffalo River will be deposited over the course of eight years gradually raising the existing bottom of the slip by 15 feet. Aquatic vegetation will then be installed to create a 6.7-acre coastal habitat. A rubble-mound breakwater will be built at the mouth of the slip to calm the water for kayaks and other small craft. A footbridge will be installed to connect the end of the slip to Wilkeson Point to prevent motorized sailboats from entering the slip and disturbing the fish habitat, and also make it more convenient for people to walk between the two areas" (Sommer 2021a, B1). ECHDC agreed to pay nearly one-third of the $14.7 million cost of the project, which is being led by the Army Corps of Engineers.

The Meadows Subarea (60.7 acres): The paved pathway along the water's edge, part of the Greenway Nature Trail ("Greenbelt") that was constructed along the Lake Erie Shoreline in 2008, will remain. Invasive species and brush will be removed, new topsoil will be added, and land-scaping improvements will be carried out to create a subarea primarily comprised of meadows, grasslands, forested areas, and pollinator fields. The shoreline will be strengthened with large stones, which will provide places for people to sit, fish, and gaze out at the water.

Bell Slip Subarea (28.2 acres): The existing 28-space paved parking lot will be relocated and the site reorganized to create a greater sense of place. A large portion of the site will receive soil amendments and will be re-landscaped to produce areas of forest, meadows, grasslands, and polli-nator fields. A comfort station with restrooms will be added. Boardwalk trails will be constructed through the large stand of cottonwood trees that overlaps with the Meadows Subarea, and invasive species will be removed.

Lakeside Complex (41 acres): The existing bike park will be expanded, three new mountain bike trails will be added for riders of dif-ferent skill levels, and an Aerial Adventure Course will be developed. An 8,000-person amphitheater will be built along the side of Terminal B. The vacant 100,000 square-foot Terminal B will be taken down to its metal frame, and a 9,000-square-foot permanent stage will be constructed on the slab of Terminal B. The balance of the floor area of the slab will be developed to accommodate the infrastructure, utilities, public restrooms, and back-of-the-house operations needed to support outdoor concerts and events.

One Last Attempt to Prevent the
Concert Pavilion from Being Built

According to the Green Code, a special use permit was required to build an amphitheater on the Terminal B portion of the Outer Harbor which was zoned N-1S (Secondary Employment). Although zoning regulations adopted by local governments are typically not enforceable against state government agencies, ECHDC nevertheless decided to apply to the Buffalo Common Council for the required special use permit. The special permit–granting authority was the Buffalo Common Council.

In advance of the meeting at which the Common Council was scheduled to consider the application, Partnership for the Public Good's Sam Magavern wrote a letter on June 9, 2021, urging Council members *not* to grant the special use permit. He reminded them that the Local Waterfront Revitalization Program (LWRP) the city adopted in July 2019 required that "water-dependent and enhanced recreation should be given priority over non-water-related uses along the coast," and that an 8,000-person amphitheater did not require a waterfront location. He also noted that constructing the concert venue would require cutting down many of the few mature trees on the Outer Harbor that migrating birds used for feeding, breeding, and resting, and reminded Council members that the LWRP required that actions not be taken that could damage the flora and fauna migrating birds depend on for feeding, breeding, and resting (figure 13.6).

On June 22, 2021, the Buffalo Common Council voted 8-1 to grant the special use permit. Two days later, the League of Women Voters of Buffalo/Niagara, 21st Century Park in the Outer Harbor, and Western New York Environmental Alliance (WNYEA) filed a lawsuit in New York State Supreme Court seeking to void the City of Buffalo's issuance of the special use permit and enjoin ECHDC from going ahead with the project. Among other things, the petitioners argued that ECHDC had violated the State Environmental Quality Review Act (SEQRA) by improperly declaring the project would have no negative impact on the environment and by failing to acknowledge that the loud noise and bright lights generated by rock concerts held at the facility could negatively affect migrating birds.

One week before oral arguments were scheduled to be heard, ECHDC held a "ground-breaking" ceremony to mark the start of construction. Instead of putting shovels into the ground, the event was held inside Terminal B and consisted of state officials taking turns pounding

Figure 13.6. Bird's-eye view of area around Terminal B showing the trees that were cut down so that the concert pavilion could be built, with Terminal A (former Ford Assembly Plant) in the background. *Source*: Derek Gee/Buffalo News. Used with permission.

a sledgehammer into a drywall inside the building. Not far away, outside the fences that surrounded Terminal B that barred them from entering, a group of activists gathered in protest.

Local television stations sent reporters and film crews to cover the protest. Speaking into a microphone in front of the protesters, Sam Magavern restated the various reasons why they believed building a concert and event facility on the Outer Harbor was a bad idea. He also hammered home the point that it would be inequitable to construct a concert facility in a location that wasn't accessible by public transit, because city residents who didn't own a car would be unable to attend and enjoy the concerts. In doing so, Magavern was reiterating one of the guiding principles that Our Outer Harbor adopted at its 2016 public meeting at RiverWorks, which was that the Outer Harbor should be used for purposes that were "truly public and inclusive."

On December 10, 2021, Supreme Court Justice Donna M. Siwek rejected all five legal arguments put forward by the plaintiffs as reasons why construction of the concert pavilion should be halted. Not long thereafter excavators and bulldozers began clearing trees from the site.

WNYEA board member Lynda Schneekloth observed: "What took 50 years of nature to generate . . . which has been feeding animals and birds was taken down . . . All of us who have been working on this project for so long and had a vision of the Outer Harbor being a wonderful green space with an ecological foundation are just devastated." "The ECHDC Grinch stole Christmas," commented Margaret Wooster (Sommer 2021m).

Before the concert pavilion was completed, ECHDC held a series of concerts between July and September 2022 on the Lakeside Event Lawn not far from Terminal B. The cost of general admission tickets was $24. VIP tickets were priced at $48. A good way to appreciate the extent to which those Outer Harbor concerts fell short of being "truly public and inclusive" is to compare them to the concerts that are offered throughout the summer at River Fest Park, which are free and much more readily accessible to the residents of inner-city neighborhoods. Once the concert pavilion is completed and a sloped grassy lawn has been created to improve spectators' views of the stage, it seems likely that tickets to the Outer Harbor concerts will be even more expensive.

By the time you read this the concert pavilion and event facility on the Outer Harbor will have been built. You might even have attended and enjoyed some of the concerts there and may therefore think that citizen activists and NGOs shouldn't have made such a big deal about the harm that building the concert facility could do to migrating birds. If so, please keep in mind that it was largely due to the efforts of these activists and NGOs that a large-scale park and recreational area have been developed on the Outer Harbor that seems destined to bring immense pleasure to the people of Buffalo and Western New York in the years and decades to come.

In 2022 Our Outer Harbor began urging people to sign a petition asking that Buffalo's Outer Harbor be officially designated as parkland and that ownership and control of the Outer Harbor be transferred from ECHDC to an agency whose mission is to manage and administer state parks. In the words of the petition: "Our Lake Erie coast is and always was Buffalo's greatest asset. It should be officially designated as parkland to protect and support the public value as our drinking water supply, our access to Lake Erie, as a globally significant fish and wildlife habitat and as crucial to Buffalo's climate resilience and recovery from the impacts of its industrial past. Declare the Outer Harbor A PARK to protect the Lake Erie Coast as a public trust that belongs to all of us in perpetuity" (www.ourouterharbor.org). As of December 2022, 42,044 individuals had signed the online petition in support of formally designating the Outer Harbor as parkland.

Figure 13.7. Bicyclists participating in a Slow Roll Buffalo bike tour of the Outer Harbor in 2021. *Source*: Photo by Fr. William Jud Weiksnar. Used with permission.

Figure 13.7. Bicyclists participating in a Slow Roll Buffalo bike tour of the Outer Harbor in 2021. *Source*: Photo by Fr. William Jud Weiksnar. Used with permission.

Governor Hochul Opens the Door
to Private Development of Terminal A

The final plan for the Outer Harbor that ECHDC adopted in November 2020 was silent with regard to what would or should take place at Terminal A because it was outside the project area covered by the plan. On December 1, 2022, roughly one month after she was elected to a full four-year term in her own right, Governor Kathy Hochul invited experienced real estate developers interested in buying and redeveloping the 550,000-square-foot former Ford Motor Company assembly plant (Terminal A) to submit proposals describing how they would redevelop the structure. The deadline set for receiving the proposal was March 30, 2023.

The Green Code zoning that applied to Terminal A (N-1S, Secondary Employment) allowed a wide variety of uses to be developed on the property, and few if any restrictions were placed on the uses that developers could incorporate in a proposed project. The request for proposals specifically invited developers to consider the possibility of accommodating housing, offices, restaurants, and cultural attractions. As Mark Sommer noted at the time, "This [was] the first time a request calling for residences and cultural attractions has been made since a more ambitious plan was unveiled in

2013 by Erie Canal Harbor Development Corp, [which was] rescinded the following year after community opposition" (Sommer 2022k, A1, A8).

Developing housing within the sprawling factory building will be difficult because of the large proportion of its floor area deep within the interior of the structure that is far removed from natural light—although designers might conceivably come up with creative ways of incorporating housing into some portion of the existing structure. It is also conceivable that some housing could be developed on vacant land elsewhere on the site, if the state were to allow it.

Many of the same arguments that activists put forward against allowing the Outer Harbor to be privately developed would seem to also apply to Terminal A. The immense scale of the project raises a particular red flag. The development of Terminal A could be "one of the largest redevelopment projects in Buffalo's history . . . with a floor space nearly 10 times the space inside the main exhibit hall at the Buffalo Niagara Convention Center . . . [and] comparable in size to the 523,000-square-foot Central Terminal, which is also seeking developers" (Sommer 2022i).

As it turned out, no private development proposals for Terminal A were received by the March 30, 2023, deadline. However, that seems unlikely to be the end of the story. I hope that what I've written so far has made you want to follow and scrutinize what the state government enables to take place at Terminal A in the future.

Part V

Conclusion

Chapter Fourteen

Summing Up and Lessons Learned

Hundreds of local citizens and scores of NGOs played key roles in helping bring about the many publicly beneficial waterfront outcomes described in this book. Thousands more were indirectly involved by virtue of their memberships in the NGOs that advocated for and helped bring about specific outcomes. The names of these waterfront heroes (individuals and NGOs) are listed in Appendix II. That so many local citizens and NGOs played important roles in advancing the renaissance should make people in Buffalo doubly proud of what has been accomplished.

Big Projects Failed to Revive
Lower Main Street and the Inner Harbor

As explained in chapter 4, the decline of lower Main Street was hastened by a number of factors: construction of the NYS Barge Canal which relocated the canal's western terminus to Tonawanda; the decay of the Canal District; the New York State Thruway Authority's taking and closure of the Lehigh Valley Railroad's passenger terminal through eminent domain to build the Niagara Section of the Thruway; the construction of the Buffalo Skyway; and the Delaware Lackawanna & Western Railroad's abandonment of its passenger terminal at the foot of lower Main Street.

In an effort to inject some activity into the area, the State of New York constructed the 140,000-square-foot Donovan State Office Building on the former site of the Lehigh Valley Railroad passenger terminal, which opened in 1962. A few years later the City of Buffalo established a ten-acre urban redevelopment district just north of where I-190 (the NYS Thruway) crossed Main Street and spent a huge amount of federal and state funding constructing Marine Midland Center. Unfortunately, the 1.2 million-square-foot office complex, which was completed in 1972, did little to revitalize what Erie County's executive had called a "rundown, disheveled, unkempt and neglected area." The Marine Midland Center project not only failed to benefit the surrounding area as much as had been expected, it undermined the importance of lower Main Street by physically and psychologically severing it from the rest of the downtown.

Years later city and state officials still seemed to believe that big projects were the best way to revitalize lower Main Street and the Inner Harbor. In July 2000, Governor George Pataki flew to Buffalo to join local and state officials in announcing that Adelphia Communications was going to build a 20–25-story office building on lower Main Street. A number of local and state government officials soon voiced support for seeking federal funding for the project. A few years later the office building project was unceremoniously scrapped when Adelphia's president and CEO was charged with corruption and securities violations and the company filed for bankruptcy. Not long thereafter in 2004, many of the same local and state government officials who had supported the Adelphia Communications project cheered Governor Pataki's announcement that a large-scale Bass Pro Outdoor World retail outlet would anchor the Inner Harbor redevelopment project—and that the company would be offered millions of dollars in subsidies to build it. Six years later in July 2010, Bass Pro officially announced that it was dropping out from the Inner Harbor project.

The State Agency Was Officially Empowered, but Citizens Were Not Powerless

Placing a state agency in charge of deciding how Buffalo's waterfront would be developed was intended to assure that waterfront redevelopment would proceed more expeditiously. However, it had the opposite effect of making waterfront planning more contentious. Because the state agency wasn't directly accountable to the local electorate, it apparently felt free to develop its plans for the Inner Harbor without considering the views of local residents and preservationists. Had they done so, they would have realized that the way they planned to develop the Inner Harbor would generate controversy. It took a lawsuit filed by the Preservation Coalition of Erie County to stop the state agency in its tracks and create the conditions that enabled preservationists and Erie Canal Harbor Development Corporation (ECHDC) to ultimately work through their contested visions of the Inner Harbor's future and achieve an outcome that most people in Buffalo and Western New York regard to be stunning success.

When ECHDC prepared its first plan for the Outer Harbor it appointed citizens and NGO representatives to an advisory committee to provide public input to the consultants who had been hired to prepare the plan. ECHDC then completely ignored and undermined what citizens and NGO representatives on the advisory committee had told the consultants by adopting a plan that called for the Outer Harbor to be extensively privately developed. ECHDC was eventually forced to walk away from that publicly unpopular plan and undertake another Outer Harbor planning process with a new team of consultants. Changes in the leadership of the agency that had taken place in the meantime had the effect of making it more receptive to inviting public input during its planning processes. As a result, ECHDC's second Outer Harbor planning process involved a considerable amount of public participation and produced a plan that was much more in tune with public sentiment.

Traditional approaches to planning and governance assume that government entities are endowed with clearly delineated powers and authorities and that they can carry out and fulfill their assigned responsibilities with little or no outside interference. As a result, government agencies such as Empire State Development Corporation (ESDC) and ECHDC, as well as public authorities such as Niagara Frontier Transportation Authority (NFTA) and the NYS Thruway Authority, don't know how to share power and collaborate with other entities. Because their authority to act in specific contexts is largely unquestioned, such entities have the power to defeat citizens' aspirations—but they do so at their peril. Citizens and NGOs have agency and *can* defeat formal power and authority when they learn how to use it. Activists and NGOs succeeded in turning public opinion against how the state agency planned to redevelop the Inner and Outer Harbors, thereby making those plans politically harder for elected officials to support, and by offering a compelling vision of the waterfront's future as an alternative to what the agency had proposed.

Among the keys to increasing activists' impact and likelihood of success in overturning the state agency's plans for the Inner and Outer Harbor were cultivating the support of those concerned about economic and social justice by establishing NGOs such as Center for Economic Justice and Partnership for the Public Good and building coalitions such as the Canal Side Community Alliance and Our Outer Harbor Coalition. One other factor that contributed to activists' success in overturning state agency plans for the Inner and Outer Harbors is important to mention: they stayed the course for as long as it took to achieve publicly beneficial outcomes in both portions of the waterfront.

Not All Preservationists in Agreement

In the lawsuit that was heard in Federal District Court the Preservation Coalition of Erie County argued that the historic importance of the Erie Canal to Buffalo and the nation made it imperative that the buried remains of the Commercial Slip be uncovered. I remain convinced that uncovering, reconstructing, and rewatering the Commercial Slip provided the key to the overall success of the Canalside project. However, in doing the research for this book I was surprised to discover that not that all preservationists agreed that uncovering and reconstructing the Commercial Slip was the most appropriate and *respectful* way of treating such a nationally significant historic artifact.

On August 6, 1999, three months after a roughly 80-foot section of the wall of the Commercial Slip had been discovered, New York's State Historic Preservation Office (SHPO) stated that it did not consider it feasible to uncover the Commercial Slip in "an exposed condition" and that it did not need to be uncovered. In rendering that judgment, the SHPO appeared to agree with ESDC that, although the stones of the Commercial Slip might be archaeologically important, they were likely "of minimal value for preservation in place." As an alternative to uncovering the walls of the Commercial Slip, the SHPO recommended that ESDC "conduct a detailed documentation of the wall that had been uncovered, rebury it, and provide for appropriate historical interpretation of the Wall through marking and signage in the project design."

Mike Vogel, who headed the *Buffalo News'* editorial board while the controversy was raging over how ESDC planned to develop the Inner Harbor, strongly agreed with ESDC's decision to leave the historic Commercial Slip buried. Having coauthored *America's Crossroads* (1993), a detailed history of Buffalo's Canal Street and District, and led the effort that saved and preserved Buffalo's historic lighthouse, Vogel clearly considered himself to be a preservationist. He might therefore have been expected to support the Preservation Coalition's efforts to uncover and publicly reveal the Commercial Slip. But that was not the case. "I was on the losing side of the argument. I thought it better to leave the artifact *in place* and not alter and mess with it. To re-create the Commercial Slip *in place* [italics added] they basically had to destroy and move the stones around to produce a rebuilt gingerbread version of the canal" (Vogel, interview, February 20, 2019).

Vogel's way of characterizing today's reconstructed and rewatered Commercial Slip has some merit. As should be evident from the photographs in chapter 7 (figures 7.1 and 7.2), a good deal of digging and moving around of the buried stones found on the site needed to be done to achieve the version of the Commercial Slip that is now on public display. The way I set Vogel's concerns to rest is by recalling what Robert Z. Melnick said when he testified in support of the Preservation Coalition's lawsuit against ESDC. As Melnick stated in court, if the Commercial Slip were not uncovered and reconstructed to a likeness of what it was in the past, the American public would be denied the opportunity to fully understand the historic importance of the site. "I always go back to what's the purpose of historic preservation, and that is to provide [members of the] public a greater sense of how this country developed over a number of years," said Melnick.

Buffalo's Local Newspaper Helps Hold the State Agency Accountable

Buffalo was extremely fortunate to have a local newspaper that kept residents well informed about how the state waterfront agency wanted to develop the Inner Harbor and why preservationists found the agency's plans so objectionable. Because the *Buffalo News* was the single most important source of local news in Buffalo and Western New York, what was reported in the newspaper had considerable impact on how positively or negatively people viewed the state agency's approach to developing the waterfront. The newspaper's blanket coverage of the ensuing Bass Pro controversy proved equally consequential in eventually causing Bass Pro to officially withdraw from the Inner Harbor redevelopment project.

Years later, despite its reduced readership, the *Buffalo News* also helped hold the state agency accountable by echoing environmentalists' concerns over a plan that ECHDC had commissioned that called for the Outer Harbor to be extensively privately developed. The more the newspaper reported on the issue the clearer it became that there was strong public support for leaving the Outer Harbor undeveloped—which eventually led ECHDC to do a major about-face and commit to developing most of the Outer Harbor for use as a park and recreational area. A total of over 175 articles, editorials, commentaries, and contributed opinion pieces that appeared in the *Buffalo News* are referenced in this book.

If and when another controversy should arise with regard to how Buffalo's waterfront should be redeveloped it seems unlikely that the newspaper's coverage of the controversy will have nearly as great an impact on the outcome. During the 1990s more than 300,000 copies of the newspaper were sold each weekday and more than 400,000 on Sundays. By 2016, the weekday circulation of the newspaper had declined to 139,000, and the Sunday circulation to 204,500. In January 2020, the newspaper was sold to Lee Enterprises, an Iowa-based company that owned a chain of 50 newspapers, most of which were in the Midwest. By 2021, the weekday circulation had fallen to 69,000; by 2023 it was 56,000. The newspaper does not disclose the number of subscribers to its online e-edition.

Margaret Sullivan grew up in Lackawanna and began working at the *Buffalo News* in 1980 as a summer intern. Nineteen years later she became the top editor at the *Buffalo News* and for the next 12 years made sure that the newspaper devoted sufficient resources and staff time to informing the public about the Inner Harbor redevelopment controversy. In September 2012, she became the fifth public editor of the *New York Times*, a position she held until April 2016.

In *Newsroom Confidential*, Sullivan observed that "study after study has shown that local news is relatively well trusted among a populace that increasingly disdains the national mainstream media" (Sullivan 2022, 232). Nevertheless, hundreds of local newspapers have gone out of business and hundreds more are now mere shells of their former selves. The diminished importance and outright disappearance of so many independent sources of local news should be matter of grave concern in a democratic society. "When local news fades, bad things happen in communities: polarization increases, civic engagement goes down, municipal costs go up. People retreat even further into political tribalism, not even able to talk to their neighbors about important concerns" (Sullivan 2022, 233).

When Sullivan began her tenure as editor of the *Buffalo News*, 200 people were employed in the paper's newsroom. By 2011 that number was down to 145. By February 2023 the full-time staff of the newsroom was down to 66 (Heaney 2023).

Two local online news outlets have helped somewhat to compensate for the *Buffalo News'* declining readership. One of those sources of local news is *Buffalo Rising*, an online publication founded in 2003 by Newell Nusbaumer. Eighteen stories that appeared on *Buffalo Rising* are referenced in this book. The other online outlet for local news, more in line with the kind of investigative reporting traditionally conducted by newspapers, is *Investigative Post*, a nonprofit news organization that was founded in 2012 by Jim Heaney, who had worked as a reporter for the *Buffalo News* for 25 years. Heaney has reportedly kept a quote of journalist Carl Bernstein taped to this side of his computer terminal that reads: "Journalism is not stenography, it is the best obtainable version of the truth." Among the journalists who joined *Investigative Post* early on was Geoff Kelly, who previously cofounded and edited *The Public*. By July 2023, the staff of *Investigative Post*'s newsroom was composed of five full-time reporters and two editors.

How Waterfront Planning *Should* Be Conducted

When ESDC developed its 1998 Inner Harbor Plan it did not involve members of the general public in its planning process, except for considering the already well-understood interests of the business community. As a result, the only course of action that ESDC seriously considered was leaving the historic western terminus of the Erie Canal permanently buried. A few years later, the state agency again showed how out of touch it was with local sentiment by unveiling a new Inner Harbor plan that called for constructing a large-scale Bass Pro Outdoor World retail outlet on the footprint of the historic Central Wharf—which caused a whole new public uproar. It was hard to avoid concluding that there was something basically wrong with the way the state agency went about developing its waterfront plans.

During the COVID-19 pandemic, I reached out to Robert Shibley, dean of the University at Buffalo's School of Architecture and Planning, and had a couple of extended conversations with him on Zoom during which he shared with me his thoughts about how planning processes *should* be conducted. The most important thing Shibley told me was that "a well-conducted planning process should expand the range of ideas and options being considered, increase peoples' imaginations regarding what might be possible, and make it possible to compare and evaluate possible outcomes from different points of view" (Shibley, February 22, 2021).

Other features of a well-conducted planning process identified by Shibley were:

- Have people with different interests and backgrounds participate in the process.

- Encourage the expression of divergent views and don't attempt to dictate the outcome.

- Don't allow any one segment of the community to dominate the process.

- Incorporate and be attuned to local values and allegiances.

- Make good use of expert knowledge and professional expertise.

- The consultants conducting the planning process need to be prepared to "speak truth to power" and tell those who are paying them things they don't want to hear.

In June 2018, Thomas Dee, who had served as ECHDC's president since 2009, retired and was replaced by Steven Ranalli, a professional engineer with a background in urban planning, who seemed to recognize that involving citizens in its planning processes might actually help the agency develop *better* plans. Under Ranalli's leadership ECHDC showed itself to be much more receptive than it had been in the past to having members of the public review the agency's plans, including at a very early stage—and much more willing to take seriously their comments and suggestions. In the words of Mike Vogel, who was appointed to ECHDC's board of directors in 2019, "There's been a sea-change at ECHDC, which is now much more open and receptive to incorporating ideas other than their own" (Vogel, interview, February 20, 2019).

On November 19, 2019, ECHDC held an open house at the Lexus Club at KeyBank Center at which attendees were shown three possible ways different portions of the Outer Harbor might be designed and developed. Attendees were asked to compare and rank the alternative design schemes in order of preference by placing colored-coded stickers alongside each scheme. They also wrote comments on Post-it notes and placed them on poster boards that displayed the alternative schemes. The feedback citizens provided appears to have been taken seriously, because the final plan that ECHDC approved called for developing the Outer Harbor into a large-scale park.

Before Ranalli became the agency's president, ECHDC had hired PPHP, an architectural firm based in the Netherlands, and T.Y. Lin International, an engineering firm headquartered in San Francisco, to develop preliminary schematic designs showing different ways that mixed-use development could be configured on the northern portion of the property formerly occupied by Memorial Auditorium (the "North Aud Block")—which was going to be more challenging and expensive to develop than the "South Aud Block" because of the significant change in elevation within the area. In August 2019, at an open house attended by about 60 people, PPHP unveiled three different ways the nearly two-acre North Aud Block might be developed—alternatives that differed significantly with regard to overall density, building heights, and amounts of underground parking. Attendees were asked to evaluate and compare the three options, indicate which one they preferred, and explain why. The transparent and participatory way in which ECHDC planned for the development of the North Aud Block was in sharp contrast to the way the state agency had developed its first plans for the Inner Harbor.

Based on the feedback the agency received at the open house, ECHDC issued a request for proposals in May 2022 inviting developers to describe how they would develop the North Aud Block if they were selected. ECHDC's preferred way of developing the site, according to the RFP, was for 425,000 gross square feet of floor space to be developed in several buildings, for historic portions of Lloyd and Commercial Streets to be reestablished, and to accommodate a mix of housing, retail, restaurants, and offices, including possibly a hotel. Governor Hochul announced that $10 million in previously committed state funding would be made available to the selected developer for the required infrastructure, such as for the construction of up to 450 below-grade parking spaces.

In April 2023, ECHDC accepted the proposal submitted by Pennrose, a Brooklyn-based company, that called for developing 367 residences complemented by ground-floor commercial storefronts, a pedestrian-friendly central public piazza, and 360 underground parking spaces. As outlined in the proposal, 4–5-story buildings will be developed overlooking the replica canal, while two other 10–14-story structures will be built further back closer to the Niagara Thruway. The way ECHDC chose to develop the North Aud Block is strikingly similar to one of the five scenarios that Friends of the Buffalo Story (Mark Goldman, Peter B. Dowd, and Scott A. Wood) presented to ECHCD's board of directors in June 2013. According to ECHDC, construction is expected to get underway sometime in 2025.

Give the State Agency Some Credit

Given how long and hard preservationists and environmentalists had to struggle to get the state agency to abandon its initial plans for the Inner and Outer Harbors, it is all too easy to portray it as the primary obstacle that stood in the way of achieving Buffalo's waterfront renaissance. However, with the benefit of hindsight it is also clear that the state waterfront agency deserves considerable credit for much of what has been accomplished.

Placing a state agency in charge of waterfront planning admittedly made it more difficult for city residents to hold waterfront planners politically accountable than if that responsibility had remained in the hands of a local government agency. However, it also meant that the state government became heavily invested in having Buffalo's waterfront successfully redeveloped.

Citizen activists and nongovernmental organizations provided the inspiration and imagination necessary to set Buffalo's waterfront renaissance into motion, but much of the money that was needed to accomplish it was provided by state agencies or by the federal government. Without that government funding, few of the major projects and improvements that significantly advanced the renaissance would have been possible. ECHDC was able to spend millions of dollars on waterfront improvements as a result of the agreement Congressman Brian Higgins negotiated with the New York Power Authority (NYPA) in connection with the relicensing of the Niagara Power project. The "Buffalo Billion" economic development program that Governor Andrew Cuomo unveiled in 2012 also provided additional millions of dollars that were able to be spent on waterfront projects and environmental improvements in the Inner and Outer Harbors and along the Buffalo River.

As described in chapter 11, the waterfront renaissance unfolded very differently along the Buffalo River than it did in the Inner and Outer Harbors because ECHDC stayed largely the background and allowed an array of other actors to take the lead in deciding how the corridor would be redeveloped. The most important action ECHDC took in that regard was to champion the redesign and reconstruction of Ohio Street and assure that new storm and sanitary sewers, water lines, and underground utilities (electric and cable lines) were installed to support the development that the agency hoped would take place after the highway project was completed.

Underappreciated Ways to Achieve Economic Development

The official mission of Empire State Development Corporation and ECHDC (a subsidiary of ESDC) is to promote economic development. Some of the standard ways ESDC, ECHDC, and local governments have gone about promoting economic development are described in this book—approaches which I generally characterize as "the corporate approach" to economic development. A good example of that approach would have been to publicly subsidize Adelphia Communications' proposed office tower project on lower Main Street because it promised to bring hundreds of new jobs. After that project failed to materialize, millions of dollars in subsidies were offered to Bass Pro to encourage it to develop one of its Outdoor World retail outlets at the Inner Harbor. ECHDC spent nearly six years defending that controversial project, during which ECHDC's then president Thomas Dee boldly stated, "If you're for Buffalo, you're for the Bass Pro project."

A particularly revealing aspect of ECHDC's corporate approach to economic development was the agency's preference for attracting national chain stores to the Inner Harbor. "Jordan Levy, the former ECHDC board chair, was committed to having national chains down there, and said so a number of times" (Kelly, interview, February 7, 2018). "Levy didn't have the slightest knowledge of urban planning and design. When he traveled abroad, he went to intimate, historic places—but in Buffalo he proposed bringing a 'Five Guys' franchise to Canalside" (Goldman, interview, February 15, 2019).

IMPROVING ENVIRONMENTAL QUALITY

Buffalo's waterfront renaissance proves there are other ways of advancing economic development in a postindustrial city than the previously described "corporate approach." Buffalo's waterfront renaissance and economic revival actually began along the Buffalo River in 1989, when a handful of citizens who had served on NYDEC's Remedial Advisory Committee formed

Friends of the Buffalo River, the nonprofit organization that evolved into Buffalo Niagara Waterkeeper.

Improving the environmental quality of the Buffalo River, restoring natural habitat along the shorelines of the river, and increasing public access to the river weren't initially conceived of as being primarily aimed at promoting economic development. However, it turned out that the improved environmental quality of the Buffalo River, in combination with the redesign of Ohio Street, caused people to view the Ohio Street corridor in an entirely new light. It didn't take long for the corridor to evolve into a prime destination for recreation as well as an appealing place to live.

"One of the most important aims of Buffalo Niagara Waterkeeper has been getting elected leaders to rethink what makes a good community and place greater value on strengthening environmental quality and quality of life, as opposed to always placing the greatest importance on the immediate economic returns of development" (Jedlicka, interview, February 13, 2019). If they did, they'd probably discover, much to their surprise, that improving environmental quality and the livability of the city is a proven way of achieving economic development. Just think how different the corridor of the Ohio Street/Buffalo River would be today if the Buffalo River hadn't been cleaned up and become an environmental attraction.

A number of projects that were developed along Ohio Street after the cleanup of the Buffalo River was completed are described in chapter 11—projects that collectively represented a huge amount of private investment. If economic development is measured by the amount of money that is invested in an area, the cleanup of the Buffalo River, the redesign and reconstruction of Ohio Street, and the development of River Fest Park would have to be judged as having been enormously successful in achieving economic development.

Not that long ago, young people who received their advanced education and professional training at the State University of New York at Buffalo, as well as those who grew up in Buffalo but graduated from other colleges and universities in the state, all too often believed they needed to move to other parts of the country to pursue their careers.[1] But as Buffalo has become a much more appealing place to live and work, and due in no small part to the transformation of the city's waterfront, local university graduates have become much more likely to choose to remain in or to relocate to Buffalo. On the day ECHDC approved its final plan for the Outer Harbor, ECHDC's President Steven Ranalli rightfully noted that "the public amenities and quality-of-life improvements provided in the Outer Harbor will attract and retain workforce and talent for the region's emerging economic sectors."

HISTORIC PRESERVATION

When Mike Vogel established the Buffalo Lighthouse Association as a nonprofit organization in 1985 to try to raise money to preserve and repair the deteriorated octagonal lighthouse at the entrance to Buffalo Harbor, the Bethlehem Steel and Republic Steel plants had recently closed and little headway was being made toward redeveloping the Inner Harbor. "Local political and business leaders in Buffalo back then had a deep disdain for anything associated with Buffalo's past, particularly as it pertained to the waterfront" (B. Fisher, interview, February 9, 2018). Nevertheless, within two years the Buffalo Lighthouse Association had received enough donations to complete the lighthouse's initial restoration, and the lighthouse was relit. Though small in scale, that successful undertaking provided an early indication that preserving historic resources and artifacts associated with Buffalo's past might be a good way to inspire and propel more momentous waterfront projects that could reenergize and revive the city.

Uncovering and rewatering the Commercial Slip provided the key to creating the authentic sense of place that drew statewide and national attention to the Canalside project and provided the impetus for the beneficial development of the area that followed. It is hard to imagine Canalside being anywhere near as successful in revitalizing the area of lower Main Street if the historic Commercial Slip had not been uncovered and made the centerpiece of the project.

The National Trust for Historic Preservation's national conference that was held in Buffalo in 2011, not long after the Commercial Slip was rewatered, marked a major turning point in how local citizens and members of the business community viewed historic preservation. Ever since then, every brochure produced by the Buffalo Convention and Visitor's Bureau has promoted the city's historic architecture and sites as reasons to visit and spend time in Buffalo—an appreciation of the economic value of Buffalo's architectural legacy that has extended to the city's iconic grain elevators.

State government officials now appreciate the economic benefits that can be achieved by underscoring Buffalo's historic significance as the western terminus of the Erie Canal, as evidenced by ECHDC's decision to finance the construction of the Longshed so that the Buffalo Maritime

Center could build a replica of the *Seneca Chief* packet boat next to the Commercial Slip. When completed, the replica *Seneca Chief* packet boat will travel across New York State on the Erie Barge Canal, playing a central role in the statewide commemoration of the October 2025 200th anniversary of the Erie Canal.

The Job Is Never Done— Even More So Because of Climate Change

On October 31, 2019, Times Beach Nature Preserve and the Outer Harbor were hit by a powerful seiche (a tsunami-like event) driven by hurricane-force winds of 90 mph that produced historically high-water levels along Lake Erie's eastern shore. The Halloween 2019 seiche didn't just destroy all the elevated boardwalks within the preserve but also breached the diked disposal area within which the US Army Corps of Engineers (USACE) had deposited dredged contaminated sediment in the 1960s and 1970s—which had serendipitously provided a unique resting and feeding place for migrating birds.

A number of seiches have occurred since then, each of which took more chunks out of the dike. "We now have a new situation where water from the pond and perhaps contaminated sediment can get outside the dike during high water events. Buffalo's drinking water intake is not far from the site. The USACE says that they believe that contamination escaping from the site is minimal, but we need to quantify that" (Burney, email, July 20, 2023).

Yet another powerful storm, this time a devastating blizzard that lasted for more than two days hit Buffalo on December 23, 2022. The huge amount of snow and the white-out conditions that were produced and sustained over a long period of time by 70-plus mph winds paralyzed the city and caused the deaths of more than 40 people. A state of emergency was declared by Governor Hochul, and the National Guard was called out to help clear city streets clogged with snow and abandoned vehicles. With a "no-drive" order in effect, it took a number of days to assess the damage that the storm inflicted on the Times Beach Preserve and other parts of the Outer Harbor.

I was back in Buffalo in July 2023 and drove across the Skyway and then north to the Times Beach Preserve at the end of Fuhrmann Boulevard where I saw that most of the large trees in the preserve had been brought down by the strong winds and the weight of the snow. However, a large proportion of the native plantings in the preserve survived. "We have milkweed and other native plant species that withstood the fury of the storm" (Burney, email, July 20, 2023).

The damage caused by the Christmas 2022 blizzard, on top of the damage caused by the Halloween 2019 seiche, forced Burney and Friends of Times Beach to rethink what the preserve should be like in the future. "It doesn't seem to make sense to repair the boardwalks when it seems likely they'll be destroyed again and again by future storms. We need to find other ways of providing people with access to the site" (Burney, email, July 20, 2023).

The somewhat more pressing and potentially more serious environmental issue of what to do about the damaged dike also remains unresolved. After the dike at Times Beach was initially damaged by the Halloween 2019 seiche, the USACE agreed to repair the dike and allocated $10 million to cover the cost of the project. However, in the aftermath of more recent storms that further damaged the dike the USACE has reconsidered that commitment. In June 2022, the USACE notified Erie County and Friends of the Times Beach Preserve that they had decided *not* to repair the dike and that the money it had previously committed had been "repurposed." "We are trying to figure out what this means in terms of the stability of the site" (Burney, email, July 20, 2023).

∽

On December 11, 2021, powerful winds tore a hole in the brick wall at the north end of the Great Northern grain elevator. Six days later, James Comerford, the city's commissioner of permit and inspection services ordered the emergency demolition of the structure.

"It's a building that is at the same scale as a great medieval cathedral, with a similar kind of monumental power," said Gregory Delaney, assistant professor at the University of Buffalo School of Architecture and Planning (McKinley 2022). Jessie Fisher, executive director of Preservation Buffalo Niagara, expressed the same sentiment more elegantly and succinctly when she said, "The Great Northern elevator is Buffalo's Notre Dame."

Prominent local developers—entrepreneurs with a definite interest in maintaining and strengthening the economic health of the city—joined preservationists in underscoring the importance of preserving the historic structure. Douglas Jemal, whose company redeveloped One Seneca and a number of other downtown buildings, offered to pay Archer Daniels Midland (ADM), the owner of the building, $100,000 toward the cost of repairing the damaged wall and also offered to buy the structure. Rocco Termini and Paul Cimenelli also decried the possibility that such an important part of Buffalo's history would be willfully destroyed.

ADM, a multinational food processing corporation based in Chicago, acquired the Great Northern Elevator in 1993, three years after the Buffalo Common Council had designated it as a local historic landmark. The structure was listed on the National Register of Historic Places in 2003. In 1996 and again in 2003, ADM sought permission from the City of Buffalo to demolish the structure. The hole in the brick wall that surrounded the steel bins of the elevator presented the company with a pretext for doing what it had wanted to do all along—this time in the name of protecting public safety.

On January 5, 2022, State Supreme Court Justice Emilio Colaiacovo denied Campaign for Greater Buffalo History, Architecture, and Culture's (C4GB) request that a temporary restraining order be issued to prevent the condemnation order from being acted upon, a ruling which C4GB immediately appealed. On January 9, a number of people gathered across the street from the Great Northern elevator to protest ADM's planned demolition of the structure (see figure 14.1). One of the protesters was a

Figure 14.1. A small group of activists gathered in January 2022 to protest ADM's planned demolition of the Great Northern Elevator. *Source*: Photo by Alan K. Oberst. Used with permission.

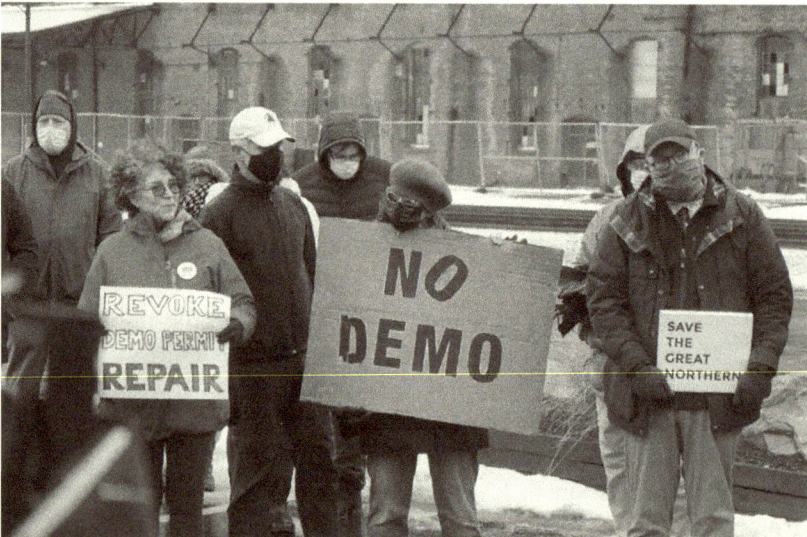

woman from Buffalo's First Ward whose grandfather had worked in the city's grain elevators (Delaney, interview, November 2, 2022).

On February 16, 2022, a panel of judges in the Appellate Division based in Rochester issued a preliminary injunction which prevented the condemnation from taking effect. In April, an appeals court agreed that Justice Colaiacovo had erred in not permitting and considering expert testimony. James Comerford, the city official who ordered the emergency demolition of the grain elevator, had previously asserted that he saw no need to seek outside opinions and saw no conflict in relying solely on ADM's engineering examination of the structure.

Five months after the hole in the outer wall of the elevator first appeared (figure 14.2), an editorial in the *Buffalo News* observed that "the longer this goes on, the more obvious it becomes that opponents of demolition are on the right side . . . There is no emergency. There is only the fixable damage that came from a 2021 storm and years of deferred maintenance" (*Buffalo News* editorial 2022a, A8).

Figure 14.2. The Great Northern Elevator in July 2022, six months after strong winds broke a hole in the wall at the northern end of the elevator. *Source*: Photo by the author.

At a hearing held at the request of the Campaign for Greater Buffalo, a number of structural engineers, contractors, architects, and developers testified that the elevator was structurally sound and that the hole in the wall could be easily repaired. But that didn't change State Supreme Court Justice Colaiacovo's opinion that ADM should be allowed to do what it wished with the Great Northern elevator. In Colaiacovo's view, the expert opinions that were offered were "outside the scope of the court's evaluation." Lawyers for ADM also made it clear that the company had no interest in the property being saved, even if it could be repaired, because of its proximity to the company's operating flour mill.

On July 5, 2022, Colaiacovo for the second time refused to issue a temporary restraining order to prevent ADM from demolishing the structure. Even more egregious, he waited ten weeks to dismiss the case, thereby preventing C4GB's lawyers from filing a timely appeal of his ruling (Sommer 2022g).

On September 16, 2022, a 165-foot-tall ultra-high demolition excavator began ripping apart and dismantling more of the north wall of the elevator (see figure 14.3). ADM issued the following statement: "The Great Northern Elevator constitutes a safety hazard and is beyond repair, a reality that has been clear to us, the City of Buffalo, and a court in its rulings upholding the city's demolition permit" (Becker 2022). A few hours after the demolition began, State Supreme Court Justice John M. Curran of the Appellate Division in Rochester quashed any remaining hope that the demolition could be halted by denying C4GB's request that a temporary restraining order be issued.

The city government's complicity in enabling ADM to demolish the Great Northern elevator was particularly galling to developer Douglas Jemal, who pointed out that the city's Department of Inspection Services never inspected the grain elevator or cited ADM for any building code violations during the three decades it owned the structure. "They're getting rewarded for being terrible citizens and terrible property owners and getting exactly what they wanted for thirty years," said Jemal (Sommer 2022a).

Throughout it all, Mayor Byron Brown remained conspicuously silent and on the sidelines. "Buffalo's mayor, Byron Brown, should [have been] one of the Great Northern's most vocal supporters. Instead, he's silent. Mayor Brown could have rescinded the demolition permit, its 'emergency' designation having been effectively refuted by both testimony and the fact of the structure's resilience. He did not" (*Buffalo News* editorial 2022b).

Figure 14.3. By October 3, 2022, the steel bins that once stored huge quantities of grain were visibly exposed as ever larger chunks of the walls that encased the Great Northern Elevator were torn down. *Source*: Photo by Douglas W. DeCroix. Used with permission.

In yet another editorial two weeks later, as the demolition of the elevator was underway, the *Buffalo News* said this: "The zeal that Buffalonians have for their historic buildings is a force unto itself and should be harnessed, not ignored. If ADM and the City of Buffalo had found a way to work together in favor of the Great Northern rather than against it, this could have been one of the city's biggest development wins. It would have restored the faith of many who have stopped looking for positive guidance from Buffalo's political leadership" (*Buffalo News* editorial 2022b).

Newell Nussbaumer, the founder and editor of *Buffalo Rising*, composed the following epitaph.

For the City to claim that it is progressive on the preservation front this is a slap in the face. It's absolutely heartbreaking to watch our great industrial heritage disappear in front of our eyes. And shame on ADM for being a terrible steward of Buffalo's architectural legacy. Future generations will look back and say, "What were they thinking?"

We are well aware that great historic architecture is a prime tourist attraction in Buffalo. Our architecture—and our position on Lake Erie—make us unique. How hard is it to protect them from further abuse, at the hands of a few? Apparently, extremely hard. This day will be remembered as another hit for a city that has been making great strides, despite the collective myopic vision of our leaders.

I always wondered how previous generations would allow so many architectural gems to be demolished. Now I understand. *(Buffalo Rising* 2022)

Despite the discouraging outcome, preservationists and NGOs can take solace in knowing that a remarkably broad public consensus has developed in Buffalo concerning the importance of preserving the city's historically and architecturally significant sites and buildings. That public consensus may well turn out to be one of the most consequential and enduring outcomes produced by Buffalo's waterfront renaissance.

Postscript: The Waterfront Renaissance Continues

When I began this book in 2019, LaSalle Park along the Niagara River just north of the Inner Harbor wasn't part of the area I expected to write about. However, as I finish the book in 2023, what is happening at LaSalle Park is likely to provide the "icing on the cake" for Buffalo's waterfront renaissance.

In the summer of 2018, the University at Buffalo's Regional Institute, in partnership with other local organizations, undertook a community-driven planning process called "Imagine LaSalle" to enable Buffalo's West Side community to forge a vision of what it wanted LaSalle Park to become in the future. The City of Buffalo's Division of Parks and Recreation, Department of Community Services and Recreational Programming, and Mayor's Office of Strategic planning assisted with the process. Nearly 1,200 local residents filled out surveys which were offered in seven languages, and the Belle Center (a multipurpose community center on Buffalo's West Side) enlisted kids from the community to take pictures and write down their thoughts about the current condition of the park and what they hoped the park would be like in the future.

On October 17, 2018, on what would have been the 100th birthday of Ralph C. Wilson Jr., the founder and long-time owner of the Buffalo Bills, the Ralph C. Wilson Jr. Foundation announced it was awarding $40 million to transform LaSalle Park into a signature park and would be putting $10 million into an endowment for the park's ongoing maintenance (Sommer 2018i).

Van Valkenburgh Associates was hired to redesign the park with a high degree of public involvement. Over two-plus years, the consultants and a team from the UB Regional Institute hosted a series of community workshops. A 22-member focus group was assembled composed of individuals who reflected the diverse backgrounds and cultures of those who regularly used LaSalle Park. The members of the focus group traveled together to Chicago, Cincinnati, and New York City to visit parks in those cities that might serve as inspirational examples and offer lessons that could be applied in redesigning LaSalle Park. An engaging video of members of the focus group describing what they learned was posted online.

Community workshops held in January, February, and March 2019 enabled area residents to review possible ways the new park could be designed. A concept plan that was publicly unveiled in May 2019 incorporated all the feedback that the designers had received from the community up to that point and provided members of the community yet another opportunity to comment on and critique the plan. "Our biggest moves [will be] to add topography to . . . make LaSalle a place that is more interesting physically . . . The park [at present] is a little too flat," said Michael Van Valkenburgh (Sommer 2019d).

Among the features incorporated into the park's final design include: a new pedestrian bridge across I-190 to better connect the park to the Lower West Side neighborhood on the other side of I-190; a berm to protect the park from the noise of traffic on I-190; a sledding hill; a reinvigorated landscape that includes 2,500 new trees; and an imaginatively designed 2.5-acre playground for children in the center of the park that provides comfortable places for parents and caregivers to sit and watch nearby. Last but not least, an inlet will be excavated into the shoreline so that visitors to the park can come directly in contact with water from the nearby Niagara River. Creating the inlet will require excavating and digging soil and rock well below the water line. Meanwhile, to minimize damage caused by flooding, a more resilient shoreline will be created by raising the elevation of the park near the shoreline and introducing changes in elevation at various points of up to 30 feet.

By the time you read this Ralph C. Wilson Jr. Centennial Park will likely have been completed. Go there to see for yourself how the extensive public participation that accompanied the replanning and redesign of the park increased the ability of people of different ages and with different interests to use and enjoy the park.

～

I've studied many other cities' efforts to reclaim and revive their postindustrial waterfronts and can't think of another city whose waterfront has undergone as wide-ranging and beneficial a transformation as what has taken place in Buffalo.[2] Nor do I know of another city where so many local citizens and nongovernmental organizations played such important roles in advancing the transformation of a postindustrial waterfront. I hope that learning what happened in Buffalo will inspire people in other cities to undertake comparable efforts aimed at reclaiming damaged and abandoned portions of waterfronts in their own respective hometowns for public use and enjoyment.

Appendix I

Timeline and Chronology

1817: New York State Governor DeWitt Clinton proposes legislation authorizing the use of state funds to build a canal west from Albany to Lake Erie. Critics call it "Clinton's Ditch."

1820: Completion of a harbor improvement project overseen by Samuel Wilkeson makes the mouth of the Buffalo River navigable, thereby enabling Buffalo to be chosen as the western terminus of the Erie Canal.

1825: Governor DeWitt Clinton comes to Buffalo to attend a ceremony marking the opening of the canal. He then boards the packet boat *Seneca Chief* and leads a parade of other boats on the canal across New York State. Upon arriving in New York City, jugs of Lake Erie water carried aboard the *Seneca Chief* are dumped into New York Harbor, signifying the "wedding of the waters."

1829: A 28-mile-long canal crossing the Niagara Peninsula in southern Ontario—the Welland Canal—is completed, enabling ships to pass between Lake Ontario and Lake Erie and avoid the barrier that Niagara Falls had long presented to such navigation.

1832: Buffalo is incorporated as a city.

1833: Octagonal lighthouse is completed at the entrance to Buffalo harbor.

1836: Work begins on enlarging and straightening the Erie Canal so that it can handle a larger volume of freight. To shorten travel times, the number of locks is reduced and double locks are added to allow boats to go in opposite directions at the same time. Due to political arguments over how to pay for the enlargement, the project is not fully completed until 1862.

1843: Joseph Dart and Robert Dunbar invent the steam-powered grain elevator, revolutionizing the grain industry by significantly cutting the time it took to unload grain from the holds of ships.

1855: The first Soo Locks are built on the St. Mary's River near Sault Ste. Marie, bypassing rapids that had prevented ships from navigating between Lake Superior and Lake Huron.

1887: The Welland Canal is expanded for a third time.

1918: In an effort to extend the useful life of the Erie Canal and increase its capacity to carry freight, the New York State legislature approves construction of the Erie Barge Canal. The western portion of the Erie Canal is enlarged and straightened to increase its capacity to carry freight, and the canal's western terminus is relocated from Buffalo's Inner Harbor to North Tonawanda. The historic Commercial Slip is filled in.

1919: The Welland Canal is expanded a fourth time.

1940: Memorial Auditorium is completed and opened to the public.

1946: Cornell University's School of Industrial and Labor Relations (Cornell ILR) establishes its first office in downtown Buffalo.

1950: Construction of a 616-unit public housing project on the edge of the former Canal District begins. Everything that previously existed in the area is cleared to make way for the project. "Blitzed London of World War II had nothing on Dante Place just off lower Main Street. . . . [where] tenements and buildings [were] reduced to rubble" (W. H. Porterfield; as quoted by Keppel, 2014b.

1954: Construction of the St. Lawrence Seaway begins.

1955: The Buffalo Skyway is completed. The pillars supporting the Skyway become a "given" that planners and designers will have to work around when attempting to redevelop the Inner Harbor.

1959: The St. Lawrence Seaway opens, allowing ocean-going cargo vessels to navigate from Duluth, Minnesota, at the western end of Lake

Superior, to the Atlantic Ocean without having to unload and transfer their cargos in Buffalo.

1961: The Dante Place public housing project is converted to a middle-income apartment development.

1962: The Buffalo Common Council designates a 12.5-acre area between lower Main Street and the Buffalo River as the Waterfront Redevelopment Area. The Donovan State Office Building is constructed on the site of the former Lehigh Valley Railroad Terminal.

1963: An urban renewal plan for the Waterfront Redevelopment Area is approved by the Buffalo Planning Board that calls for developing a new downtown neighborhood consisting of medium- and high-density housing, a marina, a community college, and an elementary school.

1967: The Buffalo River is declared to be "dead."

1969: Construction begins on a 1.2-million-square-foot office complex adjacent to and just north of where I-190 crosses Main Street. The project's 38-story office tower straddles Main Street and severs the connection between the downtown and lower Main Street.

1970: First Earth Day is celebrated, April 21, 1970.

1974: Erie Basin Marina is completed, consisting of boat docks, a waterfront promenade, and a public observatory overlooking the harbor and the city.

1976: The historic lighthouse at the entrance to Buffalo Harbor is listed on the National Register of Historic Places.

1979: The Buffalo and Erie County Naval and Military Park is created at the Inner Harbor. Initially composed of the USS *Little Rock* and USS *The Sullivans*, the USS *Croaker*, a submarine, is added to the collection in 1988.

1982: Bethlehem Steel closes its Lackawanna steel plan and lays off the 10,000 workers who had been employed at the plant.

1984: After mothballing its Buffalo River steel plant two years earlier, Republic Steel announces it will never reopen the plant.

1985: The Buffalo Lighthouse Association is established by Mike Vogel to raise money for preserving and restoring the deteriorated Buffalo Lighthouse at the entrance to Buffalo Harbor.

1987: Initial restoration of the historic circa 1833 lighthouse at the entrance to Buffalo's Inner Harbor is completed, and the lighthouse is relit.

The International Joint Commission designates 6.2 miles of the Buffalo River as an "Area of Concern (AOC)"—one of the most toxic hotspots in the Great Lakes. The AOC designation also encompasses the City Ship Canal.

1988: In September, a ceremony is held on the deck of the USS *Little Rock* to mark the creation of the Horizons Waterfront Commission.

1989: The New York State Department of Environmental Conservation (NYSDEC) adopts a Remedial Action Plan for the Buffalo River. Citizens and stakeholders that had served on NYSDEC's Remedial Action Plan Advisory Committee form Friends of the Buffalo River.

1992: In January, the Horizons Commission issues its "Action Plan for the Erie County Waterfront," which identifies a large number of projects that would increase public access to the waterfront. The Action Plan says remarkably little about what should happen in Buffalo's Inner Harbor, but a great deal about what should take place on the Outer Harbor. On the northern portion of the Outer Harbor, the Action Plan calls for developing a Great Lakes Science Research Center that would include a freshwater aquarium, a planetarium, and a weather research facility. On the southern half of the Outer Harbor the plan foresees developing up to 1,500 housing units, new retail and commercial space, and a marina in a park-like setting.

1993: Joseph E. Goodell, chairman of the Horizons Waterfront Commission, unveils the Crossroads Harbor plan for the Inner Harbor, which calls for excavating inlets to bring the waterfront close to the new downtown arena then under construction as well as up to the edge of Memorial Auditorium, which would have destroyed the Commercial Slip.

The Horizons Commission suggests that the Great Lakes Science Research Center and aquarium initially proposed to be developed on the Outer Harbor could be developed within Memorial Auditorium. Congressman Nowak secures $20 million in federal and state funding toward the cost of developing the Science Research Center within Memorial Auditorium—funding that would stay in place for a number of years and be relied upon to advance other redevelopment schemes.

1995: The Horizons Commission is dissolved by Governor Pataki. Former staff members are transferred to the Western New York regional office of Empire State Development Corporation.

1996: In July, the City of Buffalo approves a plan supported by Empire State Development Corporation that calls for inlets to be excavated to bring the waterfront close to the new downtown arena as well as Memorial Auditorium. The city's new downtown arena is completed and Memorial Auditorium is shuttered.

1998: ESDC issues a revised plan for the Inner Harbor that calls for leaving the Commercial Slip permanently buried and for constructing a replica slip not far from where the Commercial Slip lay buried. The required Federal Environmental Impact Statement (FEIS) ESDC submits for the proposed project asserts that it would have "no adverse effect" on historic resources eligible for listing on the National Register of Historic Places.

1999: Funding for the Inner Harbor redevelopment project is secured from the Federal Transit Administration (FTA).

In May, an 800-foot-long section of the long-buried wall of the Commercial Slip is discovered—the existence of which was not documented in the FEIS that ESDC had submitted.

The Preservation Coalition of Erie County files a lawsuit against Federal Transit Administration et al. in Federal District Court, contending that the FEIS was inadequate and seeking a preliminary injunction preventing ESDC from further implementing the project.

2000: Warren Barbour, whose studies provided the basis for the FEIS that ESDC submitted for the Inner Harbor project, testifies in court that the long-buried stones that lined the historic Commercial Slip could "blast apart" if uncovered and exposed to the air, after having been buried for such a long time.

On March 31, Federal District Court Judge Skretny agrees with the Preservation Coalition that historic resources eligible for listing on the National Register of Historic Place did exist on the site and that the FEIS submitted by ESDC was inadequate. The court orders ESDC to submit a Supplemental Environmental Impact Statement (SEIS) that addresses the concerns raised by the Preservation Coalition.

On June 3, the *Buffalo News* reports that the three experts that Barbour said had supported his "exploding rocks" theory said that their views had been misrepresented and that the stones that lined the walls of the Commercial Slip were much more durable than Barbour said they were.

On June 16, local and state government officials announce that Adelphia Communications is going to build a high-rise corporate office building adjacent to the recently completed downtown arena, bringing 1,000 new jobs to lower Main Street and anchoring the Inner Harbor redevelopment project.

On June 17, Erie County Executive Joel Giambra and Buffalo Mayor Masiello announce that a study will be undertaken to assess the feasibility of restoring the Erie Canal Commercial Slip and other historic resources that lie buried within the Inner Harbor Project site.

By establishing the Erie Canal National Heritage Corridor, the US Congress recognizes the Erie Canal's significance in opening the interior of the continent to settlement.

A two-day event, titled "A Canal Conversation," is held on September 11–12. Outside experts in historic preservation are brought to Buffalo to speak about the potential economic benefits of heritage tourism around the historic western terminus of the Erie Canal.

A memorandum of understanding is brokered by Erie County Executive Joel Giambra and signed by state and local officials and politicians from both parties, as well as preservationists. The signatories pledge to work toward developing a historically respectful waterfront plan that preserves the remains of the old Erie Canal and other historic resources on the site.

In October, on the 175th anniversary of the opening of the Erie Canal, Governor George Pataki comes to Buffalo to announce that the Commercial Slip will be uncovered and rewatered and that historic streets and building foundations in the former Canal District will be unearthed.

2001: Mayor Anthony Masiello begins pushing the idea that a Bass Pro Outdoor World retail outlet should anchor the Inner Harbor redevelopment project.

2002: Adelphia Communications declares bankruptcy, ending the notion that it would be building large-scale office building on lower Main Street.

A feature article in the *Buffalo News* by Sharon Linstedt (June 12, 2002) hypes the idea that a 140,000-square-foot Bass Pro Outdoor World store might be developed in Memorial Auditorium.

In the wake of Trico's announcement that it would be moving its operations to Mexico, a group of religious and labor leaders in Buffalo establish the Center for Economic Justice (CEJ) to prevent further job losses to low-wage areas.

2003: In an effort to advance the stalled 1989 Buffalo River Remedial Action Plan (RAP), the US Environmental Protection Agency issues a request for proposals allowing nonprofit organizations to apply for funding. Friends of the Buffalo River becomes the first nonprofit organization in the Great Lakes Basin to receive funding and to be authorized to manage implementation of the RAP.

2004: In November, the revised Inner Harbor plan that Governor Pataki had promised four years earlier is publicly released. Prepared by Flynn Battaglia Architects, the plan calls for uncovering, restoring, and rewatering the Commercial Slip, constructing a boardwalk promenade along the footprint of the Central Wharf, and installing a replica of the truss bridge that once spanned the Commercial Slip. Governor Pataki, Mayor Masiello, and ESDC officials use the occasion to also announce that a large-scale Bass Pro Outdoor World retail outlet would be developed within Memorial Auditorium.

ESDC signs a memorandum of understanding (MOU) with Bass Pro in which ESDC and the State of New York agree to provide Bass Pro with $35 million in direct subsidies and spend millions more on infrastructure improvements, such as by constructing a parking structure and intermodal transportation center and by constructing an off-ramp from the Thruway directly to the parking ramp and transportation center.

2005: Soon after taking office representing New York's 27th congressional district, Brian Higgins begins pushing the idea that the New York

Power Authority (NYPA) should be required to make payments to Buffalo for waterfront improvements as a condition for the federal relicensing of the Niagara Power Project. Higgins negotiates an agreement with NYPA that calls for NYPA to make annual payments of $3.5 million over a period of 50 years to advance the Canalside project and other waterfront projects.

The Donovan State Office Building on lower Main Street becomes vacant.

Erie Canal Harbor Development Corporation (ECHDC), a new subsidiary of the Empire State Development Corporation, is created by Governor Pataki to oversee the ongoing planning and redevelopment of Buffalo's waterfront.

2006: After an excessive amount of mold is discovered in Memorial Auditorium that would cost $10 million to remove with no assurance that it would not come back, a cost-benefit analysis concludes that it would be more economical to tear down the Aud and build from scratch rather than try to retrofit the building.

Work begins on removing a major section of the Hamburg Drain from the Commercial Slip in preparation for uncovering, restoring, and rewatering the Commercial Slip.

2007: The City of Buffalo transfers ownership of Memorial Auditorium to ECHDC, with the understanding that ECHDC will pay for demolishing the structure and prepare the site for private development.

On March 30, Empire State Development Corporation's Press Office announces that a 100,000-square-foot Bass Pro Outdoor World retail outlet would be built on the footprint of the historic Central Wharf. ECHDC chairman Anthony Gioia promises that an architectural review advisory committee would be appointed "to assist in the design of the new construction planned for Canal Side to ensure it is in keeping with the historic nature of the site." ECHDC would reportedly own the building, and Bass Pro would pay common area maintenance fees of $300,000 a year for an initial 20-year lease, with renewals to 50 years.

On May 13, the *Buffalo News* reports that the top issue on the minds of the 142 people who submitted letters to the editor during the prior week was that Buffalo "stick to the 2004 Erie Canal Harbor Master Plan."

In September, Congressman Brian Higgins announces that the plan to build a Bass Pro Outdoor World store on the historic Central Wharf has been scrapped.

ECHDC and Bass Pro shift back to the idea of constructing a Bass Pro retail outlet on the footprint of Memorial Auditorium after the structure is demolished and the site is cleared—with the understanding that the project would be supported by the same publicly financed infrastructure and transportation improvements previously pledged when it was expected the retail outlet would be developed *within* Memorial Auditorium.

Cornell Buffalo and other nongovernmental organizations create Partnership for the Public Good (PPG) to give nonprofit organizations in Buffalo a greater voice in public policy, particularly with regard to economic development. Cornell Buffalo helps "incubate" PPG by providing it with some of its own office space rent-free. The Center for Economic Justice serves as the fiscal sponsor for PPG's first grant application.

2008:   Demolition of Memorial Auditorium begins, paid for by ECHDC. Congressman Brian Higgins renegotiates the agreement with NYPA. NYPA agrees to pay $8.5 million for waterfront-related improvements for the next ten years.

Erie Canal Harbor opens to the public in July.

Thomas Dee replaces Charles Rosenow as president of ECHDC.

2009:   The topsail schooner *Jolly Roger*, previously based in South Carolina, is brought to Buffalo, moored in the rewatered Commercial Slip, and renamed *Spirit of Buffalo*. Buffalo Sailing Adventures begins offering visitors to Canalside the opportunity to sail out onto Lake Erie on the schooner.

The Canal Side Community Alliance (CSCA) mobilizes community opposition to the enormous public subsidies being offered to Bass Pro and begins pressing local government officials to require the signing of a community benefit agreement as a condition for allowing the project to proceed.

2010:   In March, the Buffalo Common Council unanimously approves a resolution making the transfer of the land sought by Bass Pro for its project contingent upon the signing of a community benefit agreement.

On June 2, the nonprofit Public Accountability Initiative releases "Fishing for Taxpayer Cash: Bass Pro's Record of Big-League Subsidies, Failed Promises, and the Consequences for Cities across America."

On July 19, Congressman Brian Higgins imposes a 14-day deadline for reaching a final agreement with Bass Pro. Two weeks later, Bass Pro officially announces it is dropping out from the Inner Harbor project.

Two public forums are held to chart a new direction at Canalside, the first of which is held on October 24 at the Burchfield Penney Art Center. At the second forum held on November 6, organized by Mark Goldman and titled "Imagining Buffalo's Waterfront," Fred Kent, the president and founder of Project for Public Spaces calls for rejecting the "heavy subsidy, silver-bullet, lots of parking" approach that had characterized the city's past approach to waterfront development and for embracing instead a "lighter, quicker, cheaper" approach.

On November 29, ECHDC chairman Jordan Levy announces that ECHDC has decided to indefinitely delay a vote about the construction of a parking garage on the former Memorial Auditorium site and that Fred Kent would be hired to advise ECHDC on how to implement the "lighter, quicker, cheaper" approach in the Inner Harbor.

2011:   A grassy lawn is laid down, filled with scores of multicolored Adirondack chairs, and people begin being drawn to Canalside. "The major economic development success story in our community this year involves $3,000 worth of Adirondack chairs," comments Mark Goldman.

Dredging and removal of contaminated sediment from the bottom of the Buffalo River begins.

In June, River Fest Park along the Buffalo River opens to the public.

In October, the National Trust for Historic Preservation holds its National Preservation Conference in Buffalo.

The Buffalo Lighthouse Association acquires the deed to the South Buffalo Lighthouse at the southern end of the harbor and is two-thirds of the way through a $1 million restoration of the lighthouse.

2012:   The Liberty Hound Restaurant opens adjacent to the rewatered Commercial Slip.

Jordan Levy and Larry Quinn resign from ECHDC's board of directors. Robert Gioia, president of the John R. Oishei Foundation, replaces Levy as board chair.

ECHDC invites submissions of proposed development schemes for the city-owned parcel known as the Webster block, then being used for surface parking.

Construction begins on converting the first four floors of the former Donovan New York State Office Building into a Marriott Courtyard hotel and the top four floors into office space. To pave the way for the conversion, ECHDC paid the cost of stripping the structure down to its skeleton.

Mutual Riverfront Park opens across the river from and overlooking Silo City.

2013:   HSBC Bank vacates the 38-story office tower at the foot of Main Street, the largest commercial building in the city. Not long thereafter the complex is entirely vacant.

In May, ECHDC hires Perkins&Will to prepare a "Blueprint plan" for the Outer Harbor.

Wilkeson Pointe Park opens to the public. The cost of developing the park is paid for with money obtained from NYPA in connection with the federal relicensing of the Niagara Hydroelectric Power Plant.

On June 21, ECHDC's board of directors hears a presentation by Friends of the Buffalo Story members Mark Goldman, Peter B. Dowd, and Scott A. Wood showing five different ways a mix of residential and commercial uses could be developed on the northern portion of the area formerly occupied by Memorial Auditorium.

On July 11, ECHDC's board of directors adopts "A Public Statement of Principles for High Road Development of Buffalo's Waterfront"—a document agreed to after lengthy negotiations between ECHDC and the Canal Side Community Alliance.

2014:   The redevelopment of the former Donovan State Office Building into the Marriott Courtyard Hotel and office space is completed.

A replica canal that follows the historic alignment of the old Erie Canal is constructed on the southern portion of the site formerly occupied by Memorial Auditorium.

The Congress for the New Urbanism holds its National Conference in Buffalo.

A summer concert series draws throngs of people to Canalside.

The Shark Girl sculpture is brought to Canalside from Cincinnati as part of a public art initiative undertaken by the Albright-Knox Art Gallery.

In September, NFTA transfers 350 acres of the Outer Harbor to ECHDC. Governor Andrew Cuomo authorizes ECHDC to develop the southern portion into Buffalo Harbor State Park.

An ad hoc coalition of nongovernmental organizations called Our Outer Harbor (OOH) is formed to oppose future efforts ECHDC might make to bring about the private development of the Outer Harbor.

The site of the former GLF Elevator on the Buffalo River directly across from River Fest Park is redeveloped into River-Works, a recreation and leisure-oriented facility that includes two ice-hockey rinks, a place to launch kayaks into the river, climbing walls, an indoor roller-derby rink, and a bar and restaurant. Grain silos painted to resemble a "six-pack" of Labatt Blue beer become a signature feature of the development. A Ferris wheel and zip lines are later added.

2015: HarborCenter is completed and begins hosting college hockey games, youth hockey, and semi-pro hockey.

Public ice skating and curling tournaments are held for the first time on the Ice at Canalside, the largest outdoor skating rink in New York State.

Buffalo Harbor State Park opens to the public on the Outer Harbor.

A colorful light show is projected onto the Connecting Terminal Grain Elevator across from Canalside for the first time and becomes a nightly feature.

Washington DC–based developer Douglas Jemal acquires the vacant former HSBC Center tower on lower Main Street and launches an ambitious costly project aimed at reviving the complex.

In September, Perkins&Will's "Blueprint Plan" for the Outer Harbor calls for large portions of the Outer Harbor to be privately developed.

2016: In January, the last 50 acres of the Outer Harbor controlled by NFTA (Terminals A and B of the former Ford Assembly Plant) are transferred to ECHDC.

On September 28, Our Outer Harbor holds a public meeting at RiverWorks to engage local citizens in considering the environmental value of the Outer Harbor to the city and the region. The member organizations of OOH unanimously adopt ten "shared principles" to serve as a "checklist" for evaluating projects ECHDC might propose for the Outer Harbor.

ECHDC acquires the First Buffalo Marina from the New York Power Authority.

2017: On January 3, the City of Buffalo's new Unified Development Ordinance—the "Green Code"—goes into effect.

Construction of the Explore & More Children's Museum begins at Canalside.

Trowbridge Wolf Michaels, a landscape architecture firm based in Ithaca, is hired by ECHDC to prepare a new plan for the Outer Harbor.

On October 5, the first "Day in the Life of the Buffalo River" event is held. Students from nine local schools are brought to eleven sites along the Buffalo River and its tributaries to collect samples and record environmental conditions such as water temperature, pH levels, and turbidity, and also to document the presence of species found within the watershed.

2018: On Valentine's Day, the Ralph C. Wilson, Jr. Foundation announces a $6 million grant to the Explore & More Children's Museum to assure its completion and to establish an endowment for the museum's ongoing operations. The name of the museum is changed to the Ralph C. Wilson, Jr. Children's Museum.

Shark Girl sculpture at Canalside makes the *Huffington Post's* list of "35 most Instagram-worthy subjects."

The Buffalo Maritime Center announces it plans to construct a replica of the *Seneca Chief* packet boat that Governor DeWitt

Clinton boarded in 1825 and traveled on from Buffalo to New York City to mark the opening of the Erie Canal. Assemblyman Sean Ryan seeks state money to aid the project. In August, Governor Cuomo awards $4 million in state money toward the cost of constructing the Longshed to house the building of the packet boat at Canalside.

ECHDC selects Sinatra & Co. to develop a $21 million project called Heritage Point on the South Aud Block consisting of two five-story, mixed-use buildings containing 41apartments and 71,000 square feet of retail and office space.

In August, Governor Andrew Cuomo commits $10 million in funding to support the redevelopment and transformation of the North Aud Block.

The Ralph C. Wilson, Jr. Foundation announces a $50 million gift to pay for redesigning and reconstructing LaSalle Park just north of the Inner Harbor, which is renamed Ralph C. Wilson, Jr. Centennial Park. The vision for LaSalle Park's future is shaped by more than 1,100 responses to a survey, a focus group, and by kids in the nearby West Side neighborhood being asked to share their ideas.

On October 29, Our Outer Harbor holds a public meeting in advance of ECHDC's upcoming open house in November to formulate its positions regarding what should and should not happen on the Outer Harbor.

2019: The Ralph C. Wilson, Jr. Children's Museum at Canalside opens to the public.

On July 4, tens of thousands of people line Canalside, Erie Basin Marina, and the Outer Harbor to watch 12 tall ships parade into Buffalo Harbor. As many as 125,000 people are drawn to the waterfront during the three-day festival.

The Western New York Land Conservancy invites the submission of proposed design schemes showing how an all-season nature trail could be created along the former DL&W rail line between Canalside and Riverbend. Ninety-nine design concepts are submitted in response.

2020: Construction of the Longshed is completed. The keel for the *Seneca Chief* packet boat is laid down on October 17 at a public event held in the Longshed, with everyone wearing masks and everyone in attendance signing the keel.

After owning and operating the *Buffalo News* since 1977, Berk-shire Hathaway sells the newspaper to Iowa-based Lee Enterprises.

2021: On Memorial Day weekend, the Buffalo Heritage Carousel begins operating at Canalside.

2022: In September, Lee Enterprises announces it has agreed to sell the *Buffalo News'* 160,000-square-foot headquarters building and would be moving its newsroom and administrative offices to Larkinville about a mile away. When it was built in 1973, the building, designed by Edward Durell Stone, was seen as a major commitment to downtown Buffalo by the privately owned newspaper, which was still in the hands of the founding Butler family. For 50 years, the newspapers' headquarters at the corner of Washington and Scott Streets provided its reporters with a front-row seat from which to view and write about what was happening in the Inner Harbor. With Canalside having been firmly established as a visitor and recreational destination, and with a mixture of housing and commercial space being developed at Heritage Point, the former newspaper headquarters could accommodate any of a number of different uses. *How* the building is redeveloped now becomes part of the ongoing story of Canalside.

In a deal brokered by Congressman Brian Higgins, NYPA agrees to transfer the remaining unpaid portion it agreed to pay to secure the relicensing of the Niagara Power project as a lump sum to ECHDC.

ECHDC issues an RFP inviting developers to submit proposals describing how they would redevelop the North Aud Block if they were selected for the project.

2023: In April, ECHDC selects Pennrose to develop 367 mixed-income residences, ground-floor commercial storefronts, and a pedestri-an-oriented public square on the North Aud Block. Two 4–5 story buildings will overlook the replica canal, two other 10–14 story structures will be built further back from the canal closer to the Niagara Thruway, and 360 underground parking spaces will be developed.

ECHDC awards a $14.25 million contract to construct the "Canalside Gateway Building" on the southwest corner of the North Aud Block to include public restrooms, a visitor information center, and small amount of retail space. ECHDC also plans on consolidating its waterfront operations there.

Construction begins on converting LaSalle Park into Ralph Wilson Park.

The Buffalo Maritime Center holds a "Whiskey Plank Celebration" at the Longshed on October 7 to celebrate placing the final plank on the outer shell of the replica *Seneca Chief*'s wooden hull.

Appendix II

Heroes of Buffalo's Waterfront Renaissance

Listed below are the names of individuals and nongovernmental organizations whose efforts described in this book helped advance Buffalo's waterfront renaissance. The headings under which these waterfront heroes are grouped indicate the portion of the waterfront—Inner Harbor, Buffalo River, Outer Harbor—to which they directed their efforts. Some names appear under two or more headings because they played important roles in reviving more than one portion of the waterfront. The brief thumbnail descriptions that accompany each name underscore the diverse backgrounds and interests of those who participated in and contributed to Buffalo's dramatic turnaround.

Heroes of the Inner Harbor

Preservation Coalition of Erie County: conceived of by Joan Bozer, a member of the Erie County Legislature, who saw the need for a more activist approach to advocating for preserving the historic architecture of Buffalo; established in 1981 by Tim Tielman and Susan McCartney, signaling the emergence of a citizen-led effort aimed at preserving the architectural history and fabric of Buffalo, and a willingness to be actively engaged in politically charged, controversial land-use and development issues; filed a lawsuit in 1999 in Federal District Court that forced-Empire State Development Corporation to uncover and restore the Commercial Slip, the western terminus of the Erie Canal.

"The Preservation Coalition was a citizen-based organization that changed the paradigm of genteel support for preservation as exemplified by the long-established Landmarks Society" (McCartney, interview, July 24, 2018).

Campaign for Great Buffalo History, Architecture & Culture (C4GB): established by Tim Tielman and Susan McCartney in 2002; assumed the Preservation Coalition's role as plaintiff in the legal proceedings with the state waterfront planning agency regarding the Inner Harbor redevelopment project.

"By the beginning of 2000, we were experiencing difficulties with certain board members who objected to the activist approach we were taking with regard to the Canalside project. I was president of the Preservation Coalition and still married to Tim. It became clear that Tim needed to be able to act without being constrained by those board members" (McCartney, interview, July 24, 2018).

"From shaping Canalside, to preserving the downtown buildings we're building a future on, to the Outer Harbor waterfront, to unearthing the historic Commercial Slip that fed Canalside's blossoming, Buffalo's rebirth was preservationist-driven and activist-laden. An enlightened public—in courtrooms, protests, and public meetings—battled and bent myopic politicians and power brokers into going a better way" (Esmonde 2016)

"Tim Tielman has been called an obstructionist, and he'll no doubt be called that once again. But it can be argued that no one has done more in Western New York than he to save Buffalo's history from the wrecking ball. He helped lead the fight that forced Governor George E. Pataki to reverse direction and resurrect the terminus of the Erie Canal, including the Commercial Slip, the Central Wharf, and the original [Canal Era] street network" (Sommer 2018a).

Preservation Buffalo Niagara (PBN): formed in 2008 through the merger of what remained of the Preservation Coalition of Erie County with the Landmarks Society; its membership and influence in advocating for historic preservation grew under the leadership of Jessie Fisher, who became its executive director in June 2015 after having previously been Buffalo Niagara Riverkeeper's Director of Planning.

Basil Port of Call: Buffalo 2019 tall ships event planned and organized by a Steering Committee chaired by Mike Vogel, president of the Buffalo Lighthouse Association.

Financial support for the Basil Port of Call: Buffalo tall ships event provided by Margaret L. Wendt Foundation, John R. Oishei Foundation, Buffalo & Erie County Greenway Fund, Charles and Iona Arrick Charitable

Fund at the Community Foundation for Greater Buffalo, Colligan Family Fund at the Community Foundation for Greater Buffalo, Humanities New York, and New York Canal Corporation.

Roger Allen: master boatbuilder recruited by John Montague to come to Buffalo from the Florida Maritime Center to become the first director of the Buffalo Maritime Center.

Richard G. Berger and Francis C. Amendola: the attorneys who represented the Preservation Coalition of Erie County in the 1999 lawsuit it filed against the Federal Transit Administration and Empire State Development Corporation et al.

Joan Bozer: former Erie County legislator who conceived of and was largely responsible for establishing the Preservation Coalition of Erie County; formed the Friends of Olmsted Parks organization, which later became the Buffalo Olmsted Parks Conservancy; the first public official to promote the idea of bringing a solar-powered carousel to Buffalo's waterfront.

Canal Side Community Alliance (CSCA): a network of neighborhood and faith-based organizations that included PPG, People United for Sustainable Housing (PUSH), Buffalo First!, Voice-Buffalo, minority contractors, and locally owned businesses; formed in 2009 to object to the huge taxpayer subsidies being offered to Bass Pro to develop a large-scale retail outlet at the Inner Harbor; *Allison Duwe*, executive director of CEJ and Michaela Shappiro-Shellaby led the organizing effort that created CSCA.

Center for Economic Justice (CEJ): established in the wake of Trico's announcement that it would be closing its plant in Buffalo and moving its operations to Mexico to prevent further losses of jobs to low-wage locations; mobilized community opposition to the Bass Pro project and pressured the City of Buffalo to require that a community benefit agreement (CBA) be signed as a condition for allowing any project at Canalside to go forward.

David Colligan: attorney and voting member on ECHDC's board from 2007 to 2017; originated the idea that ECHDC should construct a replica canal along the historic alignment of the Erie Canal.

Cornell Buffalo ILR: founded by Cornell University's School of Industrial and Labor Relations (ILR) in 1945, when Buffalo was one of the most heavily industrialized cities in the country; since then has provided faculty members and students a real-world context for studying industrial and labor relations in a classic postindustrial city.

Donn Esmonde: first hired by the *Buffalo News* in 1982 as a sports columnist/feature writer; had a five-year run as a Lifestyle columnist and then became the *News'* primary Metro News columnist in 1994; between

1999 and 2016 wrote scores of commentaries highly critical of the way in which ESDC and ECHDC proposed to redevelop Buffalo's Inner Harbor.

Bruce Fisher: in 2000, while serving as deputy Erie County executive in a Republican administration, encouraged Governor Pataki to recognize that he could gain politically by publicly supporting historic preservation at the Inner Harbor; as a Buffalo State College professor, organized the first public forum that was held to forge a new vision of how Buffalo's Inner Harbor could be redeveloped in the wake of Bass Pro's withdrawal from the project.

Scot Fisher: printed and distributed hundreds of "Save, Don't Pave!" posters throughout the city; launched a petition drive during the summer and fall of 2000 in support of saving and uncovering the historic Commercial Slip that garnered 14,000 signatures.

Lou Jean Fleron: joined the faculty of Cornell Buffalo/School of Industrial and Labor Relations (ILR) in 1977; codirected Partnership for the Public Good along with Sam Magavern during the first ten years of its existence.

Friends of the Buffalo Story (Mark Goldman, Peter B. Dowd, and Scott A. Wood): prepared and gave a presentation to ECHDC's board in June 2013 showing five ways a mixed-use, walkable neighborhood could be developed on the northern portion of the Inner Harbor formerly occupied by Memorial Auditorium; funding for the planning and design work that provided the basis for the presentation was provided by the *Oishei Foundation.*

Kevin Gaughan: conceived of and secured funding to hold a two-day event called *A Canal Conversation* in Buffalo in September 2000.

Significant financial support for "A Canal Conversation" provided by: The National Trust for Historic Preservation; the Baird Foundation; the Paul J. Koessler Foundation; the Western New York Foundation; Fleet Bank N. A.; and Daemen College.

"A Canal Conversation" cosponsors: American Association of University Women; American Institute of Architects, Buffalo/WNY Chapter; the Baird Foundation; Buffalo Urban League, Inc.; Buffalo and Erie County Historical Society; Chautauqua Conferences on Regionalism; City of Buffalo Public Schools; Great Lakes United, Inc.; Landmarks Society of the Niagara Frontier; Leadership Buffalo; the League of Women Voters of Greater Buffalo; the National Association for the Advancement of Colored People, Buffalo Branch; Niagara Frontier Industry Education Council; the New Millennium Group; 21st Century Club; Preservation League of New York State; Working for Downtown.

Financial support for the publication of the proceedings of the Canal Conversation event provided by: the Baird Foundation, the Paul J. Koessler Foundation, and Downtown Buffalo 2002.

Rossman Giese, Jr.: member of the Department of Geological Studies at the University at Buffalo; stood up at a public hearing conducted by ESDC and directly contradicted the agency's assertion that the stones that lined the walls of the historic Commercial Slip would break apart or explode if exposed to the air.

Mark Goldman: organized the second public forum held at City Honors School in November 2010 to reimagine Buffalo's Inner Harbor; envisioned Canalside not just as a visitor destination, but also the possibility of it becoming a mixed-use downtown neighborhood.

Laurie Hauer-LaDuca: architect and the carousel enthusiast who tracked down a "park-style" carousel in Ohio that had been manufactured in North Tonawanda in 1924 and eventually succeeded in bringing it to Canalside.

Brian Higgins: elected to Buffalo Common Council in 1988; elected to represent Buffalo and Erie County in the US House of Representatives; in 2005, negotiated an agreement with New York Power Authority whereby NYPA agreed make annual payments of $3.8 million over 50 years to advance the Canalside project and other waterfront projects in Buffalo; in 2008, renegotiated that earlier agreement to accelerate NYPA's payments by paying $8.5 million each year until 2018; forced Bass Pro to withdraw from the Inner Harbor project by imposing a 14-day deadline to commit to building the promised retail outlet.

Fred Kent: founder and president of Project for Public Spaces; keynote speaker at the November 2010 "Imagining Buffalo's Waterfront" event held at City Honors High School; urged citizens to embrace a "lighter, cheaper, quicker" approach to developing and activating the Inner Harbor.

Robert Kresse: trustee of the Margaret L. Wendt Foundation between 1984 and 2018; largely responsible for the Wendt Foundation's decision to provide $250,000 in funding to Buffalo Heritage Carousel Inc. to enable it to acquire and install a park-style carousel at Canalside.

Phil Langdon: *Buffalo News* reporter and columnist, 1973–1982; wrote numerous articles about the neglect and destruction of old buildings in Buffalo that "played a really important role in moving the needle in favor of preservation" (McCartney, interview, July 24, 2018).

Sam Magavern: first hired by Cornell Buffalo ILR in 2007 to oversee workplace compliance with the City of Buffalo's newly enacted "Living Wage Law"; organized a conference titled "The High Road Runs through the City" that gave rise to the idea of creating Partnership for the Public Good (PPG); codirected PPG along with Lou Jean Fleron, 2007–2017.

Paul McDonnell: president of the Campaign for Greater Buffalo History, Architecture & Culture; forcefully spoke out against ADM's demolition of the Great Northern grain elevator.

Robert Z. Melnick: University of Oregon School of Architecture and Allied Arts professor who flew across the country to Buffalo to testify as an expert witness on behalf of the Preservation Coalition in Federal District Court.

John Montague: established the Buffalo Maritime Center in 2007 as a nonprofit corporation and oversaw its development of a facility for building and repairing wooden boats on Arthur Street; championed building a replica of the *Seneca Chief* packet boat that Governor DeWitt Clinton traveled on to New York Harbor in 1825 to mark the opening of the Erie Canal; originated the idea that ECHDC should operate a bike ferry between Canalside and the Outer Harbor.

Partnership for the Public Good (PPG): established in 2007 as the controversy surrounding the proposed Inner Harbor Bass Pro project was reaching a fever pitch; "incubated" by Cornell Buffalo ILR, which provided it with free office space during its formative years; in 2007 had 36 partner organizations; by 2018 had over 200 partner organizations.

Rosa Patton: artist who traveled from North Carolina to Buffalo six times to train volunteers in painting the animals, chariots, decorative valences, and scenery panels of the Buffalo Heritage Carousel; volunteer painters drawn from Buffalo Snowbirds Decorative Painters and Genesee County Decorative Painters.

Public Accountability Initiative: a nonprofit, public interest research organization that in June 2010 issued "Fishing for Taxpayer Cash: Bass Pro's Record of Big-League Subsidies, Failed Promises and Consequences for Cities across America," which documented the experiences of communities across the country where large-scale Bass Pro retail outlets failed to produce promised economic benefits.

David Rogers: CEO and cofounder of Life Storage; donated $300,000 to the Buffalo Maritime Center toward the roughly $600,000 cost of building a replica of the *Seneca Chief* packet boat.

Helen Ronan: member of Buffalo Snowbirds Decorative Painters and member of Buffalo Heritage Carousel board of directors.

Russell J. Salvatore Foundation: provided $250,000 in support of Buffalo Heritage Carousel, Inc.

Frank Santuzzi: University at Buffalo School of Architecture and Planning professor; developed a model of a solar-powered carousel to demonstrate that Joan Bozer's effort to bring one to Buffalo's waterfront was feasible.

Robert Shibley and Bradshaw Hovey: secured individuals with specialized knowledge of historic preservation and heritage tourism to speak at the Canal Conversation event; compiled and edited a final report of event's proceedings.

Linda Schineller and Paula Blanchard: Basil Port of Call: Buffalo 2019 tall ships event Steering Committee members.

Patrick Stanczyk: master carver who led a team of volunteers in repairing, reassembling, and restoring the wooden animals of the Buffalo Heritage Carousel.

Margaret Sullivan: grew up in Lackawanna and began working at the *Buffalo News* as a summer intern in 1980; became the first woman editor of the newspaper in 1999; under her watch, the newspaper kept area residents well informed about the controversy that had arisen over how the Inner Harbor should be redeveloped. In September 2012, the *New York Times* hired her as its fifth public editor.

Brian Trzeciak: joined the Buffalo Maritime Center in 2016 and worked his way up to be executive director; before joining the Maritime Center, worked as a community organizer with Citizen Action.

Mike Vogel: worked at the *Buffalo News* for 43 years; first hired as a reporter in 1970; served on the newspapers' editorial board from 1998 to 2006; along with Edward Patton and Paul Redding authored *America's Crossroads: Canal Street/ Dante Place, The Making of a City* (1993); founder and president of Buffalo Lighthouse Association; member of ECHDC's Canalside History Advisory Group; appointed a voting member of ECHDC's board of directors in 2019; chairman, Basil Port of Call: Buffalo 2019 tall ships event Steering Committee.

Ralph C. Wilson, Jr. Foundation: in 2014, provided $6 million for the children's museum that was built at Canalside; made a $50 million gift to redesign and endow a newly redeveloped Ralph C. Wilson, Jr. Centennial Park (formerly LaSalle Park) along the Niagara River.

Heroes of the Buffalo River

Friends of the Buffalo River original incorporators: Lynda H. Schneekloth, University at Buffalo School of Architecture and Planning professor; Barry

Boyer, University at Buffalo Law School faculty; Margaret Wooster, Great Lakes United; Keith Martin, lawyer; Dick Jeffers, community resident; and David Reimers, community resident; Brian Shero, biology professor, Medaille College.

Others actively involved with Friends of the Buffalo River during the 1990s: Michael Hamilton, architect; Kim Irvine, Buffalo State College engineering faculty; Jill Singer, sedimentologist, Buffalo State College faculty; Betsy Trometer, US Fish and Wildlife Service. FBR board members included: Paul Dyster, mayor of the City of Niagara Falls; Tom DiSantis, City of Niagara Falls planning director; and Brian Higgins, who at the time represented South Buffalo on the Buffalo Common Council.

Timothy Bohen: grew up in the First Ward; gathered and verified much of the detailed information that was contained in his 2012 book *Against the Grain: The History of Buffalo's First Ward* at the Waterfront Memories and More Heritage Center.

Clinton Brown: preservationist and architect who was instrumental in preventing the surviving portion of the Holmes Machinery Co. factory building on Chicago Street from being demolished and oversaw its redevelopment into the Cooperage.

Friends of Reinstein Woods: in partnership with Buffalo Audubon and SUNY Fredonia, sponsored a series of annual "Day in the Life of the Buffalo River" events that brought students from area schools, their teachers, and scores of volunteers to various locations within the watershed to collect water samples and take measurements of environmental quality.

Brian Higgins: represented South Buffalo on the Buffalo Common Council between 1988 and 1993, during which time he served on the board of Friends of the Buffalo River; after being elected to the US House of Representatives, secured federal funds to transform Ohio Street from an industrial road into a landscaped, pedestrian-friendly parkway along the Buffalo River.

Jill Spisiak Jedlicka: hired by Friends of the Buffalo River in 2003 to manage and administer the multiyear cleanup of the Buffalo River; appointed executive director of Buffalo Niagara Waterkeeper in May 2012; under her leadership, the nonprofit has become the largest and most influential environmental advocacy organization in Western New York and is developing a number of Blueway sites along the Buffalo River to provide better public access.

Robert Kresse: trustee of the Margaret L. Wendt Foundation, 1984–2018; recommended that the Wendt Foundation loan the Valley Community Association $200,000 to enable it to purchase the property that became River Fest Park—a loan that was later forgiven.

Julie Barrett O'Neill: the first paid employee of Friends of the Buffalo River who helped the nonprofit prepare its successful application to EPA for funding to manage the cleanup of the Buffalo River; went on to become Buffalo Niagara Riverkeeper's full-time executive director; subsequently became general counsel and Green Program director for the Buffalo Sewer Authority; in May 2022 named as director of NYSDEC's Region 9, which includes Erie and Niagara Counties.

Margaret "Peg" Overdorf: executive director of the Valley Community Association (VCA): spearheaded VCA's development of River Fest and Mutual Riverfront parks; marshalled political support for the state and federal funding to redesign and reconstruct Ohio Street into a landscaped, pedestrian-friendly parkway; voiced strong support for habitat restoration and ongoing monitoring of water quality along the Buffalo River.

Lynda H. Schneekloth: as a University at Buffalo School of Architecture and Planning faculty member compiled *Reconsidering Concrete Atlantis: Buffalo's Grain Elevators* (2006), a 132-page report that documented the histories and physical characteristics of 16 Buffalo grain elevators eligible for listing on the National Register of Historic Places.

Western New York Land Conservancy: sponsored a competition in 2018 to generate proposed design schemes showing how the former DL&W rail corridor could be transformed into an urban nature trail and greenway; is actively pursuing the project.

Heroes of the Outer Harbor

Robert F. Andrle: founding member of Tifft Farm, Inc.; chair of Tifft Farm, Inc.'s Site Management Committee; served on the Tifft Committee of the Board of Managers of the Buffalo Society of Natural Sciences after its merger with Tifft Farm, Inc.; the first person to envision creating a nature preserve at Times Beach; developed the site management plan used as the basis for creating the Times Beach Nature Preserve.

Larry Beahan and Art Klein: long-time board members of the Sierra Club, Niagara Group; also involved with the Sierra Club at the Western New York and New York State levels.

Thomas Benjamin: Tifft Farm, Inc.'s first executive director, appointed in 1976.

Buffalo Society of Natural Sciences: merged with Tifft Farm, Inc. in 1982 to become a department of the Buffalo Museum of Science, which assumed ongoing responsibility for overseeing and managing Tifft Farm Preserve.

Jay Burney: founding member of the Times Beach Preserve and Friends of Times Beach; Our Outer Harbor Steering Committee member.

Phil Campanile: Western New York Environmental Alliance board member; Our Outer Harbor Steering Committee member.

Hugh Carmichael: South Buffalo clergyman who joined Pierzchala and others in speaking out against the Buffalo Sewer Authority's plan to dispose of a huge quantity of waste material by spreading it uniformly across Tifft Farm; member of the Citizens Advisory Committee that devised a plan that limited the disposal of waste to only a portion of the site, thereby preserving the cattail marsh and adjoining uplands.

Meghan Dye: current director of Tifft Nature Preserve, Buffalo Museum of Science.

Wayne Gall: Tifft Preserve's first administrator after it merged with the Buffalo Museum of Science in February 1983.

Zachary Goodrich: steward of Tifft Farm Preserve.

Brian Higgins: played a key role in convincing Governor Andrew Cuomo to create Buffalo Harbor State Park.

Theodore L. Hullar: Sierra Club member and University at Buffalo professor who led a delegation that presented the Tifft Advisory Committee's recommended master plan for Tifft Farm to Mayor Frank Sedita; convinced the mayor the plan was viable, thereby clearing the way for the Buffalo Common Council to approve the city's purchase of Tifft Farm from Republic Steel in 1972.

Junior League of Buffalo, Inc.: provided financial support for Lincoln Nutting's two films that documented the transformation of Tifft Farm from an industrial wasteland into a nature preserve; also provided the funding for the 1993 report *Tifft Farm: A History of Man and Nature*.

Paul MacClennan: environmental reporter for the *Buffalo News* who joined Robert Andrle in promoting the idea of establishing a nature preserve at Times Beach.

Sam Magavern: senior policy fellow, Partnership for the Public Good; author of *Buffalo's Outer Harbor: The Right Place for a World-Class Park* (August 2019).

Lincoln Nutting: naturalist, photographer, educator, and president of Buffalo Audubon Society; between 1975 and 1977; shot a 16-mm film that documented the creation of the Tifft Nature Preserve and its initial recovery from being used as a transshipment terminal and afterward as an industrial and municipal dump; produced a second film called *Through the Seasons at Tifft Nature Preserve* that focused on animal and plant life that had colonized on the recycled landscape.

Our Outer Harbor Coalition: formed in 2016 to oppose ECHDC's efforts to privately develop the Outer Harbor; other core aims included protecting the environment and fragile habitats, supporting historic preservation, enhancing opportunities for passive recreation on the Outer Harbor, and increasing climate resiliency.

Our Outer Harbor Coalition organizational members: Times Beach Nature Preserve; Pollinator Conservation Association; Western New York Environmental Alliance (WNYEA); Buffalo Niagara Waterkeeper; League of Women Voters of Buffalo Niagara; Preservation Buffalo Niagara; Sierra Club Niagara Group; Partnership for the Public Good; 21st Century Park Outer Harbor; the Public; Wellness Institute of Greater Buffalo; Trout Unlimited; Erie County Federation of Sportsmen's Clubs.

Preservation Buffalo Niagara: organizational sponsor of the 2018 report *The Buffalo Outer Harbor as a Cultural Landscape*.

Tony Pierzchala: resident of South Buffalo neighborhood and member of South Buffalo Valley Association who spearheaded community opposition to the Buffalo Sewer Authority's plan to dispose of two million cubic yards of waste material at Tifft Farm; canals carved into the site by the Lehigh Valley Railroad when it was used as a transshipment terminal were eventually reconfigured into lakes which were named after Pierzchala's daughters Kirsty, Beth, and Lisa.

Lynda H. Schneekloth: WNYEA board member; member of Our Outer Harbor Coalition Steering Committee.

Slow Roll Buffalo: nonprofit organization founded in 2014 by volunteers to promote public health and connect communities by providing inclusive free bicycle tours of different parts of Buffalo for people of all ages and skill levels; each year since it was formed has brought groups of bicyclists to the Outer Harbor, thereby enabling many of them to experience a part of Buffalo's waterfront they had previously known very little about.

David Spiering: former ecologist of Tifft Farm Preserve.

Lynda Stephens, Ellen Gibson, and Gladys Gifford: League of Women Voters Buffalo Niagara representatives on Our Outer Harbor Coalition.

Tifft Farm Citizen Advisory Committee organizational members: South Buffalo Valley Association, Buffalo Ornithological Society, Buffalo

Audubon Society, Sierra Club Niagara Group, Erie County Federation of Sportsmen's Clubs.

Kerry Traynor, Annie Shentag, and Camden Miller: authors of *The Buffalo Outer Harbor as a Cultural Landscape* (August 2018).

Margaret Wooster: WNYEA board member; Our Outer Harbor Coalition Steering Committee member; executive director of Great Lakes United, a binational (US/Canada) nongovernmental organization, 1996–2004.

Honorary Hero: *Buffalo News* Reporter Mark Sommer

To be able to play a meaningful role in shaping how Buffalo's waterfront was redeveloped and used, citizens needed to stay well informed about what was being planned and contemplated for portions of the waterfront. Mark Sommer made that possible by writing scores of waterfront-related articles that were published in the *Buffalo News* that told residents what was happening and likely to happen if local citizens didn't get involved. Over 60 of Sommer's articles are referenced in this book.

Sommer began working at the *Buffalo News* in August 1999 as the paper's Arts editor and wrote numerous articles at the time about citizen-led efforts aimed at saving old buildings in the city. "There wasn't much recognition of the importance of preserving old buildings, particularly among those who had the greatest power and deepest pockets" (Sommer, interview, April 27, 2019). In 2021–2022, Sommer would find himself once again writing articles about preservationists' efforts to prevent the demolition of the Great Northern Elevator.

Especially consequential in terms of what ended up happening at Canalside are the articles Sommer wrote about the Buffalo Maritime Center's announced intention to build a replica of the *Seneca Chief* packet boat at Canalside, and about Buffalo Heritage Carousel's efforts to bring a park-style carousel to Canalside, which produced an outpouring of public support and contributions that assured the success of both those citizen-led initiatives.

Appendix III

Interviewees

The following individuals were either interviewed in person, spoken to on the phone, or contacted and asked questions via email in connection with the research for this book. Extended back-and-forth email conversations were conducted with some of these individuals.

Roger Allen: master boatbuilder; first director of the Buffalo Maritime Center.

Chris Andrle: son of Robert F. Andrle, who helped establish the Tifft Nature Preserve and the Times Beach Nature Preserve; participated in cleanups of the Outer Harbor organized by Buffalo Niagara Riverkeeper/Waterkeeper; Buffalo Maritime volunteer; researched how packet boats that shipped goods on the Erie Canal were designed and constructed for the Buffalo Maritime Center; built the model of the *Seneca Chief* packet boat that was displayed at the entrance to the Longshed.

Richard Berger: attorney for the Preservation Coalition of Erie County in its lawsuit against ESDC; subsequently a member of the board of Campaign for Greater Buffalo Architecture and Culture.

Paula Blanchard: member of the Steering Committee that organized the July 2019 Port of Call: Buffalo tall ships event.

Thomas D. Blanchard, Jr.: former president, Horizons Waterfront Commission, 1989–1995; director of Research and Planning, Empire State Development Corporation, Western New York Region, 1995–2007.

Jay Burney: founder and chair of Friends of Times Beach Nature Preserve; WNYEA board member; Our Outer Harbor Coalition Steering Committee.

David Colligan: lawyer and voting member of ECHDC's board of directors, 2007–2017.

Thomas Dee: president of ECHDC, 2009–2018.

Greg Delaney: clinical assistant professor, School of Architecture and Planning, University at Buffalo.

Hilary Epes-Oballim: executive director, Buffalo Scholastic Rowing Association.

Donn Esmonde: reporter and commentator for the *Buffalo News*, 1982–2015.

Bruce Fisher: self-described preservationist; deputy Erie County executive, 2000–2007; Buffalo State College faculty member.

Jessie Fisher: executive director, Preservation Buffalo Niagara.

Scot Fisher: former board member of the Preservation Coalition of Erie County.

Lou Jean Fleron: emerita faculty member, Cornell at Buffalo ILR.; codirector of Partnership for the Public Good for ten years.

Peter T. Flynn: architect, Flynn Battaglia Architects.

Wayne Gall: Tifft Nature Preserve's first administrator.

Mary Beth Giancarlo: EPA manager for the cleanup of contaminated sediment of the Buffalo River conducted under the Great Lakes Legacy Act.

Zachary Goodrich: steward, Tifft Nature Preserve.

Vicki Hass: project manager, Natural Habitat Parks, Erie County Department of Environment and Planning.

Chris Hawley: senior planner, City of Buffalo Office of Strategic Planning; member of the Smart Growth Committee of the New Millennium Group that urged the City of Buffalo to adopt a new Unified Development Ordinance (the "Green Code").

Jim Heaney: worked as a reporter for the *Buffalo News* for 25 years; in 2012, founded *Investigative Post* as a nonprofit online news organization to conduct the kind of investigative reporting traditionally conducted by newspapers.

Bradshaw Hovey: research associate professor, School of Architecture and Planning, University at Buffalo.

Jill Jedlicka: hired by Friends of the Buffalo River in 2003 to administer and manage the cleanup of the Buffalo River; went on to become Buffalo Niagara Waterkeeper's executive director.

Geoff Kelly: former editor of *ArtVoice*; in 2014 launched and became editor of *The Public*; later joined Jim Heaney at *Investigative Post*.

Renata Kraft: deputy executive director, Buffalo Niagara Waterkeeper.

Philip Langdon: staff reporter/writer, the *Buffalo News*, 1973–1982.

Jeff Lebsack: Riverline director, Western New York Land Conservancy.

Sam Magavern: senior policy fellow, Partnership for Public Good (PPG); codirected PPG along with Lou Jean Fleron, 2007–2017.

Susan McCartney: president of the Preservation Coalition of Erie County for 20 years; director, Buffalo State College Small Business Development Center.

John Montague: founder of the Buffalo Maritime Center.

Margaret "Peg" Overdorf: executive director, Valley Community Association.

Steven Ranalli: professional engineer employed by ECHDC beginning in 2008; in March 2019 appointed president of ECHDC; in March 2023 named president of the Erie County Stadium Corporation—the entity overseeing the construction of the new Buffalo Bills stadium.

Jajean Rose-Burney: deputy executive director, Western New York Land Conservancy.

Lynda H. Schneekloth: emeritus professor, School of Architecture and Planning, University at Buffalo; incorporator of Friends of the Buffalo River; WNYEA board member; Our Outer Harbor Coalition Steering Committee.

Robert Shibley: dean, School of Architecture and Planning, University at Buffalo.

Josh Smith: Silo City ecologist.

Rick Smith: president of Rigidized Metals; owner of a number of the grain elevators at Silo City.

Mark Sommer: staff writer, the *Buffalo News*.

Tim Tielman: cofounded the Preservation Coalition of Erie County along with Susan McCartney and later the Campaign for Greater Buffalo History Architecture & Culture.

Richard Tobe: former Erie County director of planning; staffed the Horizons Waterfront Commission, 1997–2005.

Brian Trzeciak: director, Buffalo Maritime Center.

Michelle Urbanczyk: CEO of Explore & More Children's Museum.

Mike Vogel: employed by the *Buffalo News* 1970–2011; member of the newspaper's editorial board 1998–2006; president, Buffalo Lighthouse Association and chairman of the Steering Committee for the July 2019 Port of Call: Buffalo tall ships event.

William Jud Weiksnar O.F.M., priest, Ss. Columba-Brigid Catholic Church; member of Our Outer Harbor Coalition.

Barbara Wilks: founding principal, W-Architecture & Landscape Architecture; headed the team of designers that prepared the concept plan for the Riverline nature trail on the former DL&W rail corridor.

Margaret Wooster: executive director of Great Lakes United, 1996–2004; WNYEA board member; Our Outer Harbor Coalition Steering Committee; author of *Meander: Making Room for Rivers* (2021).

Jerry Young: architect and principal, Young + Wright Architectural; convinced his partner Shawn Wright that their firm should purchase the abandoned former Kreiner & Sons Malting Company grain elevator on Elk Street at a city auction for $5,000 in October 2015 and move their firm's offices there; the top three floors of the five-story drying house, where no floors previously existed, were redeveloped into 1,500-square-foot-apartments; other uses incorporated include a landscape architecture firm, a craft brewery, and a barber shop.

Notes

Chapter Two

1. The original incorporators of FBR were: Ken Sherman, an ordained Lutheran minister; Lynda H. Schneekloth, University at Buffalo School of Architecture and Planning faculty member; Barry Boyer, University at Buffalo Law School faculty member; Margaret Wooster, Great Lakes United; Keith Martin, lawyer; Brian Shero, Medaille College biology professor; and Dick Jeffers and David Reimers, community residents.

Chapter Three

1. Louis Fuhrmann was mayor of Buffalo between 1910 and 1917.

Chapter Four

1. Completion of the Barge Canal failed to reverse the decline in the amount of freight being shipped on the canal. Construction of the New York State Thruway in the 1950s and the increased share of freight being shipped on trucks by the 1970s sealed its fate. By the 1990s, the canal was primarily used for private recreation. In 1992, the New York State Canal System was transferred to the New York State Thruway Authority, which became responsible for maintaining 524 miles of canals, 57 locks, and 17 lift bridges. On January 1, 2017, operation of the New York Canal System became the responsibility of the New York Power Authority.

2. The 400 low-income families who still lived at Dante Place attempted to fight the conversion. However, the New York State Supreme Court ruled in October 1960 that the conversion was not in violation of New York Public Housing Law.

Chapter Five

1. Federal funding came with strings attached—namely that the planning process had to be conducted to assure a maximum amount of citizen participation.

2. In addition to operating the city's bus system, NFTA functioned as Buffalo's Port Authority.

3. The principals of the Caucus Partnership were Robert Shibley and Lynda Schneekloth.

4. James Griffin was mayor of Buffalo from 1978 to 1993.

5. The New York State Urban Development Corporation was created in 1968 by the state legislature to carry out major housing and economic development projects.

6. Nowak represented Western New York congressional districts from 1975 to 1992.

7. Joseph E. Goodell, president and chief executive of Buffalo-based American Brass Company, replaced Edward Cosgrove as chairman of the Horizons Commission in January 1992.

8. Memorial Auditorium was the premier venue for large-scale events of all kinds beginning in 1940 and was the home of the NHL Buffalo Sabres between 1970 and 1996.

9. After the Horizons Commission was dissolved in 1995, Thomas Blanchard, who had served as president of the Horizons Commission, was transferred to the Western New York regional office of Empire State Development Corporation.

Chapter Six

1. Warren Barbour was a professor of anthropology at the University at Buffalo.

2. What Deputy County Executive Bruce Fisher told Tielman in 2000 about ESDC not having enough money to construct the docks and slips into the shoreline was probably true at the time, because that was well before Congressman Brian Higgins negotiated the agreement with New York Power Authority in 2005 that provided the state waterfront agency with millions of dollars with which to redevelop Canalside.

Chapter Seven

1. In 2003, the Buffalo Sabres NHL franchise was sold to a consortium headed by Tom Golisano, the founder/owner of Paychex, Inc.

2. *The Buffalo News* benefited from a long period of stable ownership. After being locally owned and operated by the Butler family for decades, the newspaper was purchased in 1977 by Warren Buffet's Berkshire Hathaway Co., which operated it quite profitably for the next 43 years. In January 2020, the newspaper was sold to Lee Enterprises, an Iowa-based company that owned a chain of 50 newspapers, most of which were in the Midwest.

Chapter Eight

1. Julie Barrett O'Neill was appointed to ECHDC's board of directors in November 2011 but resigned a few months later in March 2012 when she was hired as general counsel and Green Program director for the Buffalo Sewer Authority. She subsequently served as executive director for Local Initiatives Support Corporation and in May 2022 was named by NYSDEC as regional director for Region 9, which includes Allegany, Cattaraugus, Chautauqua, Erie, Niagara, and Wyoming counties.

2. Artist Casey Riordan Millard's creation of the Shark-Girl statue was funded by a $6,000 grant through Cincinnati's Arts Ambassador Fellowship program.

3. Ric Hilliman died of complications from pneumonia in March 2020. Buffalo Sailing Adventures continues to operate the *Spirit of Buffalo* and *Queen City Bike Ferry* as before, under the direction of his wife Kathy and son Richard J. Hilliman II.

Chapter Nine

1. The music of the Heritage Carousel's band organ is generated by paper rolls similar to those of a player piano.

2. The model of the *Seneca Chief* packet boat that was displayed at the Longshed was built by BMC volunteer Chris Andrle, the son of Robert F. Andrle, whose role in helping establish the Tifft Farm and Times Beach Nature Preserves is described in chapter 12.

Chapter Eleven

1. The Lake Erie-Niagara River Ice Boom is strung across the mouth of the Niagara River during the winter to protect against ice jams further downriver.

2. The *Canadiana* began operating between downtown Buffalo and Crystal Beach, Ontario, in 1910. The *Canadiana's* final trip between Buffalo and Crystal Beach was on Labor Day 1956.

Chapter Twelve

1. See chapter 1 for earlier history of Tifft Farm.

2. A study conducted for the NY State Department of Environmental Conservation reported that the drums discovered in 1975 and excavated from Lake Kristy, Lisa Pond, and the east side of the mounded area at Tifft Farm likely contained acid sludge from the Chevrolet plant in Buffalo.

Chapter Thirteen

1. ECHDC agreed to pay NYPA $1.00 for the property. Prior to transferring the First Buffalo Marina to ECHDC, NYPA had installed a new roof on the Connecting Terminal elevator, stabilized the structure, and removed asbestos and other hazardous materials from the structure.

2. A seiche is a change in the water level of a lake caused by a rapid change in atmospheric pressure and strong onshore winds. The huge waves often caused by a seiche can overtop shorelines and any structures therein.

3. Construction of the first course for mountain bikes on the Outer Harbor was approved by ECHDC in November 2015 and completed by 2017.

Chapter Fourteen

1. The University at Buffalo is the largest institution of higher education in the 64-campus State University of New York system, with a total student enrollment of approximately 32,000.

2. In *Making Places Special: Stories of Real Places Made Better by Planning* (2002), I described waterfront transformations brought about in Chattanooga, Tennessee, Providence, Rhode Island, and Duluth, Minnesota. In *Transforming Providence: Rebirth of a Post-Industrial City* (2017), I provided an updated and more comprehensive account of changes brought about along Providence's waterfront.

References

Andrle, Robert F. 1973. "Times Beach: Buffalo's Harbor for Wildlife." *Science on the March* 55 (4): 48–50.

Andrle, Robert F. 1976. "Tifft Farm Nature Preserve." *Science on the March* 53 (3): 38–40.

Archibold, Randal C. 2002. "Company's Ills Further Deflate Buffalo's Hopes" *New York Times*, June 17, 2002.

Ashby, Donna. 2000. "A Place with a Story to Tell: Experts, Public Call for Doing the Real Canal Thing." *ArtVoice*, September 28, 2000.

Becker, Maki. 2022. "Judge Denies Restraining Order to Stop Demolition of the Great Northern Grain Elevator." *Buffalo News*, September 17, 2022.

Besecker, Aaron. 2017. "Skating Opens for Season at Icc at Canalside." *Buffalo News*, November 24, 2017.

Besecker, Aaron, 2019. "Tall Ships Headed to Buffalo Comes with a Dose of History" *Buffalo News*, July 2, 2019, A1.

Besecker, Aaron, and Stephen T. Watson. 2019. "Fleet of Tall Ships Parade into Buffalo Harbor as Holiday Revelers Flock to Revived Waterfront." *Buffalo News*, July 5, 2019, A1, A6.

Bohen, Timothy. 2012. *Against the Grain: The History of Buffalo's First Ward.* Buffalo, NY: Bohane Books.

Brown, Richard C., and Bob Watson. 1981. *Buffalo Lake City in Niagara Land.* Buffalo, NY: Buffalo and Erie County Historical Society.

Brown, William J. 2015. *American Colossus: The Grain Elevator, 1843 to 1942.* Brooklyn, NY: Colossus Books.

Buffalo News editorial. 2000. "Inner Harbor, A Canal Conversation," September 14, 2000.

Buffalo News editorial. 2010. "Lighter, Quicker, Cheaper." *Buffalo News*, November 11, 2010.

Buffalo News editorial. 2017a. "Waterfront Has Undergone Remarkable Evolution." *Buffalo News*, November 30, 2017.

Buffalo News editorial. 2017b. "Jemal Moves to Rescue One Seneca Tower and to Preserve the City's Revival." *Buffalo News*, January 30, 2017.

Buffalo News editorial. 2018a. "Build the Boat," *Buffalo News*, June 9, 2018.

Buffalo News editorial. 2018b. "Canalside Thrives." *Buffalo News*, August 23, 2018, A10.

Buffalo News editorial. 2022a. "The Emergency That Isn't." *Buffalo News*, May 9, 2022, A8.

Buffalo News editorial. 2022b. "Great Northern in Peril." *Buffalo News*, September 14, 2022.

Buffalo News editorial. 2022c. "It Didn't Need to Happen." *Buffalo News*, September 20, 2022.

Buffalo News staff. 2004. "Luring Bass Pro . . . State Casts Its Offer and Gets Down to Some Serious Fishing." *Buffalo News*, April 20, 2004.

Buffalo News staff. 2014. "Winter Hot Spot—Exciting New Ice Rink Turning Canalside into a True Year-Round Destination," *Buffalo News*, December 28, 2014.

Buffalo News staff. 2015. "1885 Street Map Sparked the Idea to Re-Create History at Canalside." *Buffalo News*, January 3, 2015.

Buffalo Niagara Riverkeeper. 2006. "Buffalo River Greenway: Vision & Implementation Plan," prepared for Riverkeeper by Lynn Mason, ASLA, assisted by Julie Barrett O'Neill, Jill Spisiak Jedlicka and Lynda Schneekloth.

Buffalo Rising. 2010. "Lighter, Quicker, Cheaper!" November 6, 2010.

Buffalo Rising. 2011. "Peg's Park Will Soon Be Our Park." May 9, 2011.

Buffalo Rising. 2013. "New Outer Harbor Park, Wilkeson Pointe, Now Open." June 1, 2013.

Buffalo Rising. 2015. "Planning the Future of the Outer Harbor." September 16, 2015.

Buffalo Rising. 2016. "Public Forum: Habitat Restoration on the Buffalo River." June 9, 2016.

Buffalo Rising. 2017a. "Red Jacket—Connecting Key Parks along the Waterfront," July 9, 2017.

Buffalo Rising. 2017b. "A Closer Look at Red Jacket Park," October 12, 2017.

Buffalo Rising. 2018. "ECHDC Seeks Public Input for Three Projects Focusing on the Improvement of Access And Activation of Outer Harbor," July 6, 2018.

Buffalo Rising. 2019. "The Biggest Celebration in the History of the Buffalo Waterfront Sails in This Summer, April 19, 2019.

Buffalo Rising. 2021. "Redevelopment of Barcalo Factory on Louisiana Street," January 5, 2021.

Buffalo Rising. 2022. "UPDATE: TOO LATE!!! Demolition Commences, Preservation Efforts Thwarted," September 16, 2022.

Burney, Jay. 2019. "Another Voice: Climate Change Demands We Preserve Outer Harbor." *Buffalo News*, November 23, 2019.

Cichon, Steve. 2015. "Dante Place Public Housing Becomes Marine Drive Apartments." *Buffalo News*, June 22, 2015.

Cichon, Steve. 2019. "Torn-Down Tuesday: Buffalo's Biggest Landowners, 1965." *Buffalo News*, October 22, 2019.

Ciotta, Rose. 1986. "Attractions Projected for Waterfront Called Lure to Falls Tourists." *Buffalo News*, April 30, 1986.

Ciotta, Rose. 1987. "Griffin Has No Taste for Pie in the Sky." *Buffalo News*, July 12, 1987, A1.

Collison, Kevin 1998. "Poised for Private Funds." *Buffalo News*, October 31, 1998, A1, A6.

Collison, Kevin. 1999a. "Ceremony Will Launch Inner Harbor project." *Buffalo News*, September 17, 1999, B1, B13.

Collison, Kevin. 1999b. "Preservationists Take Inner Harbor Plan to Court." *Buffalo News*, October 7, 1999, B1, B4.

Collison, Kevin. 2000a. "Commercial Slip Find Hailed as 'Holy Grail.'" *Buffalo News*, May 11, 2000, B1.

Collison, Kevin. 2000b. "The Hard Facts: The Stone Walls of the Old Erie Canal Terminus Are More Durable Than a Consultant's Report Says." *Buffalo News*, June 3, 2000, A1, A4.

Collison, Kevin. 2000c. "Inner Harbor Project OK'd." *Buffalo News*, October 26, 2000, A1, A11.

Collison, Kevin. 2000d. "New Life Will Flow Into Old Canal Slip." *Buffalo News*, October 27, 2000.

Conlin, John H. 2002. "The Famous Central Wharf of the Buffalo Waterfront, Part I." *Western New York Heritage* 5 (2): 20–31.

Conlin, John H. 2008. "Old Photo Album: A Forgotten Atlantis." *Western New York Heritage* 11 (1): 28–35.

Conlin, John H. 2016. "The Famous Central Wharf of the Buffalo Waterfront: Part II." *Western New York Heritage*, April 5, 2016. https://www.wnyheritage.org/content/the_famous_central_wharf_of_the_buffalo_waterfront_part_ii/index.html.

Dabkowski, Colin. 2018a. "Silo City to Host Site-Specific Performance 'In the Dark.'" *Buffalo News*, April 10, 2018.

Dabkowski, Colin. 2018b. "Experimental Artists Find an Intriguing Canvas in the Post-Industrial Complex." *Buffalo News*, June 10, 2018, D1.

Davis, Henry L., and Sharon Linstedt. 2005. "Bass Pro Agreement Is Described as 'a Work in Progress.'" *Buffalo News*, March 7, 2005.

Davis, Henry L., and Sharon Linstedt. 2006a. "Aud to Be Razed for Bass Pro Store." *Buffalo News*, September 3, 2006.

Davis, Henry L., and Sharon Linstedt. 2006b. "Bass Pro Gets 30 Days to Make a Deal: Ultimatum Comes as $200 Million Plan Is Unveiled for Waterfront Development." *Buffalo News*, December 18, 2006.

DeCroix, Douglas W. 2021. "Full Circle: The Amazing Journey of the Buffalo Heritage Carousel." *Western New York Heritage* 24 (2): 26–37.

DeCroix, Douglas W. 2022. "Buffalo's Great Northern Elevator-Beginnings." *Western New York Heritage* 25 (1): 24–27.

Dewey, Caitlan. 2019. "How Once Desolate Canalside Turned into Buffalo's Pride: Canalside Transformed into Hub For Events That Draw Thousands." *Buffalo News*, July 4, 2019, A1.

Eberle, Scott, and Joseph A. Grande. 1987. *Second Looks: A Pictorial History of Buffalo and Erie County*. Norfolk, VA: The Donning Company.

Egan, Dan. 2017. *Death and Life of the Great Lakes*. New York: W. W. Norton & Co.

Epstein, Jonathan D. 2013. "Erie Canal Harbor Site Work Modified." *Buffalo News*, November 13, 2013.

Epstein, Jonathan D. 2015. "$200 Million Later, Harborcenter Is Among City's Biggest Projects." *Buffalo News*, September 20, 2015.

Epstein, Jonathan D. 2018. "Defining One Seneca's New Character Builds upon Familiar Artistic Symbol." *Buffalo News*, June 1, 2018, B1.

Epstein, Jonathan D. 2019. "Silos at Elk Street Opens." *Buffalo News*, May 7, 2019, C3.

Epstein, Jonathan D. 2020a. "Queen City Landing Builder Planning to Develop Rest of Outer Harbor Peninsula." *Buffalo News*, February 19, 2020, B1, B2.

Epstein, Jonathan D. 2020b. "Barcalo Redevelopment Ready to Start with $1 Million in Tax Breaks." *Buffalo News*, February 27, 2020.

Epstein, Jonathan D., 2020c. "Work Begins on Project to Bring Historic Silo City Site Back to Life." *Buffalo News*, November 18, 2020, B4.

Epstein, Jonathan D. 2022a. "After Repeated Delays, Sinatra Starts Work on Heritage Point Apartments." *Buffalo News*, March 15, 2022, B1.

Epstein, Jonathan D. 2022b. "Barcalo Living & Commerce Taking Shape in Old First Ward." *Buffalo News*, May 27, 2022.

Epstein, Jonathan D. 2023a. "BMHA Plans to Tear Down and Replace Marine Drive Apartments Towers." *Buffalo News*, February 10, 2023 (updated July 3, 2023).

Epstein, Jonathan D. 2023b. "Construction to Begin on Ralph Wilson Park in June, Officials Say," *Buffalo News*, April 27, 2023.

Esmonde, Donn. 1999a. "Burying City's Past Is Not the Way to Build Its Future." *Buffalo News*, August 17, 1999.

Esmonde, Donn. 1999b. "Groundbreakers Ignore History at Inner Harbor." *Buffalo News*, September 21, 1999.

Esmonde, Donn. 1999c. "Reburying History of Inner Harbor Makes No Sense." *Buffalo News*, November 22, 1999.

Esmonde, Donn. 2000a. "Court Testimony Argues We Need to Do Canal Right." *Buffalo News*, March 13, 2000.

Esmonde, Donn. 2000b. "Judge Gives City Another Chance to Salvage Canal." *Buffalo News*, April 6, 2000, C1.

Esmonde, Donn. 2000c. "State's Arrogance Evident at Hearing on Harbor Plan." *Buffalo News*, May 26, 2000.

Esmonde, Donn. 2000d. "State's Big Lie on Canal Shows Aim to Kill History." *Buffalo News*, July 5, 2000.

Esmonde, Donn. 2000e. "It's a No-Brainer: The Erie Canal Site Is a Piece of History and Must Be Preserved." *Buffalo News*, June 11, 2000, H1.

Esmonde, Donn. 2000f. "Positive Signs but Real Canal Is Still in Dispute." *Buffalo News*, June 16, 2000.

Esmonde, Donn. 2000g. "For Many Slaves, Inner Harbor Was Step to Freedom." *Buffalo News*, September 4, 2000, B1.

Esmonde, Donn. 2000h. "Take the Time to Do the Canal Right, Experts Say." *Buffalo News*, September 13, 2000.

Esmonde, Donn. 2000i. "County's Study on Canal Says: Just Do It!," *Buffalo News*, October 2, 2000.

Esmonde, Donn. 2000j. "From the Brink of Disaster, Canal Is Born." *Buffalo News*, October 27, 2000, B1.

Esmonde, Donn. 2000k. "Unsung Heroes Saved a Piece of Our History." *Buffalo News*, October 28, 2000.

Esmonde, Donn. 2007a. "History Says 'No' to Hosting a Bass Pro." *Buffalo News*, March 2, 2007, B1.

Esmonde, Donn. 2007b. "Bass Pro Plan Puts History in Back Seat." *Buffalo News*, April 1, 2007, C1.

Esmonde, Donn. 2007c. "No Reason to Bait Hook for Bass Pro." *Buffalo News*, April 15, 2007.

Esmonde, Donn. 2007d. "Waterfront Board Needs New Mind-set." *Buffalo News*, June 1, 2007, D1.

Esmonde, Donn. 2008a. "'Wow' Factor Proves We Did History Right." *Buffalo News*, June 4, 2008.

Esmonde, Donn. 2008b. "2nd Chance for Us to Get History Right." *Buffalo News*, October 17, 2008, D1.

Esmonde, Donn. 2009. "Questioning Bass Pro Isn't Anti-Buffalo." *Buffalo News*, October 21, 2009, B1.

Esmonde, Donn. 2010a. "Do Business without Using Power Brokers." *Buffalo News*, August, 1, 2010.

Esmonde, Donn. 2010b. "Time for Shift to Reality at Canal Side." *Buffalo News*, August 22, 2010.

Esmonde, Donn. 2010c. "Bass Pro's Ghost Still Haunting Us." *Buffalo News*, November 14, 2010, C1.

Esmonde, Donn. 2010d. "We Have Time to Get It Right on Waterfront." *Buffalo News*, November 17, 2010.

Esmonde, Donn. 2010e. "Downsizing to Saner Plan for Waterfront." *Buffalo News*, December 5, 2010.

Esmonde, Donn. 2011a. "Quinn's Exit Didn't Come Soon Enough." *Buffalo News*, February 13, 2011, C1.

Esmonde, Donn. 2011b. "It Is Now the People's Waterfront." *Buffalo News*, March 16, 2011.

Esmonde, Donn. 2011c. "Giving Public What It Wants on Waterfront." *Buffalo News*, July 13, 2011, B1.

Esmonde, Donn. 2011d. "We Have Two to Thank for Preservation." *Buffalo News*, October 21, 2011, D1.

Esmonde, Donn. 2012. "Turnaround of Levy Serves as a Model." *Buffalo News*, March 2, 2012.

Esmonde, Donn. 2013a. "Dedication to Preservation Has Spurred Buffalo's Revival." *Buffalo News*, October 5, 2013.

Esmonde, Donn. 2013b. "We Finally Found Our Resurgence Hiding in Plain Sight." *Buffalo News*, November 30, 2013.

Esmonde, Donn. 2015. "Catalyst of Canalside Basks in the Glow of Its Progress." *Buffalo News*, June 19, 2015.

Esmonde, Donn. 2016. "Demise of Bass Pro Was Turning Point for 'New Buffalo.'" *Buffalo News*, July 16, 2016

Federal Transit Administration. 2000. Draft Supplemental Environmental Impact Statement, Buffalo Inner Harbor Development Project, May 10, 2000.

Federal Transit Administration. 2004. Supplemental Final Environmental Impact Statement, Erie Canal Harbor Project, December 2004.

Fink, James. 2014. "ECHDC Hires Perkins+Will for Outer Harbor Work." *Buffalo Business First*, May 12, 2014.

Fink, James. 2016. "Ithaca Firm to Design Outer Harbor Blueprint." *Buffalo Business First*, September 12, 2016.

Flynn Battaglia Architects. 2004. "Erie Canal Harbor Project Master Plan," November 2004.

Gall, Wayne. 1990. "Breaking the Barriers: Restoration of an Urban Green Space." In *Ecologically Sound Approaches to Urban Space*, edited by D. Gordon, 169–176. Montreal, Quebec: Black Rose Books.

Gall, Wayne. 2014. "A Memorial Tribute to Lincoln P. Nutting, 1922–2014." (unpublished).

Goldman, Mark. 1983. *High Hopes: The Rise and Decline of Buffalo, New York*. Albany: State University of New York Press.

Goldman, Mark. 1990. *City on the Lake*. Amherst, NY: Prometheus Books.

Goldman, Mark. 2007. *City on the Edge*. Amherst, NY: Prometheus Books.

Goldman, Mark. 2021. *City of My Heart*. Buffalo, NY: Friends of the Buffalo Story.

Graebner, William. 2007. "A Cultural Biography of the Buffalo Skyway (1955)." *American Studies* 48 (1): 77–100.

Heaney, Jim. 2012. "Big Projects, Small Returns." *Buffalo News*, March 17, 2012.

Heaney, Jim. 2014. "The Buffalo News Is Hemorrhaging Journalists." *Investigative Post*, February 5, 2023.

Higgins, Brian. 1990. "From Rust Belt to Greenbelt," 1990 Report to Buffalo Common Council (unpublished).

Horizons Waterfront Commission. "Action Plan for the Erie County Waterfront," January 1992.

Hovey, Bradshaw. 1991. "Taken in Again—Citizen Participation in the Buffalo Waterfront Plan 1982–1987." Master of urban planning thesis, State University of New York at Buffalo (unpublished).

Howe, Nicholas. 2003. *Across an Inland Sea: Writing in Place from Buffalo to Berlin.* Princeton, NJ: Princeton University Press.

Hughes, C. J. 2022. "Buffalo's 'Other Story' Is Told in Redevelopment and Growth." *New York Times*, July 3, 2022.

Keppel, Angela. 2014a. "Canal Street—The Wickedest Street in the World." *Discovering Buffalo, One Street at a Time.* buffalostreets.com/2014/03/31/canal part1.

Keppel, Angela. 2014b. "Canal District Part 3—Marine Drive-Public Housing and Canalside." *Discovering Buffalo, One Street at a Time.* buffalostreets.com/tab/dante-place.

Keppel, Angela. 2023. "Fuhrmann Blvd—Settle a 50 Year Old Lawsuit, Get a Street Named after You." *Discovering Buffalo, One Street at a Time.* buffalostreets.com/2023/09/04/fuhrmann/.

LaKamp, Patrick. 1999. "Mayor Unveils Latest Plan for Waterfront Project." *Buffalo News*, October 15, 1999, C1, C4.

LaKamp, Patrick, and Mark Sommer. 2022. "Preservationists Race to Halt Razing of ADM Elevator." *Buffalo News*, September 17, 2022, A1, A7.

Leary, Thomas F., Elizabeth C. Sholes, and the Buffalo and Erie County Historical Society. 1997. *Buffalo's Waterfront.* Charleston SC: Acadia Publishing.

Kowsky, Francis R. 2006. "Monuments of a Vanished Prosperity: Buffalo's Grain Elevators and the Rise and Fall of the Great Transnational System of Grain Transport." In *Reconsidering Concrete Atlantis: Buffalo Grain Elevators*, edited by Lynda H. Schneekloth, 18–44. Buffalo, NY: University at Buffalo School of Architecture and Planning Urban Design Project.

Langdon, Philip. 1980. "Bank Plaza at a Loss." *Buffalo Evening News*, November 17, 1980.

Langdon. Philip. 1981a. "A City without Plans." *Buffalo Evening News*, March 23, 1981.

Langdon, Philip. 1981b. "Good Progress in Preservation—And Plenty More to Be Done." *Buffalo Evening News*, May 11, 1981.

Licata, Elizabeth. 2021. *Secret Buffalo: A Guide to the Weird, Wonderful and Obscure.* St. Louis, MO: Reedy Press.

Linstedt, Sharon. 1988. "Signatures on Agreement Launch Horizons Waterfront Commission." *Buffalo News*, September 23, 1988, B1.

Linstedt, Sharon. 2002. "Aud May Be Reborn as Sport-Store Complex." *Buffalo News*, June 12, 2002.

Linstedt, Sharon. 2007a. "Bass Pro Landed—At Last: Central Wharf Site Will Be the Location of Multilevel Store." *Buffalo News*, March 30, 2007, A1, A2.

Linstedt, Sharon. 2007b."Bass Pro Plan Shifts Back to Aud Site." *Buffalo News*, September 7, 2007, A1, A2.

Linstedt, Sharon. 2008. " 'Lake & Rail' Grain Elevator Purchased by Minnesota Firm." *Buffalo News*, June 13, 2008, D4, D7.

Lord Cultural Resources, Ralph Appelbaum Associates & Robert Coles Architect. 2010. "Buffalo Canal Side Cultural Master Plan."

McKinley, Jesse. 2022. "Fighting to Preserve Towering Testament to Buffalo's History." *New York Times*, January 23, 2022, 22.

McNeil, Harold, Sharon Linstedt, and Margaret Hammersley. 2004. "State Offers $80 Million to Attract Bass Pro to City." *Buffalo News*, April 23, 2004.

Magavern, Sam. 2019. "Buffalo's Outer Harbor: The Right Place for a World-Class Park." *Partnership for the Public Good*, August 2019. ppgbuffalo.org/files/documents/environment/buffalos_outer_harbor_the_right_place_for_a_world-class_park.pdf.

Montague, John. 2018. "Erie Canal Bicentennial Offers New Opportunities." *Buffalo News*, May 29, 2018.

Mroziak, Michael. 2019. WBFO *Takeaway*. "Jemal Buying Former Buffalo Police HQ, Loaning Money to Get Main Street Work Moving," February 15, 2019.

Neville, Anne. 2017. "Recalling a Buffalo Disaster; 1959 Tewksbury Freighter Crash." *Buffalo News*, January 24, 2017.

Norton, Schuyler. 2017. "Making Waves: The Buffalo Maritime Center." *Buffalo Rising*, February 7, 2017.

Nussbaumer, Newell. 2010. "Bass Pro to Buffalo: Good Luck." *Buffalo Rising*, July 10, 2010.

Nussbaumer, Newell. 2014a. "Ohio Street and Inner Harbor Infrastructure Improvement Project." *Buffalo Rising*, April 2, 2014.

Nussbaumer, Newell. 2014b. "Riverkeeper Offers Alternative Vision for Buffalo's Outer Harbor." *Buffalo Rising*, September 17, 2014.

Nussbaumer, Newell. 2015. "The Future of LaSalle Park: Bring a Real Park Planner into This Conversation." *Buffalo Rising*, July 1, 2015.

Nussbaumer, Newell. 2016. "A Visit to Tewksbury Lodge." *Buffalo Rising*, July 18, 2016.

Nussbaumer, Newell. 2017. "Ohio Street Habitat Restoration Project Will Bring Pollinator Garden and Amenities to NYSDEC Boat Launch." *Buffalo Rising*, October 17, 2017.

NYS Governor's Office Press Release. 2018. "Governor Cuomo Announces $24 Million Investment to Support Three New Projects as Part of Buffalo's Waterfront Transformation." August 14, 2018.

O'Connell, Francis J., 1972. "A Blow to Buffalo's Milling Prestige." *Buffalo Courier-Express Magazine*, March 12, 1972, 4–5.

Palen, Frank S., 1983. "City Planning in Buffalo, New York: A History of Institutions." School of Law, State University of New York at Buffalo, November 1983 (unpublished).

Pignataro, T. J. 2018a. "At Outer Harbor, Visions of an 'Ecological Playground.'" *Buffalo News*, February 24, 2018, A1.

Pignataro, T. J., 2018b. "Decades Later, Buffalo River Habitat Restoration Is Complete." *Buffalo News*, July 30, 2018.

Pignataro, T. J., 2019a. "From Scrap Metal Art to Sledding Hills, 20 Designs for Buffalo's High Line Park." *Buffalo News*, April 8, 2019.

Pignataro, T. J., 2019b. "Winning Designs: Jury, Community Picks for Linear Park along Old Rail Corridor." *Buffalo News*, June 14, 2019.

The Public. 2015a. "Looking Backward: Port of Buffalo, 1939." January 28, 2015.

The Public. 2015b. "Looking Backward: Hanna Furnace," February 24, 2015. dailypublic.com/articles/02242015/looking-backward-hanna-furnace.

The Public. 2015c. "Looking Backward: Ford Motor Co., Fuhrmann Assembly Plant," August 4, 2015. www.dailypublic.com/articles/08042015/looking-backward-ford-motor-co-fuhrmann-assembly-plant.

The Public. 2015d. "Looking Backward: Buffalo River 1918," December 16, 2015.

Quinn, Larry. 2007. "Waterfront Plan Offers Tremendous Opportunity." *Buffalo News*, April 22, 2007.

Ray, J., 2010. "Don't Box in Waterfront, Forum Told." *Buffalo News*, November 7, 2010.

Schneekloth, L. H., ed. 2006a. *Reconsidering Concrete Atlantis: Buffalo Grain Elevators*. Buffalo, NY: University at Buffalo School of Architecture and Planning Urban Design Project.

Schneekloth, L. H. 2006b. "Unruly and Robust: An Abandoned Industrial River." In *Loose Space: Possibility and Diversity in Urban Life,* edited by K. A. Frank and Q. Stevens, 253–269. New York: Routledge.

Shibley, R., and B. Hovey, eds. 2001. "A Canal Conversation: A Community Forum on Buffalo's Inner Harbor Development and the Erie Canal." Urban Design Project, School of Architecture and Planning, University at Buffalo, State University of New York.

Sommer, Mark. 2002. "A Grain of Respect." *Buffalo News*, December 7, 2002, A1.

Sommer, Mark. 2005. "Senecas to Raze Historic H-O Oats Grain Elevator as Part of Casino Project." *Buffalo News*, December 5, 2005.

Sommer, Mark. 2010. "Re-creating Erie Canal Wins OK." *Buffalo News*, November 30, 2010.

Sommer, Mark. 2011. "Revelations of Grain Elevators." *Buffalo News*, October 21, 2011.

Sommer, Mark. 2013. "Canalside Carousel Called a Perfect Fit as Waterfront Attraction." *Buffalo News*, August 30, 2013.

Sommer, Mark. 2014. "Grain Elevator Will Provide Canvas for Waterfront Light Show." *Buffalo News*, August 12, 2014.

Sommer, Mark. 2016a. "Waterfront Agency Buys 14 Acres on Outer Harbor." *Buffalo News*, September 12, 2016.

Sommer, Mark. 2016b. "Canalside Envisioned as a Place to Work, Play—and Live." *Buffalo News*, December 16, 2016.

Sommer, Mark. 2016c. "Buffalo's Zoning Code Steps into the 21st Century." *Buffalo News*, December 27, 2016.

Sommer, Mark. 2017a. "Mayor Signs Buffalo's Green Code into Law." *Buffalo News*, January 3, 2017.

Sommer, Mark. 2017b. "Resignation May Cripple Harbor Board, Already Plagued by Absences." *Buffalo News*, January 22, 2017.

Sommer, Mark. 2017c. "A Neighborhood, Not Open Space, in Canalside's Future." *Buffalo News*, May 23, 2017.

Sommer, Mark. 2017d. "Backers Want Historic Grain Elevators Turned into National Park." *Buffalo News*, May 15, 2017.

Sommer, Mark. 2017e. "What to Do with Port Terminal A Is a Multi-Million Dollar Question." *Buffalo News*, October 9, 2017.

Sommer, Mark. 2018a. "2017 Outstanding Citizen: Tim Tielman, Force in Buffalo Preservation." *Buffalo News*, April 7, 2018.

Sommer, Mark. 2018b. "A Maritime Mission." *Buffalo News*, May 17, 2018, D1.

Sommer, Mark. 2018c. "After 30 Years of Abandonment, Grain Elevator Getting New Life as Offices." *Buffalo News*, June 20, 2018.

Sommer, Mark. 2018d. "Two New Buildings Expected to Spur Canalside Neighborhood." *Buffalo News*, August 8, 2018, A1.

Sommer, Mark. 2018e. "$24 Million from State to Boost Buffalo Waterfront's Build-Out: Effort to Restore Original Fabric of the Neighborhood." *Buffalo News*, August 15, 2018, A1.

Sommer, Mark. 2018f. " 'Sort of a Boat Guy': Life Storage CEO to Foot the Bill for Packet Boat at Canalside." *Buffalo News*, August 25, 2018.

Sommer, Mark. 2018g. "Canalside Carousel Called a Perfect Fit as Waterfront Attraction." *Buffalo News*, August 30, 2018.

Sommer, Mark. 2018h. "Canalside Carousel Menagerie One Step Closer to Final Home." *Buffalo News*, September 25, 2018, B1.

Sommer, Mark. 2018i. "Ralph Wilson's Biggest Gift Year: $100M to Transform LaSalle Park Trails." *Buffalo News*, October 17, 2018.

Sommer, Mark. 2018j. "Sky-High Views among Ideas Pitched for Light-Show Grain Elevator." *Buffalo News*, December 11, 2018.

Sommer, Mark. 2019a. "Plans for Outer Harbor Bridge May Be Tied to Skyway's Future: Opportunity Seen to Dismantle Skyway." *Buffalo News*, February 2, 2019.

Sommer, Mark. 2019b. "$125 Million Master Plan for Outer Harbor Is Unveiled: In Contrast to Canalside, Outer Harbor Seen as Passive Recreation Area." *Buffalo News*, May 2, 2019, A1.

Sommer, Mark. 2019c. "Getting First Peek Inside Explore and More." *Buffalo News*, May 3, 2019, A1.

Sommer, Mark. 2019d. "Ambitious Plan Would Elevate Character of LaSalle Park: A Community-Driven Process in Many Ways." *Buffalo News*, May 4, 2019, A1.

Sommer, Mark. 2019e. "Period Building for Packet Boat Projects at Maritime Center Wins Agency's Approval." *Buffalo News*, May 15, 2019, B1–B2.

Sommer, Mark. 2019f. "Public Offers Feedback on 3 Options for Revitalizing North Aud Block; Taller Buildings Block Noise, Allow More Housing." *Buffalo News*, August 3, 2019, C1.

Sommer, Mark. 2019g. "Construction of Long-Awaited Longshed Underway at Canalside." *Buffalo News*, August 13, 2019, A1.

Sommer, Mark. 2019h. "Proposed LaSalle Park Playland 'Beyond Anything We Have Seen': Kids, Parents Wowed by Waterfront Plan." *Buffalo News*, October 1, 2019, A1.

Sommer, Mark. 2019i. " 'The Riverline' Brings New Identity, Momentum to DL&W Corridor Project." *Buffalo News*, November 20, 2019.

Sommer, Mark. 2020a. "Longshed at Canalside Is Complete, Making Way for Packet Boat Replica." *Buffalo News*, October 16, 2020, B1.

Sommer, Mark. 2020b. "Outer Harbor Master Plan Includes Amphitheater." *Buffalo News*, November 11, 2020, B1–B2.

Sommer, Mark. 2021a. "Outer Harbor Habitat Plan Is Designed to Bring Fish Back." *Buffalo News*, March 21, 2021, B1.

Sommer, Mark. 2021b. "Design of the Riverline Nears Completion." *Buffalo News*, April 28, 2021.

Sommer, Mark. 2021c. "After 63 years in Storage, a New Era Begins for Amusement Ride Made in 1924." *Buffalo News*, May 29, 2021, A1.

Sommer, Mark. 2021d. " 'Water Will Define Our Future': Buffalo Blueway Is Showing How." *Buffalo News*, June 12, 2021, A1, A3.

Sommer, Mark. 2021e. "Canalside Concerts Headed for Outer Harbor Pavilion." *Buffalo News*, June 23, 2021, B1.

Sommer, Mark. 2021f. "Lawsuit Filed to Stop Music Pavilion Planned at Outer Harbor." *Buffalo News*, June 28, 2021, B3.

Sommer, Mark. 2021g. "Grant Will Allow Explore & More to Fill Jobs, Extend Operating Days." *Buffalo News*, June 29, 2021, B1.

Sommer, Mark. 2021h. "Nature as Refuge: Final Design for the Riverline Is Unveiled." *Buffalo News*, July 19, 2021.

Sommer, Mark. 2021i. "Funds Approved for Music Pavilion on Outer Harbor." *Buffalo News*, October 12, 2021.

Sommer, Mark. 2021j. Wilson Foundation to Donate $100 Million to Boost Arts, Cultural Institutions." *Buffalo News*, December 2, 2021, A1.

Sommer, Mark. 2021k. "Judge Rejects Amphitheater Challenge on Outer Harbor." *Buffalo News*, December 10, 2021.

Sommer, Mark. 2021l. "Great Northern Grain Elevator Damaged by Buffalo Windstorm." *Buffalo News*, December 11, 2021

Sommer, Mark. 2021m. "Outer Harbor Site Cleared of Trees for Amphitheater Project." *Buffalo News*, December 23, 2021.

Sommer, Mark. 2022a. "Judge Allows Demolition of Great Northern Elevator." *Buffalo News*, January 5, 2022.

Sommer, Mark. 2022b. "Great Northern Grain Elevator Case Renews Calls for Local Landmark Reforms." *Buffalo News*, January 15, 2022.

Sommer, Mark. 2022c. "Great Northern Grain Elevator Gets Another Reprieve from Court." *Buffalo News*, February 16, 2022, B1–B2.

Sommer, Mark. 2022d. "Appellate Court Orders New Hearing on Great Northern Demolition Request." *Buffalo News*, April 29, 2022.

Sommer, Mark. 2022e. "Demolition of Great Northern to Start Thursday; Preservationists Running Out of Time." *Buffalo News*, September 14, 2022.

Sommer, Mark. 2022f. "Demolition Expected to Begin Today at Great Northern Site." *Buffalo News*, September 15, 2022, B1–B2.

Sommer, Mark. 2022g. "Demolition of Great Northern Proceeds Slowly as Court Appeals Still Sought." *Buffalo News*, September 23, 2022.

Sommer, Mark. 2022h. "Demolition of Great Northern Moves Ahead as Appeal Looms." *Buffalo News*, September 24, 2022.

Sommer, Mark. 2022i. "State Looks for Big Development at Outer Harbor: Empty Terminal Building Offered to Developers for Housing, Other Uses." *Buffalo News*, December 2, 2022, A1, A8.

Sommer, Mark. 2023a. "Group Gives Up Fight for Great Northern as Demolition Continues. *Buffalo News*, February 20, 2023, A1, A7.

Sommer, Mark. 2023b. "Developer Chosen to Remake Old Aud Site, Reshape Waterfront." *Buffalo News*, April 18, 2023, A1, A4.

Sommer, Mark. 2023c. "Riverline Project Gets Funding Boost from New York State." *Buffalo News*, June 20, 2023.

Sommer, Mark, and Brian Meyer. 2010. "Delays Asked on Vote for Waterfront Canals, Underground Parking." *Buffalo News*, November 11, 2010, B5.

Sorensen, Jon R., and Sharon Linstedt. 2007. "Bass Pro Plan Shifts Back to Aud Site: New Structure Proposed for Sporting Goods Store." *Buffalo News*, September 7, 2007.

State of New York, Executive Chamber, George E. Pataki, Governor. 2000. Press Release: "State, County, City Announce Agreement at 175th Anniversary of Erie Canal Opening." October 26, 2000.

Stecker, Andrew, and Kevin Connor, and Public Accountability Initiative. 2011. "Fishing for Taxpayer Cash: Bass Pro's Record of Big-League Subsidies, Failed Promises, and the Consequences for Cities Across America." public-accountability.org/wp-content/uploads/2011/09/fishing-for-taxpayer-cash.pdf.

Sullivan, Margaret. 2022. *Newsroom Confidential*. New York: St. Martin's Press.

Telvock, Dan. 2014. "Unfinished Business for Buffalo's Outer Harbor." *Investigative Post*, October 9, 2014.

Terriri, Jill. 2012. "Sabres Win Webster Block." *Buffalo News*, August 30, 2012, B1–B2.

Thomas, Amy. "36 Hours in Buffalo New York." *New York Times*, July 8, 2018, 10.

Traynor, Kerry, kta preservation specialists. *The Buffalo New York Outer Harbor as a Cultural Landscape*, August 2018.

"Trico Products Corporation." *Encyclopedia.com*. February 21, 2024. https://www.encyclopedia.com/books/politics-and-business-magazines/trico-products-corporation

US District Court, Western District of New York. 2000. Decision and Order filed by District Judge William M. Skretny, Preservation Coalition of Erie County vs. Federal Transit Administration, et al., March 31, 2000.

US Department of Transportation, Niagara Frontier Transportation Authority, New York State Urban Development Corporation (d/b/a Empire State Development Corporation) et al. 2004. "Supplemental Final Environmental Impact Statement for the Erie Canal Harbor Project," December 2004.

Utter, Brad L., Ashley Hopkins-Benton, and Karen E. Quinn. 2020. *Enterprising Waters: The History and Art of New York's Erie Canal*. Albany: State University of New York Press.

Vielkind, Jimmy. 2012. "Media Coverage of Major Land Use and Development Issues." Masters research paper, Department of Geography and Planning, University at Albany.

Vogel, Mike. 1993. "$800 Million Overhaul Readied for Waterfront: Crossroads Harbor Plan Unveiled." *Buffalo News*, August 11, 1993, A1, A7.

Vogel, Mike. 1998. "Launching the Waterfront: Pataki to Unveil Final Inner Harbor Plan." *Buffalo News*, June 15, 1998, A1.

Vogel, Michael N., Edward J. Patton, and Paul F. Redding. 2009. *America's Crossroads: Buffalo's Canal Street/Dante Place, The Making of a City*. Derby, NY: Acorn Books.

Walkowski, Jennifer. 2012. "Roll Out the Barrels." *Western New York Heritage*, Fall 2012, 8–17.

Warner, Gene. 2000. "Judge Orders Another Hearing on Canal Slip." *Buffalo News*, June 3, 2000.

Western New York Land Conservancy. 2018. "Reimagining the DL&W Corridor: An International Design Ideas Competition." 2018 Invitation and Solicitation of Design Ideas.

Wolfe, Teresa L., and the Tifft Farm Committee. 1983. *Tifft Farm: A History of Man and Nature."* Buffalo, NY: Buffalo Museum of Science.

Wooster, Margaret 2021. *Meander: Making Room for Rivers*. Albany: State University of New York Press.

Zach, John. 2020. "Mister Buffalo River: The Environmental Advocacy of Stan Spisiak." *Western New York Heritage*, Fall 2020, 62–69.

Zhao, Michelle. 2017. "Taking the High Road to Canalside: How Community Activism Has Shaped Buffalo's Waterfront." Partnership for the Public Good Policy Brief, ppgbuffalo.org/files/documents/171026_canalside_policy_brief.pdf.

Index

Page numbers in *italics* refer to figures.

271

Tonawanda, New York, 33
Torn Space Theater Company, 142
Traynor, Kerry, 28, 248
Trellis, 144
Trico Corporation, 38, 239
Trico Products Corporation, 84
Trometer, Betsy, 244
Trout Unlimited, 179, 247
Trowbridge Wolf Michaels, Landscape
    Architects (TWM), 179–80
Trzeciak, Brian, 111–12, 114, 243, 251
Tutuska, B. John, 39
T.Y. Lin International, 207

Unified Development Ordinance
    (Green Code), 183–84, 191, 194
University at Buffalo, 144, 218–19
Urban Development Corporation
    (UDC), 48, 51. *See also* Empire
    State Development Corporation
    (ESDC)
Urbanczyk, Michelle, 104–6, 251
US Army, 23
US Army Corps of Engineers
    (USACE)
  1833 lighthouse and, 42
  cleanup efforts and, 123–25, 128
  contamination of Buffalo River and,
    24–25
  General Project Plan (GPP) and,
    190
  Outer Harbor and, 27–28, 31
  waste disposal and, 31, 171–73,
    212, 213
US Department of Housing and
    Urban Development, 39
US Department of the Navy, 37
US Fish and Wildlife Service, 128
US Treasury Department, 10, 170
Utter, Brad L., 15

Valley Community Association
    (VCA), 126, 131–39, 245

Van Valkenburgh Associates, 219
Vielkind, Jimmy, 2, 88–90
Vogel, Michael N.
  on Canal District, 33–34
  ECHDC and, 206
  on ESDC's plan for Inner Harbor,
    55, 202–3
  Lighthouse Association and, 211
  restoration of lighthouse and, 42
  role of, 238, 243, 251
  on Times Beach Nature Preserve,
    170
Voice-Buffalo, 85, 239
Vuong, Ocean, 142–43

W Architecture & Landscape
    Architecture, 161
Walkowski, Jennifer, 149
Wallace Roberts Todd (WRT), 44–
    46
War of 1812 (1812–1815), 7
watercraft design, 110
Waterfront Development Advisory
    Committee, 176
Waterfront Greenway Trail, 77
Waterfront Memories and More
    Heritage Center, 137–38, *138*
Waterfront Planning Board (WPB),
    43–47
Waterfront Redevelopment Area,
    35–36, 37, 43–51
Webster Block, 51
Weiksnar, William "Jud," xix–xxi, 251
Wellness Institute of Greater Buffalo,
    179, 247
Wendt Foundation, 107, 108, 132,
    238–39, 241, 244–45
Western New York Environmental
    Alliance (WNYEA), 178, 179,
    181–82, 183, 191, 247
Western New York Foundation, 240
Western New York Land Conservancy
    (WNYLC), 159–61, 245

Milton Keynes UK
Ingram Content Group UK Ltd.
UKHW041911040924
447908UK00005B/45

9 781438 499086